Building Kotlin Applications

A comprehensive guide for Android, Web, and Server-Side Development

Mounir Boussetta

www.bpbonline.com

Copyright © 2024 BPB Online

All rights reserved. No part of this book may be reproduced, stored in a retrieval system, or transmitted in any form or by any means, without the prior written permission of the publisher, except in the case of brief quotations embedded in critical articles or reviews.

Every effort has been made in the preparation of this book to ensure the accuracy of the information presented. However, the information contained in this book is sold without warranty, either express or implied. Neither the author, nor BPB Online or its dealers and distributors, will be held liable for any damages caused or alleged to have been caused directly or indirectly by this book.

BPB Online has endeavored to provide trademark information about all of the companies and products mentioned in this book by the appropriate use of capitals. However, BPB Online cannot guarantee the accuracy of this information.

First published: 2024

Published by BPB Online
WeWork
119 Marylebone Road
London NW1 5PU

UK | UAE | INDIA | SINGAPORE

ISBN 978-93-55516-336

www.bpbonline.com

Dedicated to

My daughter:
Inas
&
My son **Saad**

About the Author

Mounir Boussetta a highly accomplished and dedicated software engineer with a passion for the ever-evolving world of technology. As a co-founder and a project manager at FIRETHUNDER, a leading company in medical information systems, Mounir brings an exceptional level of expertise and leadership to his role.

Mounir's journey in the IT industry began after he graduated with a degree in electronics and telecoms engineering in 2013. Driven by his love for programming, he transitioned into the IT domain, where he has thrived ever since. With over 13 years of experience in Java development, starting from version 1.6, and 6 years of experience with Kotlin, Mounir has an extensive understanding of the language and its applications.

Prior to his role at FIRETHUNDER, Mounir worked as a software developer at Vivace Consulting SARL, where he honed his skills in AngularJS/Angular, Java, Spring Boot, Spring Data, Spring Security, Hibernate, and REST APIs. His proficiency in IHE Framework standards such as DICOM 3.0 and HL7, which he gained through five years of experience, has been instrumental in his success in the field.

About the Reviewer

Devnath Jha is a seasoned Android developer with nearly a decade of experience in both Java and Kotlin.

In addition to his extensive work in the Android realm, Devnath has embarked on an exciting journey in the world of Java backend development with Spring Boot and MongoDB.

He is currently contributing his expertise to a forward-thinking IT startup company based in Bangalore.

His passion for technology extends beyond the confines of his workspace.

When he isn't immersed in code, he dedicates his time to staying updated with the latest advancements in both Android and backend technologies.

Devnath Jha's unique blend of Android expertise, coupled with his burgeoning backend development skills, positions him as a versatile and invaluable asset in the realm of software engineering.

Acknowledgement

I wish to extend my profound appreciation to my family and friends for their consistent support and motivation throughout the process of writing this book.

Additionally, I'd like to express my thanks to BPB Publications for their invaluable guidance and expertise in bringing this book to fruition. The journey of revising this book was a lengthy one, and I am immensely thankful for the valuable contributions and collaboration of reviewers, technical experts, and editors.

I would also like to acknowledge the significant contributions of my colleagues and coworkers from my years of working in the tech industry. They have not only taught me a great deal but have also provided valuable feedback on my work.

Lastly, I want to convey my gratitude to all the readers who have shown interest in my book and supported its realization. Your encouragement has been truly priceless.

Preface

Building applications is a multifaceted endeavor that demands a comprehensive grasp of cutting-edge technologies and programming languages. Kotlin has emerged as a powerful and increasingly popular tool in the realm of software development.

This book is meticulously crafted to serve as your all-encompassing guide to constructing enterprise applications with Kotlin. It delves into a vast array of topics, beginning with the fundamentals of Kotlin programming, progressing to advanced concepts like object-oriented programming, and culminating in the utilization of the Kotlin ecosystem to forge robust and scalable applications.

As you traverse the pages of this book, you will immerse yourself in the essential attributes of Kotlin and its ecosystem, equipping you to fashion enterprise applications that are not only efficient and reliable but also easily maintainable. You will glean insights into best practices and design patterns tailored to the unique demands of enterprise application development, and you will encounter a plethora of real-world examples that will solidify your comprehension of these concepts.

Whether you are a newcomer to Kotlin and the world of enterprise application development or an experienced developer seeking to fortify your command of these technologies and elevate your proficiency in crafting resilient and dependable applications, this book is your compass on this journey.

With this book as your companion, you will acquire the knowledge and expertise needed to flourish as an adept developer in the sphere of multiplatform applications development using Kotlin. I sincerely hope that you discover this book to be enlightening and invaluable on your path to mastery.

Chapter 1: Java and Kotlin - In this first chapter, we will put you in the context of the language, and you will be introduced to the history of Kotlin, why this new programming language has appeared, who created Kotlin, and what was their intention behind Kotlin. We will also learn about Kotlin in comparison to Java; we will learn about the advantages and disadvantages of each and what makes the Kotlin language the right choice for your future development and maybe your career.

Chapter 2: Kotlin Basics - The readers will get an understanding of the basics of the Kotlin programming language. They will be able to deal with variables, data types, the creation of functions, the basic control structures, and also how to work with some Kotlin features like smart casting, class extensions, and operator overloading.

Chapter 3: OOP with Kotlin – This presents how to create some basic real-world applications in Kotlin by following an object-oriented way, and this goal will be possible by following this chapter's sections on object-oriented programming. It examines and discovers what makes a language object-oriented by learning about the pillars of this concept.

Chapter 4: Generics – The learners will be able to use generics in your programs to be more concise in writing code by getting most of the advantages they offer. They will explore some new concepts that are introduced in Kotlin, such as reified-type parameters and declaration-site variance. They will be taught some issues with generics in Java that are resolved in Kotlin in a very concise way.

Chapter 5: Annotations and Reflection – The readers will learn about annotations and reflection and how to be able to use and define their custom annotations, and will be able to use reflection to introspect classes at runtime as well.

Chapter 6: Functional Programming with Kotlin and RxKotlin - This will give learners some understandings about the functional programming paradigm, reactive programming, functional data structures, higher order functions, how error handling is done, and many other concepts.

Chapter 7: Observables, Observers, and Subjects – It will make readers understand the concepts of observables, observers, and subjects in the context of reactive programming. Learn how to create observables and observers in Kotlin using the RxKotlin library. Explore the various factory methods and operators the RxKotlin library provides for working with observables. Understand the different types of Subjects available in the RxKotlin library and how they can be used. Learn how to use observables, observers, and subjects to create asynchronous and event-based programs in Kotlin.

Chapter 8: Flowables and Backpressure - Flowables and observables are types of data streams that are used in reactive programming. They allow developers to represent asynchronous data streams and react to changes in the data over time. Flowables are a type of data stream designed to handle large volumes of data, known as backpressure. They allow developers to control the rate at which data is emitted and processed, ensuring that it can be processed efficiently and without overloading the system. On the contrary, observations are a simpler type of data stream that does not have built-in support for backpressure. They are often used for smaller data volumes or cases where backpressure is unnecessary.

Chapter 9: Data Transformers and Async Operators - This chapter aims to provide a comprehensive understanding of the various Rx operators and how they can be used to work with streams of data in a reactive programming paradigm. Understanding these operators and their use will help developers create powerful, efficient, and responsive data flows that can handle real-world scenarios.

Chapter 10: Concurrency and Parallel Processing - This chapter covers the concepts of concurrency, schedulers, and their usage in RxKotlin. We will start by understanding the basics of concurrency and how it can be applied in our systems. Then, we will delve into the world of schedulers, which are responsible for scheduling the execution of our tasks. We will learn how to use schedulers with the subscribeOn and observeOn operators in RxKotlin to achieve concurrency and parallel processing.

Chapter 11: Testing Reactive Applications - Testing reactive applications in Kotlin requires a different approach than testing traditional applications. Reactive applications are asynchronous and often handle concurrency, which can make them more difficult to test. However, there are several testing tools and techniques that can be used to make testing reactive applications easier.

Chapter 12: Spring Reactive for Kotlin - Spring Boot is a popular framework for building JVM-based applications, and Kotlin, as we already know, is a modern programming language that has gained popularity in recent years due to its concise syntax and powerful features. Together, they provide a powerful combination for building efficient and scalable applications.

Chapter 13: Asynchronous Programming and Coroutines - It will explore the concepts of multithreading, callbacks, coroutines, jobs, and UI threads. It discuss why multithreading is important in modern software development, including the benefits of improved performance, scalability, and responsiveness. And then dive into the topic of handling work completion using callbacks, which are a powerful mechanism for signaling the completion of asynchronous tasks.

Chapter 14: Suspending Functions and Async/Await- In the real world, suspending functions can be used to write code that performs network requests, database queries, and other asynchronous operations. For example, you could use suspending functions to write code that fetches data from a web service, updates a database, or plays a sound file.

Chapter 15: Contexts and Dispatchers - This chapter focuses on the management and control flow aspects of Kotlin coroutines. It will explore how coroutines are scheduled and executed, the different types of dispatchers available, and how exceptions propagate within coroutines. Additionally, It will delve into the critical topic of coroutine cancellation, understanding the mechanisms behind it and exploring techniques to effectively manage and handle cancellations.

Chapter 16: Coroutines Channels - The concept of channels is an important part of Kotlin coroutines. Channels can be used to implement communication patterns between coroutines, allowing data to be passed between them in a safe and efficient way. This chapter will explore the various features of channels, including generators, pipelines, and broadcast channels.

Chapter 17: Coroutine Flows – The chapter delve into the powerful concept of Coroutine Flows in Kotlin. Asynchronous programming often involves handling data streams that require efficient processing and management. Traditional approaches to stream processing may have limitations when it comes to handling backpressure, composing operators, and maintaining concurrency. Coroutine Flows offers a comprehensive solution to these challenges by providing a declarative and efficient way to work with data streams.

Chapter 18: Multiplatform and Kotlin - This final chapter of the book, will delve into the realm of multiplatform development with Kotlin. Multiplatform development has emerged as a powerful approach to building applications that can run on multiple platforms, enabling code sharing and reducing development effort, It will explore the principles and benefits of multiplatform development and guide readers through the process of setting up development environment for multiplatform projects.

Code Bundle and Coloured Images

Please follow the link to download the
Code Bundle and the *Coloured Images* of the book:

https://rebrand.ly/wq5ve66

The code bundle for the book is also hosted on GitHub at **https://github.com/bpbpublications/Building-Kotlin-Applications**. In case there's an update to the code, it will be updated on the existing GitHub repository.

We have code bundles from our rich catalogue of books and videos available at **https://github.com/bpbpublications**. Check them out!

Errata

We take immense pride in our work at BPB Publications and follow best practices to ensure the accuracy of our content to provide with an indulging reading experience to our subscribers. Our readers are our mirrors, and we use their inputs to reflect and improve upon human errors, if any, that may have occurred during the publishing processes involved. To let us maintain the quality and help us reach out to any readers who might be having difficulties due to any unforeseen errors, please write to us at :

errata@bpbonline.com

Your support, suggestions and feedbacks are highly appreciated by the BPB Publications' Family.

> Did you know that BPB offers eBook versions of every book published, with PDF and ePub files available? You can upgrade to the eBook version at www.bpbonline.com and as a print book customer, you are entitled to a discount on the eBook copy. Get in touch with us at :
>
> **business@bpbonline.com** for more details.
>
> At **www.bpbonline.com**, you can also read a collection of free technical articles, sign up for a range of free newsletters, and receive exclusive discounts and offers on BPB books and eBooks.

Piracy

If you come across any illegal copies of our works in any form on the internet, we would be grateful if you would provide us with the location address or website name. Please contact us at **business@bpbonline.com** with a link to the material.

If you are interested in becoming an author

If there is a topic that you have expertise in, and you are interested in either writing or contributing to a book, please visit **www.bpbonline.com**. We have worked with thousands of developers and tech professionals, just like you, to help them share their insights with the global tech community. You can make a general application, apply for a specific hot topic that we are recruiting an author for, or submit your own idea.

Reviews

Please leave a review. Once you have read and used this book, why not leave a review on the site that you purchased it from? Potential readers can then see and use your unbiased opinion to make purchase decisions. We at BPB can understand what you think about our products, and our authors can see your feedback on their book. Thank you!

For more information about BPB, please visit **www.bpbonline.com**.

Join our book's Discord space

Join the book's Discord Workspace for Latest updates, Offers, Tech happenings around the world, New Release and Sessions with the Authors:

https://discord.bpbonline.com

Table of Contents

1. Java and Kotlin 1
   Introduction 1
   Structure 2
   Objectives 2
   Overview 2
   History of Kotlin 2
      Who is behind Kotlin, and when did it appear? 3
      Why Kotlin? 4
      What is Kotlin? 4
      The name Kotlin 5
   Kotlin versus Java 5
   Kotlin 9
      Advantages 9
      Disadvantages 13
   Java 13
      Advantages 14
      Disadvantages 15
   Next in Kotlin 15
   Conclusion 15
   Points to remember 16

2. Kotlin Basics 17
   Introduction 17
   Structure 17
   Objectives 18
   Overview 18
   Variables 19
      Declaration and initialization 19
   Types and cast 20
      Integer types 20

- *Floating-point types* 21
  - *Numbers representation on the JVM* 22
- *Character* 22
- *String* 23
  - *String functions* 24
- *Boolean* 26
- *Arrays* 27

Null safety 28

Creating functions 29
- *Creating and using a function* 29
- *Function arguments* 30
- *Variable number of arguments (varargs)* 32

Choices and conditions 32
- *if/else-if/else* 32
- *when* 33

Loops 34
- *repeat* 35
- *for loop* 35
- *while and do .. while loops* 36

Returns and jumps 37
- *Return* 37
- *Break* 38
- *Continue* 39

Smart cast with Kotlin 39

Work with extensions 40
- *Extension functions* 40
- *Extension properties* 41

Overloading operators 41

Handle exceptions 43

Conclusion 44

Points to remember 44

3. OOP with Kotlin 45

Introduction 45
Structure 45
Objectives 46
Overview 46
Classes and objects 46
    Kotlin class 47
    Objects 50
Inheritance 52
    Inheritance in Kotlin 52
        Overriding parent class methods 57
    Abstract classes 59
Properties 61
    Getters and setters 61
    Backing fields 62
Interfaces 63
    Properties in interfaces 63
    Interfaces inheritance 64
Visibility modifiers 65
    Packages 65
    Class and interface visibility modifiers 66
Types of classes 67
    Simple class 67
    Open class 67
    Data class 68
    Nested class 68
    Inner class 69
    Sealed class 70
Delegation 71
Type aliases 72
Conclusion 73
Points to remember 73

4. Generics 75
Introduction 75
Structure 75
Objectives 75
Overview 76
Generics 76
    Generic classes 76
        Generic advantages 77
    Generic functions 78
    Generic constraints 79
        Upper bound constraint 79
        Type erasure 81
Variance 81
    Declaration-site variance 82
        out keyword 82
        in keyword 82
    Use-site variance: type projection 83
Reified-type parameters 84
    Type reification 85
    Type checking and type casting 86
Conclusion 87
Points to remember 87

5. Annotations and Reflection 89
Introduction 89
Structure 89
Objectives 90
Overview 90
Annotations 90
    Usage 90
    Define custom annotation 91
    Annotation constructor 93
        Instantiation 94

| *Use-site target* 95
   Reflection 95
        JVM reflection dependency 96
            In a Gradle project: 96
            In a Maven project: 96
            Reference to a Kotlin class 96
            Callable references 97
        Serialization and deserialization 98
            Serialization 99
            Deserialization 103
   Conclusion 103
   Points to remember 103

6. **Functional Programming with Kotlin and RxKotlin** 105
   Introduction 105
   Structure 105
   Objectives 106
   Overview 106
   Introduction to reactive programming 106
        Why adopt a functional reactive programming paradigm? 108
        Reactive Manifesto: reactive principles 108
   Lambda expression 110
        Declaring a lambda 110
        Lambda type declaration 110
   Pure function 111
   Higher-order functions 111
   Inline functions 113
        noinline 114
   Polymorphic functions 114
   Functional data structures 115
        Definition and declaration of the singly linked list data structure 115
   Handling errors 119

    Conclusion 122

    Points to remember 123

7. Observables, Observers, and Subjects **125**

    Introduction 125

    Structure 125

    Objectives 125

    Overview 126

    How do observables work? 126

    Observable factory methods 127

    Subjects 131

        BehaviorSubject 131

        PublishSubject 133

        ReplaySubject 135

    Conclusion 137

    Points to remember 138

8. Flowables and Backpressure **139**

    Introduction 139

    Structure 139

    Objectives 140

    Overview 140

    Flowables and observables 140

        Difference between observables and flowables 141

        When to use flowables and not observables? 142

    Flowable from observable 142

    Backpressure 143

    Flowable with backpressure 144

    Conclusion 149

    Points to remember 149

9. Data Transformers and Async Operators **151**

    Introduction 151

    Structure 152

Objectives 152
Overview 152
Rx-operators 153
Filtering operators 153
Transforming operators 159
Reducing operators 161
Processors 163
Grouping operators 165
Mapping operators 167
Error handling 168
Example 170
Conclusion 171
Points to remember 171

10. Concurrency and Parallel Processing 173
Introduction 173
Structure 173
Objectives 174
Overview 174
Concurrency 174
Schedulers 177
Schedulers with subscribeOn and observeOn 178
Conclusion 181
Points to remember 181

11. Testing Reactive Applications 183
Introduction 183
Structure 183
Objectives 184
Overview 184
Importance of unit testing 184
JUnit tests 185
   Setting up Junit *185*

　　　　Writing your first JUnit test 186
　　　　Using assertions 186
　　　　Writing tests for reactive applications 192
　　RxKotlin testing 193
　　　　Observables 193
　　　　Operators 194
　　　　Subjects 195
　　TestSubscriber 196
　　TestScheduler 197
　　TestObserver 198
　　Conclusion 200
　　Points to remember 200

12. Spring Reactive for Kotlin **201**
　　Introduction 201
　　Structure 201
　　Objectives 202
　　Overview 202
　　Introduction to Spring Boot 203
　　　　Overview of Spring framework 203
　　　　Key features of Spring Boot 204
　　　　Support of reactive programming 205
　　Gradle 207
　　Getting started with Spring Boot 211
　　　　Spring Boot and the n-tier architecture 212
　　　　　　Creating a basic Spring Boot application 213
　　Flux and Mono 221
　　Spring Data Reactive 224
　　Conclusion 230
　　Points to remember 230

13. Asynchronous Programming and Coroutines **231**
　　Introduction 231

Structure 231
Objectives 232
Overview 232
Why multithreading? 232
 Reason behind multithreading use 233
 Challenges 233
 Solutions 234
  Use thread-safe data structures and synchronization mechanisms 234
  Use atomic operations 235
  Use thread pools 235
  Use message passing 236
  Use profiling and debugging tools 237
Handling work completion using callbacks 237
 Asynchronous programming 238
 Asynchronous file I/O using CompletableFuture 240
Understanding coroutines 241
Jobs   243
UI threads 244
Conclusion 246
Points to remember 246

14. Suspending Functions and Async/Await 247
Introduction 247
Structure 247
Objectives 248
Overview 248
Suspending versus non-suspending 249
 Non-suspending functions 249
 Suspending functions 249
 Some real-world examples 250
Creating suspendable API 251
 Understanding suspendable APIs 252
 Advantages of suspendable APIs 252

   Thread safety 255
   Testing and debugging 257
 Async/await 260
  Understanding Async/Await 260
  Benefits of async/await 261
 Deferred values 262
  Creating a Deferred value 262
  Error handling with Deferred values 263
 Combination of deferred values 264
 Conclusion 267
 Points to remember 267

15. Contexts and Dispatchers 269
 Introduction 269
 Structure 269
 Objectives 270
 Overview 270
 Task scheduling 270
  Understanding coroutine scheduling and execution flow 270
  Coroutine contexts and their role in determining the execution context 273
  Coroutine builders and their impact on scheduling 274
 Dispatcher's types 275
  Dispatchers.Default 275
  Dispatchers.IO 275
  Dispatchers.Main 275
  Dispatchers.Unconfined 276
 Exception propagation and its handling 277
 Coroutine cancellation 279
  Coroutine cancellation is cooperative 280
   How to cancel a coroutine? 282
 Manage cancellation 284
  Using a try-catch block 284
   Using a finally block 285

Conclusion 287

Points to remember 288

16. Coroutines Channels 289

Introduction 289

Structure 289

Objectives 290

Overview 290

Generators and sequences 290

Pipelines 292

Send and offer (trySend) 295

Receive and poll (tryReceive) 297

Channels versus Java queues 299

Broadcast channels 300

Producers and actors 302

Conclusion 303

Points to remember 304

17. Coroutine Flows 305

Introduction 305

Structure 306

Objectives 306

Overview 306

Data streams 307

Streams limitations 310

Handling backpressure and cancellation 310

Backpressure 310

Cancellation 313

Inefficient resource utilization 314

The need for a coroutine flows approach 316

Flows constraints 316

Conclusion 319

Points to remember 319

18. Multiplatform and Kotlin 321

Introduction 321
Structure 322
Objectives 322
Overview 323
Setting up the development environment 323
  Creating a simple Android application with Jetpack Compose 324
  Setting up the Compose multiplatform project structure 325
    Setting up the common module 327
    Setting up the Android module 330
    Setting up the desktop module 332
Todo app in Compose Multiplatform 334
Conclusion 358
Points to remember 358

Index 361-368

CHAPTER 1
Java and Kotlin

Introduction

You probably heard about Kotlin, the new programming language that competes with Java and the other JVM-based languages, and you might also heard that Kotlin is now used by the biggest IT companies such as Google, Amazon, Netflix, Uber, Trello, Pinterest, Foursquare, and others.

You need to know that most of these companies had been using Java for a long time until the appearance of Kotlin, then they had chosen to migrate to this one because of the power it gives them and the interoperability with the existing Java code, which makes the switching to the new programming language gradually easy and not starting the process from scratch.

Taking Google as an example, in 2017, they announced that Kotlin will be the main programming language for Android applications over Java. Coursera, Uber, Duolingo, and other popular Android applications are now using Kotlin for their development.

Kotlin, as a multi-platform programming language, is used almost everywhere, from mobile development and Web applications to scripting, machine learning, and data science, thanks to the concise, expressive style and full interoperability with Java.

This will give you some confidence to go ahead with your choice to this journey of learning Kotlin language over Java and other JVM-based languages for your future IT career.

Structure

In this chapter, we will cover the following topics:
- History of Kotlin
- Kotlin versus Java
- Kotlin
    o Advantages
    o Disadvantages
- Java
    o Advantages
    o Disadvantages
- Next in Kotlin

Objectives

After reading this chapter, you will know the reasons behind creating Kotlin programming language, the differences between Kotlin and Java, and the advantages of using Kotlin over Java as a main programming language for building applications.

Overview

In this first chapter, we will put you in the context of the language, and you will be introduced to the history of Kotlin, why this new programming language has appeared, who created Kotlin, and what was their intention behind Kotlin. We will also learn about Kotlin in comparison to Java; we will learn about the advantages and disadvantages of each and what makes the Kotlin language the right choice for your future development and maybe your career.

History of Kotlin

First of all, we need to get to know a little bit of the history of any language we intend to learn; by that, we will get some understanding of the philosophy behind that language. At this very first stage, we will try to answer the following questions:
- Who is behind Kotlin, and when did it appear?
- Why another JVM-based language?
- What is Kotlin?
- The name Kotlin?

Who is behind Kotlin, and when did it appear?

JetBrains is a Czech software development company that makes tools for software developers and project managers. Initially called IntelliJ Software, it was founded in 2000 in Prague by three Russian software developers: *Sergey Dmitriev*, *Valentin Kipyatkov*, and *Eugene Belyaev*. The company's first product was IntelliJ Renamer, a tool for code refactoring in Java.

Figure 1.1: *JetBrains logo from 2000 to 2016*
(source: https:// wikipedia.com)

The beams that stem from the Black Box in our logos and icons represent our boundless energy, innovation, and our drive to develop. Combined with the Black Box, it is the perfect visual representation of what JetBrains is and a unique visual element.

Figure 1.2: *Current JetBrains logo from 2016*
(source: https://www.jetbrains.com/company/brand/)

The company offers many **integrated development environments (IDE)** for the programming languages Java, Groovy, Kotlin, Ruby, Python, PHP, C, Objective-C, C++, C#, Go, JavaScript, and the domain-specific language SQL.

InfoWorld magazine awarded the firm Technology of the Year Award in 2011 and 2015.

JetBrains announced Project Kotlin in 2011, a new JVM-based language that had been under development for a year. The first officially stable version of Kotlin was released on February 15, 2016. JetBrains has committed to long-term backward compatibility, starting with this version.

At Google I/O 2017, Google announced first-class support for Kotlin on Android.

Kotlin 1.2 was released on November 28, 2017. The sharing code between JVM and JavaScript platforms feature was newly added to this release (as of version 1.4 multiplatform programming is an alpha feature upgraded from *experimental*). A full-stack demo has been made with the new Kotlin/JS Gradle Plugin.

Kotlin 1.3 was released on October 29, 2018, bringing coroutines for asynchronous programming.

On May 7, 2019, Google announced that the Kotlin programming language is now its preferred language for Android app developers. Kotlin 1.4 was released in August 2020, with for example, some slight changes to the support for Apple's platforms, that is, to the Objective-C/Swift interop.

Kotlin 1.5 was released in May 2021. Kotlin 1.6 was released in November 2021.

At the time of writing this book, the latest version of Kotlin is 1.6.10.

Why Kotlin?

JetBrains development lead *Dmitry Jemerov* said that most existing languages lack the features they are looking for, with the exception of Scala, but Scala has one deficiency, which is the slow compilation time.

One of the targets of a new JVM-based language is to compile as quickly as Java and have the feature set of Scala and the other languages benefits. The other reason behind the investment in a new JVM-based programming language, as explained by Dmitry Jemerov in the JetBrains Blog, is their own productivity; he said that they need to be more productive by switching to a more expressive language; the other reason is to drive the IntelliJ IDEA (Integrated development environment for JVM-based languages) sales.

What is Kotlin?

Kotlin is an open-source, general-purpose, and statically typed programming language that runs on the Java Virtual Machine and also compiles to JavaScript and Native code, and it is concise, safe, and interoperable with other languages.

According to the Kotlin development lead Andrey Breslav, Kotlin is designed to be an industrial-strength object-oriented language and a better language than Java, but keeping the interoperability with Java code, which will give the companies interested in the language to gradually migrate their project from Java to Kotlin.

Figure 1.3: Current Kotlin logo

Kotlin is also influenced by other languages like Python, Groovy, Scala, C#, Gosu, Eiffel, and JavaScript, which make the Kotlin language gain the benefits of these languages and implement them in one language that will be more expressive and easier to work with.

The name Kotlin

The name behind Kotlin comes from Kotlin Island, where most employees of JetBrains; it is a Russian island located near the head of the Gulf of Finland, 32 kilometers (20 mi) west of *Saint Petersburg* in the Baltic Sea (*Figure 1.4*), *Andrey Breslav* (Kotlin development lead) mentioned that the team decided to name it after an island, just like Java was named after the Indonesian island of Java (though the programming language Java was perhaps named after the coffee rather than the island).

Figure 1.4: *Kotlin Island on Google Maps*

Kotlin versus Java

You may be wondering: It is okay! You said that Kotlin is better than Java and that most IT companies migrated from Java to Kotlin, but what are the differences between the two languages that make one better than the other if they both work on top of the **Java Virtual Machine (JVM)** and what Kotlin has that Java does not or vice versa.

Figure 1.5: *Java logo*

Java was originally developed by *James Gosling* at Sun Microsystems and released in May 1995 as a core component of Sun Microsystems' Java platform. It is a high-level, class-based, object-oriented programming language, and it is a general-purpose programming language that lets the programmers write the code once and run it everywhere on all the platforms that support Java without the need to recompile.

At the time of writing these lines of the book, the latest version of Java is Java 17, which is a **Long-Term Support** (**LTS**) version. Java has many issues that Kotlin comes to address and fix; for example, Null references, which were the most common pitfalls in Java, raw types, invariant arrays, function types, exceptions, and more.

Among the best features Kotlin comes with is its concise and expressive syntax; let us take this example of a **Patient** class in both Java and Kotlin. In Java, this data class will be like the following:

Patient class in Java:

```java
public class Patient {
    private Long id;
    private String firstName;
    private String lastName;
    private LocalDate dateOfBirth;
    private String phoneNumber;
    private String email;

    public Patient() {
    }

    public Patient(Long id, String firstName, String lastName, LocalDate dateOfBirth, String phoneNumber, String email) {
        this.id = id;
        this.firstName = firstName;
        this.lastName = lastName;
        this.dateOfBirth = dateOfBirth;
        this.phoneNumber = phoneNumber;
        this.email = email;
    }
```

```java
    public Long getId() {
        return id;
    }

    public void setId(Long id) {
        this.id = id;
    }

    public String getFirstName() {
        return firstName;
    }

    public void setFirstName(String firstName) {
        this.firstName = firstName;
    }

    public String getLastName() {
        return lastName;
    }

    public void setLastName(String lastName) {
        this.lastName = lastName;
    }

    public LocalDate getDateOfBirth() {
        return dateOfBirth;
    }

    public void setDateOfBirth(LocalDate dateOfBirth) {
        this.dateOfBirth = dateOfBirth;
    }
```

```java
    public String getPhoneNumber() {
        return phoneNumber;
    }

    public void setPhoneNumber(String phoneNumber) {
        this.phoneNumber = phoneNumber;
    }

    public String getEmail() {
        return email;
    }

    public void setEmail(String email) {
        this.email = email;
    }

    @Override
    public boolean equals(Object o) {
        if (this == o) return true;
        if (o == null || getClass() != o.getClass()) return false;
        Patient = (Patient) o;
        return Objects.equals(id, patient.id) &&
                Objects.equals(firstName, patient.firstName) &&
                Objects.equals(lastName, patient.lastName) &&
                Objects.equals(dateOfBirth, patient.dateOfBirth) &&
                Objects.equals(phoneNumber, patient.phoneNumber) &&
                Objects.equals(email, patient.email);
    }

    @Override
    public int hashCode() {
```

```
            return Objects.hash(id, firstName, lastName, dateOfBirth, phoneNumber, email);
    }
}
```

The same data class in Kotlin would be as follows, without all that boilerplate and with less frustration, which makes Kotlin more readable and clearer:

Patient class in Kotlin:

```
data class Patient (
    val id: Long,
    val firstName: String,
    val lastName: String,
    val dateOfBirth: LocalDate,
    val phoneNumber: String,
    val email: String
)
```

That is one of many features that Kotlin is offering.

Next, you will learn about the pros and cons of each language and what makes one better than another for your future projects. Do not worry if you do not understand something right now, and in the coming comparison section, you will learn all about these features in the upcoming chapters.

Kotlin

So far, you know the *who is* and the *why is* behind Kotlin; now, we will look at the advantages of adopting Kotlin as the main programming language for your future projects and what are the disadvantages it has in comparison with Java.

Advantages

Kotlin comes with many pros and features to compete with the other JVM-based programming languages. The following are the main advantages of Kotlin:

- **Code conciseness**: As you saw earlier, the same Java class with dozens of lines can be written in a few lines in Kotlin without missing any required operations; if you have to create a **Hello World** program in Kotlin, you will do it like the following:

    Main function in Kotlin:

```
fun main() {
    println("Hello World!")
}
```

While the same program in Java would be written as follows:

Main function in Java:

```
public class Main {
    public static void main (String[] args) {
        System.out.println("Hello World!");
    }
}
```

This is a case where Kotlin can reduce the total amount of the boilerplate of Java and demonstrate the conciseness of Kotlin.

- **100% Java-interoperable**: Kotlin works with existing Java code, which means you can work with Kotlin alongside any existing Java code, which makes the transition from Java to Kotlin very easy; if there is a Framework or an API that is written with Java, you can work with Kotlin and consume the already existing code as if it was written in Kotlin, as easy as that.

- **Easy maintenance**: Kotlin is supported by many IDEs, if not the most; Android Studio and IntelliJ IDEA, the most dominant IDEs for Android development and JVM-based languages, respectively, are made by the same company behind Kotlin (JetBrains); they both fully support Kotlin and the use many implicit tools that can be used easily to migrate your existing Java code to Kotlin in a few seconds.

- **Learning Kotlin is easy**: Many Java developers who work with Java on Android mobile applications have made the transition to Kotlin without the need to learn much, and this is thanks to the expressive syntax of Kotlin.

  In addition, JetBrains has made the learning of Kotlin as many other languages and concepts easy and accessible in their IDEs by launching the JetBrains Academy with the possibility to gain certificates.

- **Kotlin comes with support for functional and procedural programming**: You may find some languages that support procedural programming and others that support functional programming, but Kotlin has the two at once, which gives it an advantage over other languages.

- **Data classes**: On any project, you will find classes that are meant to hold data; in Java, a developer will need to define many fields to store the data, getters, and setters functions to set and get the field data, constructors, equal, **hashCode**, and **toString** functions (see the code for **Patient class in Kotlin**), In Kotlin, you do not need to do so, all you need is to add the data keyword before your class, and the compiler will deal with all the boilerplate for you.

- **Extension functions**: Kotlin provides a way to extend a class with new functionalities without the need to inherit from the class; it means you can write new functions an any third-party library class that you cannot modify and call them on that class as if they were methods of the original class.
- **Higher-order functions and lambdas**: Higher-order function is a function that takes as arguments another function or returns a function.

  Lambda expressions and anonymous functions, or function literals as known, are functions that are not declared but passed immediately as expressions.
- **Inline functions**: Variables that are accessed in the body of the function are known as closures. The use of higher-order functions can impose several runtime penalties. Every function in Kotlin is an object, and it captures a closure. A closure is a scope of variables that can be accessed in the body of the function. Both functions and classes memory allocation and the virtual calls can introduce a runtime overhead.

  But in many cases, inlining the lambda expression can eliminate this kind of overhead.
- **Native support for delegation**: Kotlin supports the Delegation pattern natively in order to be a good alternative to implementation inheritance requiring zero boilerplate code.

  Class delegation is an alternative to inheritance in Kotlin.

  For example, a derived class Circle can implement an interface Shape by delegating all of its public members to a specified object (do not worry, this example is for explanation; you will learn it all in the coming chapters):

  Delegation example:

  ```kotlin
  interface Shape {
      fun print()
  }

  class ShapeImpl(val area: Float) : Shape {
      override fun print() { print(area) }
  }

  class Circle(s: Shape) : Shape by s

  fun main() {
      val shape = ShapeImpl(10.0f)
      Circle(shape).print()
  }
  ```

The **by** clause in the supertype list for **Circle** indicates that "s" will be stored internally in objects of **Circle**, and the compiler will generate all the methods of **Shape** that forward to "s."

- **Null safety**: **NullPointerException** (NPE for short), is the most infuriating issue of Java for developers, or the Billion Dollars Mistake as called by *Tony Hoare*, one of the computer scientists who has made foundational contributions to programming languages, algorithms, and operating systems.

    Java lets developers assign null values to any variable, but when they try to access that variable with a null reference, they face this **NullPointerException**! Kotlin type system distinguishes between nullable references (references that can hold null values) and non-nullable references (those that cannot hold null values).

    For example, a regular variable of type **Int** cannot hold null:

    Non-null reference

    ```
    var x: Int = 2022
    x = null // compilation error
    ```

    To allow nulls, you can declare a variable as a nullable by writing Int?:

    Nullable reference

    ```
    var x: Int? = 2022
    x = null // It's Ok! the compiler is happy now!!
    print(x)
    ```

- **Coroutines**: Kotlin has opened the door to asynchronous programming by introducing coroutines, in addition to a wealth of other possibilities, such as concurrency and actors.

    Asynchronous or non-blocking programming is an important part of development; when developing any application, you not only need to provide a user experience that is fluid but also make the application scalable if needed.

    Kotlin solves this problem with coroutines in a flexible way at the language level. Android is single-threaded by default; as a result, the UI thread will get completely frozen as the main thread is blocked.

    Kotlin, with coroutines, allows the creation of additional threads to perform long-running or intensive operations by suspending execution without blocking the main thread and resuming the execution at a later time, all this in a clear and concise way.

- **Smart Casts**: In Java, when you need to cast an object, you must check for its type before; otherwise, you might result in a **ClassCastException** if the object is not of the target type.

Kotlin comes with a Smart Cast feature that automatically handles such redundant casts, and the smart cast returns a null value that you can check if the cast attempt was unsuccessful.

- **Support for constructors**: A Kotlin class can have one or more secondary constructors in addition to the primary constructor, whereas Java allows this by constructor overloading.

Disadvantages

Every programming language has its advantages and disadvantages; let us see what are some disadvantages of using Kotlin.

- **Different from Java**: Kotlin is a relatively new language compared to Java, which has a huge community. However, some developers are not willing to make any switch to a new language or make an effort to learn any new language as they have already mastered the Java language.
- **Compilation speed**: When it comes to compilation time, Java beats Kotlin for clean builds, but those are rare cases; when it comes to incremental compilation, which is the most cases, Kotlin compiles as quickly as Java.
- **Less Kotlin professionals**: Kotlin programmers need to have in-depth knowledge; since Kotlin is a relatively new language, it can be difficult to find experienced developers in the field domain.
- **Limited sources to learn**: For every new language, the first thing it will suffer from is the sources to learn from other than the language documentation, which, in most cases not clear to everybody. Kotlin does not make the exception, but still not like the other languages thanks to its interoperability with Java, its resemblance to Java, and its concise syntax that makes the language a little bit familiar and easy to learn.

Java

On the other hand, Java, which has been a big part of the JVM-based programming language community for decades, also has its advantages; let us see what are the most common pros and cons of working with Java.

Advantages

Among the advantages of Java language:

- **Checked exceptions**: Even some Kotlin developers consider the omission of try/catch blocks a welcome change and that there is no need to declare or catch any exceptions, but most see that checked exceptions are a need, and it encourages error recovery and the creation of a robust code.

- **Implicit widening conversions**: Java has support for implicit widening conversion; smaller types can be converted to bigger types in this direction: `byte` => `short` => `int` => `long` => `float` => `double`.

  Automatic conversion is only possible for numeric data types and not from numeric to `Char` or `Boolean`.

- **Non-private fields**: To achieve a desirable level of maintainability in any program, we usually adopt Encapsulation. Encapsulation is a mechanism of restricting direct access to some components of an object such that users cannot access state values for all of the variables of a particular object. Encapsulation can be used to hide both data members and data functions or methods associated with an instantiated class or object.

  Non-private fields or public fields in Java are useful in scenarios where the callers of an object need to change according to its representation. It simply means that such fields expose the representation of an object to the callers.

- **Primitive types**: Java has primitive types like `char`, `double`, `float`, and `int`; variables of primitive types are not objects in Java; they are not instantiated from a class or a struct, whereas in Kotlin the equivalent types are only objects; however, the Kotlin compiler uses primitive types but implicitly.

- **Static members**: In programming languages, the keyword static means that one and only one static member is created and used across all instances of the class.

- **Wildcard types**: When working with generics, the special character **?** refers to an unknown type; this character is known as the wildcard. Unlike Java, Kotlin does not offer wildcard types but has declaration-site variance and type projection as alternatives.

- **Ternary operator**: In many programming languages, the ternary operator is like a basic if statement; its syntax is as follows:

  (condition) ? (value if condition is true): (the other value if condition is false)

Disadvantages

We can list the following disadvantages of Java:
- **Verbose and complex code**: Java codes are verbose; there are a lot of words and many complex sentences that are hard to use, remember, and memorize, which can reduce

the readability of the code. It requires more coding, which makes it prone to errors and bugs.

- **Java consumes memory space**: Java garbage collection requires a big amount of memory space, which can affect the efficiency and the system's performance.
- **Old language**: Java is considered as an ancient language and no longer a modern one like Kotlin or Go, which implies certainly that it has many limitations, especially for Android development.
- **Lack of functional programming features**: Java does not have support for functional programming. Functional programming is a paradigm where programs are constructed by applying and composing functions.

Unlike Java, Kotlin supports functional programming in an elegant way.

Next in Kotlin

Kotlin was conceived as a statically typed language, which makes the code statically checkable during compilation time to make sure your code works, is maintainable, and has fewer bugs. Kotlin will work on the improvement of type-safe nullability and many other features that are already implemented to make the language robust and the most stable.

Kotlin will focus a lot on the multiplatform infrastructure; actually, it is already supporting multiplatform by releasing the **Kotlin multiplatform mobile** (**KMM**) and also the release of Compose multiplatform 1.0 in December 2021, the declarative UI framework for Kotlin, which supports all different platform (Web, Desktop, Mobile, and so on) and provide a wide range of different abstractions and utilities to developers.

Kotlin still works to make it easier for the community to build their domain-specific things for the big Kotlin ecosystem. Data science is also a focus for the Kotlin programming language because working with data is an important aspect for many professionals.

Conclusion

So far, you have been introduced to Kotlin's history and the philosophy behind this amazing, concise, and expressive programming language. You also learned what makes Kotlin a better choice over Java for many programming aspects.

In the upcoming chapter, you will be introduced to Kotlin language by learning its basics, starting from variables declaration and initialization, functions and nullable reference to smart casting and handling exceptions.

Points to remember

- Kotlin is an open-source programming language, meaning its source code is freely available for anyone to use, modify, and contribute to.
- Kotlin is recognized as a modern and cutting-edge programming language, designed to address many of the shortcomings of older languages.
- Kotlin was first developed by JetBrains, a software development company, and was introduced to the public in July 2011.
- Kotlin was officially released as a stable version in 2016, marking a significant milestone in its development.
- In 2017, Google announced official support for Kotlin as a first-class language for Android app development, boosting its popularity in the mobile app development community.
- In May 2019, Google declared Kotlin as the preferred language for Android app developers, further solidifying its status in the Android development ecosystem.
- Kotlin is a cross-platform language, which means it can be used to develop applications for various operating systems, including Windows, Linux, Mac, and even JavaScript for web development.
- Kotlin is fully compatible with Java, allowing developers to seamlessly interoperate with existing Java codebases and libraries.
- Kotlin is known for its concise syntax, which reduces boilerplate code, and its strong type system, which enhances code safety.
- Kotlin is considered relatively easy to learn, especially for those with prior experience in Java or other programming languages. Its simplicity and readability make it accessible to a wide range of developers.

Join our book's Discord space

Join the book's Discord Workspace for Latest updates, Offers, Tech happenings around the world, New Release and Sessions with the Authors:

https://discord.bpbonline.com

CHAPTER 2
Kotlin Basics

Introduction

Now, Kotlin is widely used around the world, and its community is constantly growing; many developers who use Kotlin confirm that their work is now faster and more exciting.

Kotlin is a general-purpose language for many platforms; JetBrains releases many versions a year; you can find the latest version on **https://kotlinlang.org**.

Structure

This chapter will cover the following topics:
- Declaration and initialization of variables
- Types and cast
- Null safety
- Create functions
- Choices and conditions
- Loops
- Returns and jumps
- Smart cast with Kotlin

- Work with extensions
- Overloading operators
- Handle exceptions

Objectives

After reading this chapter, you will get an understanding of the basics of the Kotlin programming language. You will be able to deal with variables, data types, the creation of functions, the basic control structures, and also how to work some Kotlin features like smart casting, class extensions, and operator overloading.

Overview

Kotlin is a multiplatform language, and learning Kotlin allows developers to write not only Android mobile applications but also server-side and desktop applications, as well as frameworks and libraries. Kotlin can be used in many fields, such as financial services, telecommunications, embedded systems, medicine, data science, and so on. Kotlin is also designed as a pragmatic language, which means that its main purpose is solving real-world problems.

Kotlin supports multiple programming paradigms, such as imperative programming, object-oriented programming, functional programming, and more. Kotlin is also supported by many development tools such as IntelliJ IDEA, Android Studio, and Eclipse.

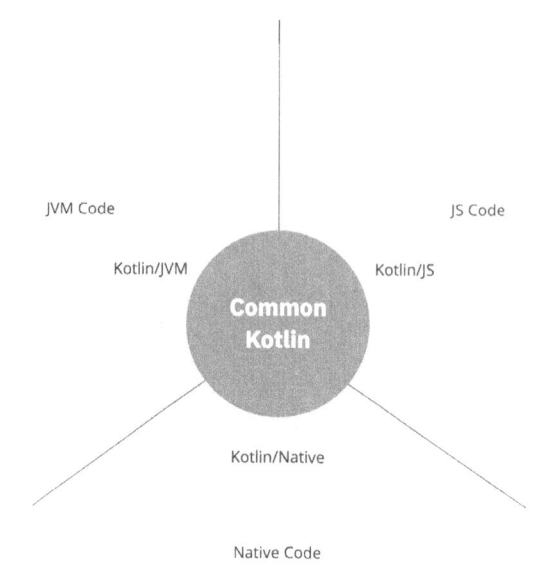

*Figure 2.1. Kotlin multiplatform
(source: https://kotlinlang.org/docs/multiplatform.html)*

Variables

In this section, we will explore one of the building blocks of programming languages: variables. A variable in Kotlin is like a virtual unique container that holds information of a specific type that can be referenced and used throughout the program.

A *variable* can eventually be associated with or identified by a memory address. The variable name is the usual way to reference the stored value. You can think of variables as many named boxes where we can put on each box a different type of product.

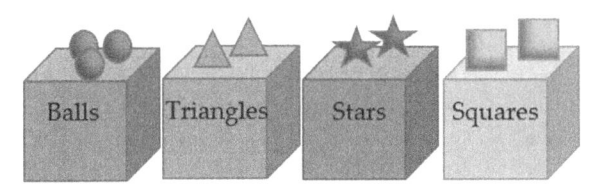

Figure 2.2: Variable illustration

In *Figure 2.2*, you can consider each colored box as a variable, and each box can accept only a certain shape; the shape in this example is the data type the variable can hold. The variable's value can be changed during the execution of the program based on how we declare that one and how we intend to work with, sometimes we need to declare a variable, and we will not need to change its value like the mathematical PI constant ($\pi = 3.14...$).

Declaration and initialization

To declare and initialize a variable of type **String** in Java, you would do it as follows:

```
String myVar = "This is my Java variable";
```

In Kotlin, it is a little bit different, to declare and initialize a variable of type **String** in Kotlin, you do it like the following:

```
val myVar = "This is my Kotlin variable"
```

The keyword **val** lets you ensure that the variable will be assigned only once.

```
val age = 25 // Int
age = 45 // Error
```

For variables that can be reassigned, we use the keyword **var** instead:

```
var x: Int = 0
x = 100 // Ok
```

Note that you do not need to add the semi-colon at the end of the statement, whereas in Java, it is mandatory.

Types and cast

Data types are another building block of a programming language; a data type represents the type of value a variable holds, which tells the compiler or interpreter how the programmer intends to use the data. Based on the data type, we can define the operations allowed on the data, its meaning, and the ways we can store that type of data.

Most programming languages, including Kotlin, allow the programmer to define new data types by combining multiple elements of other types and defining the valid operations on the new data type. For example, in mathematics, a programmer can create a new data type like a complex number, which will include a real part and a complex part.

In computer science, data type is used by the type system to check the correctness of computer programs that access and manipulate the data. The most common data types in programming languages are as follows:

- Integer
- Floating-point types
- Character
- String
- Boolean
- Arrays

Integer types

Numbers in Kotlin are represented by a set of built-in types, and there are four types of integer types for numbers with different sizes and ranges.

Type	Size(bits)	Min value	Max value
Byte	8	−128	127
Short	16	−32,768	32,767
Int	32	−2,147,483,648	2,147,483,647
Long	64	−9,223,372,036,854,775,808	9,223,372,036,854,775,807

Table 2.1: Integer types and their ranges

If you initialize a variable with a numeric value that does not exceed the max value of the `Int` type, this variable will be of type `Int`. If you need to declare the variable as `Long`, you need to append the letter `L` to the value, or you can specify the variable data type by specifying its type.

Example:
```
val age = 25 // Int
val worldPopulation = 7_953_952_577 // Long
val area = 12200L
val engineMaxSpeed: Short = 240
```
In Kotlin, you can make big numbers more readable by using the underscore (_).

Floating-point types

For real numbers (evocative of mathematic real numbers), Kotlin provides floating-point types **Float** and **Double**; floating-point types differ by their decimal place, that is, how many decimal digits they can store. They usually have predefined limits on both their maximum values and their precision. Typically stored internally in the form **significant** × **base**^{**exponent**} (where significant and base are integers), but displayed in familiar decimal form.

For example,

$2.022 = 2022 \times 10^{-3}$

In this example, the significance is **2022**, the base is **10**, and the exponent is **-3**.

Type	Size(bits)	Significant bits	Exponent bits	Decimal digits
Float	32	24	8	6-7
Double	64	53	11	15-16

Table 2.2: *Floating-point types*

Numbers having fractional parts are initialized as **Double** or **Float** variables; fractional part and integer part are separated by a period (**.**); if you do not specify the variable data type explicitly, the compiler will infer the **Double** type.

If you specify the variable type as **Double** and you initialize it with a value without period (**.**), you will get a mismatch type error.

Example:
```
val PI = 3.14 // Double
val bmi = 23.0 // Double
val price: Double = 12000 // Error
```

To explicitly specify the **Float** type, you need to add the suffix **f** or **F** to the value; otherwise, it will be inferred as a **Double**.

Example:

```
val pi = 3.14159265358979 // Double
val piFloat = 3.14159265358979f // Float, actual value is 3.1415926
```

If the value contains more than 6-7 decimal digits, it will be rounded.

Numbers representation on the JVM

On the JVM, numbers are stored as primitive types, such as `int`, `double`, `float`, `byte`, and so on, but when using nullable number references such as `Double?` or using generics, in these cases, numbers are boxed in Java classes `Integer`, `Double`, and so on.

Character

Characters are represented by the type `Char`, the `Char` data type is used to store a single character, and the `char` value must be surrounded by single quotes like `c` or `C`;

Example:

```
val degree: Char = 'A'
println(degree) // Prints A
```

In Java, we could use ASCII values (see the following table) to display certain characters. In Java, 65 will print the character `A`, whereas in Kotlin will display an error.

```
val letterA: Char = 65
println(letterA) // Error
```

ASCII	Hex	Oct	Binary	HTML Code	Character	Description
65	41	101	01000001	&#65;	A	Upper Case Letter A
66	42	102	01000010	&#66;	B	Upper Case Letter B
67	43	103	01000011	&#67;	C	Upper Case Letter C
68	44	104	01000100	&#68;	D	Upper Case Letter D
69	45	105	01000101	&#69;	E	Upper Case Letter E
70	46	106	01000110	&#70;	F	Upper Case Letter F
71	47	107	01000111	&#71;	G	Upper Case Letter G
72	48	110	01001000	&#72;	H	Upper Case Letter H
73	49	111	01001001	&#73;	I	Upper Case Letter I
74	4A	112	01001010	&#74;	J	Upper Case Letter J
75	4B	113	01001011	&#75;	K	Upper Case Letter K
76	4C	114	01001100	&#76;	L	Upper Case Letter L

ASCII	Hex	Oct	Binary	HTML Code	Character	Description
77	4D	115	01001101	&#77;	M	Upper Case Letter M
78	4E	116	01001110	&#78;	N	Upper Case Letter N
79	4F	117	01001111	&#79;	O	Upper Case Letter O
80	50	120	01010000	&#80;	P	Upper Case Letter P
81	51	121	01010001	&#81;	Q	Upper Case Letter Q
82	52	122	01010010	&#82;	R	Upper Case Letter R
83	53	123	01010011	&#83;	S	Upper Case Letter S
84	54	124	01010100	&#84;	T	Upper Case Letter T
85	55	125	01010101	&#85;	U	Upper Case Letter U
86	56	126	01010110	&#86;	V	Upper Case Letter V
87	57	127	01010111	&#87;	W	Upper Case Letter W
88	58	130	01011000	&#88;	X	Upper Case Letter X
89	59	131	01011001	&#89;	Y	Upper Case Letter Y
90	5A	132	01011010	&#90;	Z	Upper Case Letter Z

Table 2.3: ASCII codes for alphabetic letters
(source: https://www.lookuptables.com/text/ascii-table)

String

To work with text in Kotlin, we use the data type **String**, and **String** is a sequence of characters in a double quote (").

In Java, you need to specify the **String** data type to represent a text variable, whereas Kotlin is smart enough to understand that the greeting variable in the following example is a **String** because of the double quote, but if you need to, you can specify the type.

Example:
```
val greeting = "Hello World!" // Inferred as String
val country: String = "Morocco"
```

Elements of a string are characters; you can access them via indexing operation: the character at the index **i** of a string s will be **s[i]**. Note that the indexing starts from 0, which means the first character has an index 0, the second is **1**, and so on.

Example:
```
val s = "You are doing well, keep up the good work."
println(s[4]) // Prints a
```

Hence, you can iterate over the string character using a **for** loop (we will see loops in this chapter).

Example:

```
// Iterate over characters of a string
val str = "ABCD"
for (c in str) println(c)
// Output:
//  A
//  B
//  C
//  D
```

Note that strings are immutable, which means you cannot change a **string** variable once it is initialized. All operations you perform on a **String** variable are stored in a new **String** object, but the original **String** remains the same.

Example:

```
//String immutability
val name = "abc"
println(name.uppercase()) // Prints ABC
println(name) // Prints abc
```

String functions

There are many string functions that you can perform on a **String** object, but remember, the transformation result is stored in a new **String** object because of String immutability.

The most common **String** functions are as follows:

- **length**: The **length** function returns the length of a **String** variable. It counts the number of characters in a **String**, including spaces.

    Example:

    ```
    // String length function
    val myStr = "Kotlin is awesome"
    println(myStr.length) // Prints 16
    ```
- **Lowercase and uppercase**: We already see the uppercase function, which converts the value of a **String** object to uppercase and returns the value result in a new **String** object.

The same thing for the lowercase function, which converts a **String** value to lowercase and returns a new lowercase **String** object.

```
//String lowercase function
val name = "Hello WORLD"
println(name.lowercase()) // Prints hello world
```

- **get**: The **get** function is used to access a string characters by their indexes, and it returns the character of a string at the given index passed to the get function.

```
// String get function
val id = "ID_1"
println(id.get(3)) // Prints 1
```

- **compareTo**: The **compareTo** function compares two strings and returns 0 if both are equal, a negative number if the first string is less than the other string, and a positive number if greater than the other string.

```
// Comparing strings
val str1 = "ABC"
val str2 = "DEF"
println(str1.compareTo(str2)) // Prints negative number
```

- **indexOf**: To check if a string is included in another string, you would like to use the **indexOf** function. It returns the index of the searched string to the string container, if it is not found it returns **-1**.

```
// Search string in a string
val bookText = "Building Kotlin Applications from beginner to advanced"
println(bookText.indexOf("Kotlin")) // Prints 9, text found
println(bookText.indexOf("Java")) // Prints -1
```

- **plus**: To concatenate multiple strings, we use the plus function. The result string will be a new **String** object and not a change of the first string. The same thing would be done with the plus operator (**+**).

Example:

```
// Concatenate strings
val a = "Hello"
val b = "World"
println(a.plus(" ").plus(b)) // Prints Hello World
println(a + " " + b) // Prints Hello World
```

- **String templates**: String templates are another easy way to concatenate and add variables insides inside a **String**. You need to add the dollar sign (**$**) before the value of the variable inside the string to reference its value.

  Example:
  ```
  val fullName = "Adam Smith"
  val rank = 2
  val message = "Hello $fullName, your rank in this contest is $rank"
  println(message) // Prints: Hello Adam Smith, your rank in this contest is 2
  ```
  If you did not add the dollar sign before the name of the variable, it will be considered as a simple text and not reference the variable's value.

- **split**: The **split** function splits a text into a sequence of parts based on a delimiter passed to the function.

  Example:
  ```
  // Split string
  val str3 = "Hello World"
  println(str3.split(" ")) // Prints: ["Hello", "World"]
  ```
  The delimiter in this example is the white space " ", and the result is an array of strings.

Boolean

The type Boolean represents objects that can only have two values, true and false; in Kotlin, a Boolean has a nullable counterpart, Boolean? that also has the null value.

The common built-in operations on booleans include the following:
- **||**: disjunction (logical OR)
- **&&**: conjunction (logical AND)
- **!**: negation (logical NOT)

|| and **&&** work lazily, which means if the first condition is true, the second condition will not be checked.

```
//Booleans
val isTrue: Boolean = true
val isFalse: Boolean = false
val isNull: Boolean? = null
```

```
println(isTrue || isFalse) // Prints: true
println(isTrue && isFalse) // Prints: false
println(!isFalse) // Prints: true
```

Arrays

We use arrays to store multiple values in a single variable instead of creating multiple variables for each value; in Kotlin, arrays are represented by the **Array** class. To create an array, we use the function **arrayOf()** and pass the item values to it, or by using the **Array** constructor with size as a parameter.

To access an element in the array, we use the get function or **[ ]**, and to change the value in the array, we use the **set** function by indicating the index of the element to change and the new value as an argument of the **set** function.

Example:
```
//Arrays
val array1 = arrayOf(1,2,3,4) // array1 = [1,2,3,4]
//print the second element in the array
println(array1.get(1)) // Prints: 2
println(array1[1]) // Prints: 2
// update the value of an element at the given index
array1.set(0, 5) // array1 = [5,2,3,4]
//Using Array constructor
val array2 = Array(4) {"ID_${it+1}"} // array2:["ID_1","ID_2","ID_3", "ID_4"]
```

- **Primitive type arrays**: Kotlin can represent arrays of primitive types without boxing overhead among the primitive type arrays **IntArray**, **ByteArray**, and so on.

    Example:
    ```
    // Primitive type arrays
    val intArr = IntArray(4) // intArr = [0,0,0,0], the same as intArrayOf(0,0,0,0)
    // Initialize an array with a constant
    val intArr2 = IntArray(4) { 2022 } // intArr2 = [2022,2022,2022,2022]
    ```

Null safety

In the Kotlin-type system, we need to distinguish between references that can hold null values (nullable references) and those that cannot accept null values (non-nullable references).

For example, if you intend that a variable can hold a null value, you must add the interrogation mark at the end of the type name. Suppose you need to declare a variable to store an integer number, and you know that this variable can have a null value during the execution of your program. To do so, you need to declare it as **Int?**; otherwise, you will get a compilation error.

Example:

```
//Nullable reference
var age: Int? = 35
age = null //ok


var balance: Int = 100
balance = null // Compilation error
```

In this example, you will not get a **NullPointerException** when you try to perform an operation on the balance or access its properties. But in the case of the age variable, you need to make some checks before accessing it.

```
//Convert the integer value to Double
println(age.toDouble()) // Error NPE
println(balance.toDouble()) // ok
```

However, you need to access nullable reference properties, and to do so, you have many ways:

- **Safe calls**: Kotlin has a safe call operator (**?.**) to handle null references; it executes any action on the reference when it has a non-null value; otherwise, it returns a null value.

    Example:

    ```
    // Safe call operator
    var country: String? = "Morocco"
    println(country?.length) // Prints: 7
    country = null
    println(country?.length) // Prints: null
    ```

- **Check for null in conditions**: Like most programming languages, we can check nullable variables with the **if...else** expression explicitly.

Example:
```
// Null check with if-else expression
val city: String? = "Casablanca"
val cityLength = if (city != null) city.length else null
println(cityLength)
```
- **Elvis operator (?:)**: The Elvis operator expression is as follows:

  `var a = b ?: c`

  The value of a will be **b** if **b** is not null; otherwise, it will be the value of **c**. The right-hand side of the Elvis operator expression is evaluated only if the value of the left-hand side is null.

  Example:

  `val l = text?.length ?: -1`

  In this example, the value of **l** is the text length; if the text value is not null, else **l** value will be **-1**.

- **The !! operator**: The not-null assertion operator (**!!**) converts any null value to a non-null type and throws an NPE if the value is null.

  `val l = text!!.length`

Creating functions

A function in computer science is a block of code that only runs when it is called, and it can take data as inputs, known as parameters, to perform some work. Functions are also known as methods.

Some already seen functions are `main()` and `println()`.

Creating and using a function

In Kotlin, functions are declared with the keyword `fun`. To create your own function, you would like to do it as follows:

```
fun functionName(parameters): returnType {
    body of the function
}
```

Where

- `functionName`: The name of the function; it needs to be expressive as a best practice.

- **parameters**: The input data passed to the function; you can pass as many parameters as you want, separated by a comma and specifying the data type of each parameter.
- **returnType**: The data type that will be returned by the function.

Example:

```
//Calculate the volume of a sphere
fun calculateSphereVolume(radius: Double): Double {
    return 4 * Math.PI * radius.pow(3) / 3
}
```

Function arguments

When you call a function that has parameters inside your code, the data passed to the function as a parameter is called an argument. For example, the function **calculateSphereVolume** has a parameter **radius**; when you want to calculate the volume of a sphere that has a radius of 5.0 m, the value **5.0** is an argument of the function.

Example:

```
// Calculate the sphere volume with 5.0 m radius
val volume = calculateSphereVolume(5.0)
println(volume)
```

- **Default arguments**: In Kotlin, function parameters can have default values set at the function declaration step; the corresponding arguments can be skipped when you call the function, which can reduce the number of overloads.

    Example:

    ```
    // Read data from a CSV file
    fun readCSVFile(filename: String, delimiter: String = ","): Unit {
        /** code here */
    }
    ```

    The default value is defined using the equal sign (=) after the type. So, in this example, when you call the function **readCSVFile** without specifying the argument for the delimiter parameter, the default value will be used ("," in this case):

    ```
    // Read CSV file
    readCSVFile("data.csv") // delimiter = ","
    ```

    But when you have a different delimiter, you need to pass its corresponding argument:

    ```
    // Read CSV file
    ```

```
readCSVFile("data.csv", ";") // delimiter = ";"
```
- **Positional arguments**: Positional arguments are function arguments that must be passed in the same order they are declared.

    Let us consider the following function example:
    ```
    fun openWindow(width: Int, height: Int, resizable: Boolean) {
        // code here...
    }
    ```
    To invoke this function using positional arguments, you do it like the following:
    ```
    openWindow(1000, 800, false)
    ```
    When you have a function with several mixed-type parameters, it will be hard to understand which argument for which parameter without looking at the function declaration; otherwise, you will get them in the wrong order. The named arguments come as a neat solution to this problem.

- **Named arguments**: In Kotlin, when you invoke a function, you can name its arguments; each argument name should be the same as the corresponding parameter name specified in the function declaration.

    To invoke the **openWindow** function using named arguments, you may do it as follows:
    ```
    openWindow(width = 1000, height = 800, resizable = false)
    ```
    If all parameters are named, you can pass them in any order you want;
    ```
    openWindow(resizable = false, height = 800, width = 1000)
    ```

- **Mixing named and positional arguments**: You might notice that named arguments add more text to your code, but wait, there is a way to mix—in a single call—positional arguments for conciseness and named arguments for clarity when it is needed.

    To call a function with mixed arguments, you can do it in different ways; just remember to maintain the order of positional arguments. For example, you can call the **openWindow** function in different ways, like the following:

    o **openWindow(resizable = false, 1000, 800)**

    o **openWindow(1000, height = 800, false)**

    o **openWindow(height = 1000, width = 800, resizable = false)**

Also, when it is combined with default arguments, named arguments become a great way to deal with functions in your code.

Variable number of arguments (varargs)

You can pass a variable number of arguments to a function. To make this possible, you need to mark the last parameter (if the function has many many) using the keyword **vararg** as follows:

```
fun readInputs(vararg args: Int) {
    // consider args as a list
}
```

Then you can use the function with any number of arguments like the following:

```
val userInputs = readInputs(1, 2, 3)
val otherInputs = readInputs(5, 6, 9, 8, 20)
```

Choices and conditions

To handle choices and conditions, we use control structures. Kotlin, as any programming language, has the basic control structures you would expect to find, including the following:

- **if/else-if/else**
- **when**

if/else-if/else

In Kotlin, if statements are just like Java, but in Kotlin, they are expressions; they always return a value. Therefore, there is no need for a ternary operator in Kotlin because a simple if can make this role.

- **If statement**: The **if** statement executes one or more statements when a condition is met; if the condition is **TRUE**, the statement is executed else nothing happens.

    The **if** statement syntax is like the following:

    ```
    if (condition) statement
    ```

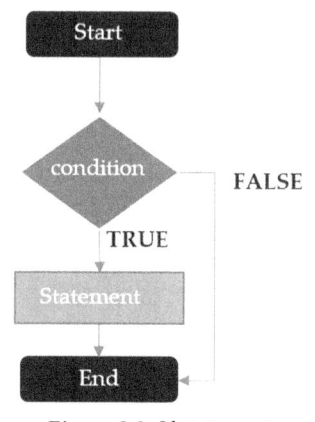

Figure 2.3: If statement

- **If-else statement**: When an **if** condition is met, statements inside the **if** block will execute; otherwise, statements inside the **else** block will execute instead, or else nothing will happen.

    The **if-else** statement syntax is like the following:

    ```
    If(condition) {
        Statements
    } else {
        Other Statements
    }
    ```

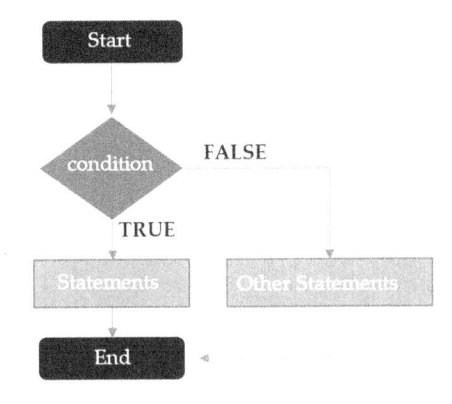

    Figure 2.4: If-else statement

- **If as expression**: The **if** expression always returns a value, which means you can assign its result to a variable.

    Example:

    ```
    val max = if (a > b) a else b
    ```

    In this example, we return the **max** value between two numbers.

when

The **when** statement defines a condition expression with multiple branches, it is similar to the **switch** statement in C-like languages. Its simple form looks like the following:

```
when(gender) {
    "M" -> print("Male")
    "F" -> print("Female")
    else -> print("Unknown")
}
```

The **when** statement compares its argument with all branches one by one until some conditions are met, then it executes the block next to the matched branch and finishes the **when** block.

The **when** can be used in two different ways: as a statement or as an expression.

- **when as a statement**: If **when** is used as a statement, it will be similar to **if** statement; the values for individual branches are ignored, each branch can be a block, and its value will be the last expression in the block.
- **when as an expression**: If **when** is used as an expression, the value of the first matching branch becomes the value of the overall expression. The **else** branch is mandatory in this case.

Unlike switch statement in Java, when branch condition can combine multiple cases in a single line with a comma, like in the following example:

```
when (language) {
    "en", "fr" -> println("Supported")
    else -> println("Not supported")
}
```

You can check if a value in or not in a range:

```
fun isAuthorized(age: Int): Boolean = when(age) {
    in 18..30, !in restrictedAges -> true
    else -> false
}
```

You can also check if a value is or not of a specified type:

```
when(value) {
    is String -> true
    else -> false
}
```

Using **when** does not require a break statement at the end of each case.

Loops

Loops are one of the basic control structures in any programming language, and they allow the execution of a block of code repeatedly until a condition is met.

Kotlin supports many types of loops, which are given as follows:

- **repeat**
- **for** loop
- **while** and **do..while** loops

repeat

In Kotlin, to repeat a statement or a block of statements n times, you can rely on the basic **repeat** loop as follows:

```
repeat(100) { idx ->
    println(idx)
    println("This line will be printed many times")
}
```

You can also get access to the index of the current iteration.

for loop

The **for** loop is used to iterate over a sequence of values or anything that provides an iterator, such as a range, an array, or a collection; it executes a block of statements for each value in the sequence.

In Kotlin, the **for** loop syntax is like the following:

```
for (item in collection) {
    // block of statements
    println(item)
}
```

Example (calculate the sum of squared even numbers less or equal 20):

```
// calculate the sum of squared even numbers less or equal 20
var sum = 0
for (x in 1..20) {
    if (x % 2 == 0) sum += x*x
}
println("Sum = $sum")
```

In Kotlin, you can iterate over a range of numbers in many ways. Let us see some examples:

```
for (i in 100 downTo 0 step 2) {
    println(i)
}
```

In this example, we use the **downTo** function to iterate over a range of numbers in reverse order with a step of 2, which means we decrement by **2** after each iteration. To iterate over a range of numbers in ascendant order using the **until** function, you would do it the following way:

```
for (i in 5 until 50 step 5) {
    println(i)
}
```

The **until** function excludes the last value from iteration; in the preceding example, 50 is not included. To loop through an array or a list with an **index**, the following example shows how:

```
val array = arrayOf("Eat", "Code", "Sleep")
for (index in array.indices) {
    println(array[index])
}
```

Or you can do it using **withIndex** function as follow:

```
for ((index, value) in array.withIndex()) {
    println("The value at index $index is $value")
}
```

while and do .. while loops

The **while** and **do..while** executing their body continuously while their condition is satisfied. The difference between the two is the condition checking time:

- The **while** checks the condition and, if it is satisfied, executes the body and then returns to the condition check.
- The **do...while** executes the body and then checks the condition. If it is satisfied, the loop repeats. So, the body of **do...while** executes at least once regardless of the condition.

The syntax of the **while** and **do...while** loops are as follows:

```
do {
    val x = performSomeWork()

} while (x != -1)

while (answer != "No") {
    answer = continueTheSurvey()
}
```

Returns and jumps

Kotlin supports the following three types of jump expression:
- `Return`
- `Break`
- `Continue`

Return

The **return** expression, by default, returns from the nearest enclosing function or anonymous function; to return from an outer function, we can use a qualified return expression.

As any expression in Kotlin can be marked with a label, the label has a form like **abc@**, **func2@**, **loop10@**, and so on; it is a text followed by the **@** sign. You can qualify the return expression with a label (**return@label**), so when the return invoked, the execution returns from the labeled function (**label@**).

The most important use case is returning from a lambda expression. Let us take a look at the following example:

```
fun doSomething() {
    (1..10).forEach {
        if (it == 5) return // return from the outer function doSomething
        println(it)
    }
    println("This line will not execute!")
}
```

In this example, the return expression will return from the outer function **doSomething** and not from the function **forEach**; hence, the code after the **forEach** will not execute.

If you need to return only from the lambda expression called by the **forEach** function, you need to do it the following way:

```
fun doSomething() {
    (1..10).forEach innerLoop@ {
        if (it == 5) return@innerLoop // return from the forEach loop and
                                      not from the outer function doSomething
        println(it)
    }
```

```
        println("This line will be printed!")
    }
```

Or you can replace the lambda expression inside the **forEach** function with an anonymous function without using labels as follows:

```
fun doSomething() {
    (1..10).forEach(fun (value) {
        if (value == 5) return // return from the forEach loop and not
        from the outer function doSomething
        println(value)
    })
    println("This line will be printed!")
}
```

Break

The **break** expression is used to terminate the execution of the nearest enclosing loop, it is usually used with an **if** condition.

Example:

```
for (x in 1..10) {
    if (x == 7) break
    println(x)
}
```

The **for** loop terminates execution when the break is invoked.

We suppose that we have a nested **for** loop, and we want to terminate the outer loop when a condition is met in the inner **for** loop; in this case, we will need to use a labeled break expression.

Example:

```
outer@ for (col in columns) {
    inner@ for (row in rows) {
        if (row > col) break@outer
        println("$row, $col")
    }
}
```

Continue

The **continue** construct is used to skip the current iteration of a loop and jump to the end of the loop body. It is always used with an **if/else** construct.

For example:
```
while (i > 0) {
    // code here
    if (i == 10) continue
    // code continue here
}
```

In this example, when the **i** is equal to **10**, **continue** is executed and skips all code inside the while loop block and goes to the next iteration. The **continue** can also be used with labels; continue with labels works the same way as return with labels.

Example:
```
here@ for (col in columns) {
    for (row in rows) {
        if (row > col) continue@here
        println("($row, $col)")
    }
}
```

Smart cast with Kotlin

In many cases, you need to work with mixed data types, so you will need to know the type of an object at runtime before working with it and maybe call its methods and access its properties. In Java, we use the instance of operator to check if an object is an instance of a given type before working with it; then, we need to explicitly cast to the target type.

Here is an example of how it can be implemented in Java:
```
private int getSize(Object obj) {
    if (obj instanceof String) {
        return ((String) obj).length();
    } else if (obj instanceof Integer) {
        return ((Integer) obj).intValue();
```

```
    } else if (obj instanceof List<?>) {
        return ((List) obj).size();
    }
    return 0;
}
```

Kotlin, on the other hand, is smart enough to deal with these scenarios. The operator is and its negation !is are used to check the type of an object, then the cast is done implicitly. The next example shows the implementation of the previous example of the **getSize** function in Kotlin using smart casting.

```
fun getSize(obj: Any): Int = when(obj) {
    is String -> obj.length
    is Int -> obj
    is List<*> -> obj.size
    else -> 0
}
```

It is more elegant and concise than Java.

Work with extensions

Kotlin has come with many features, among these features the **extension functions**. It allows us to extend the functionality of a class with our user-defined functions without the need to inherit from the class or decorate it in any way.

The idea behind extension functions is to add new functions to third-party library classes that we cannot modify and call them in a usual way. There are also the extension properties, which are new properties we define for an existing function.

Extension functions

To create an extension function for an existing class, either it is a Java class or a Kotlin class, we use the class as a receiver followed by a period (.) and the function name, like the following:

```
Reciver.functionName(parameter) {/* .. */}
```

For example, let us look at the following simple example of a String print extension function:

```
fun String.print() {
    println(this)
}
```

The **this**, in the example, corresponds to the receiver object. To call this extension function in your code, all you need to do is the following:

```
"Hello world".print() // will print Hello world on the console
```

Now, every **String** instance has a **print()** function, as simple as that.

But how do Kotlin extensions work? Kotlin extensions are resolved statically, which means that the extended function is determined by the type on which it is invoked at compile-time.

Let us take a look at the following example to better understand how that works:

```
open class Animal
class Cat: Animal()

fun Animal.getType() = "Animal"
fun Cat.getType() = "Cat"

fun printClassType(a:Animal) {
    println(a.getType())
}

fun main() {
printClassType(Cat()) // Prints: Animal
}
```

This will print **Animal** because the extension function called depends only on the declared type of the parameter **a**, which is the **Cat** class.

Extension properties

Kotlin support for extension properties is much like the extension functions.

Example:

```
val <T> List<T>.lastIndex: Int?
    get() = if (size > 0) size - 1 else null
```

Overloading operators

Kotlin has many features, and one of these is the operator overloading. The idea here is to apply some arithmetic operations to any object. Kotlin documentation says that by convention, if your class defines a special method named **plus**, then you can use the **+** operator on instances of this class.

Example:

```
fun main() {

    val z = Complex(1f, -1f) + Complex(2f, -3f)
    println(z) // Prints: Complex(3, -4)


}

data class Complex(val x: Float, val y: Float) {
    operator fun plus(o: Complex) :Complex{
        return Complex(x+o.x, y+o.y)
    }

    override fun toString(): String {
        return "Complex($x, $y)"
    }
}
```

In this example, we just overridden the **plus** function, and then we could use the **+** operator to add two objects.

There are many other special functions that we can override for the other arithmetic operations.

The following table lists some common special functions and their equivalent arithmetic operations. Let us suppose **c1** and **c2** are two instances of **Complex** class:

Expression	Function called
c1 + c2	c1.plus(c2)
c1 - c2	c1.minus(c2)
c1 * c2	c1.times(c2)
c1 / c2	c1.div(c2)
c1 % c2	c1.rem(c2)
c1 ++	c1.inc()
c1 --	c1.decT()

Table 2.4: Special functions for arithmetic operations

There are many other special functions you can override depending on the use case you are dealing with.

Handle exceptions

Exception handling is the operation of gracefully dealing with problems that occur during the execution of a program without disrupting the conventional flow.

In Kotlin, we do not support checked exceptions like Java does; fortunately, it is considered as a controversial feature in Java by most developers because it just increases the boilerplate code without any additional increase in the quality code.

All exception classes in Kotlin inherit from the **Throwable** class. To throw an exception in Kotlin, we use the **throw** expression:

```
throw Exception("I am an exception")
```

And we use **try…catch** expression to catch an exception:

```
try {
    // code here
} catch (e: Throwable) {
    // handle exception here
} finally {
    // Optional block
}
```

Try is an expression that means it can have a return value. The returned value will be the last value in the **try** block; if an exception occurs, it will be the last value in the **catch** block. The **finally** block does not affect the result of the expression.

Example:

```
val userInput = "12"
//Try expression
val age: Int? = try {
    userInput.toInt()
} catch (e: Throwable) {
    null
}
```

Conclusion

So far, you have learned the basics of Kotlin programming language and some of its key features, like nullable reference, smart cast, and class extensions. But you might have some ambiguous points you had seen in this chapter about classes, objects or instances, and so for.

In the upcoming chapter, you will be taught all about these points and learn a new programming paradigm, which is **object-oriented programming (OOP)**.

Points to remember

The following are some key points to remember:

- To declare a variable, use **val** if the variable is assigned only once and **var** if you want to reassign it.
- Kotlin is smart enough to cast types implicitly when the instance is checked as an instance of a given type, to check if an instance is of a specified type, we use the "is" or "!is" operators.
- Kotlin distinguishes between references that can hold null (nullable reference) and those that cannot (non-nullable reference).
- Use safe call operator (**?.**) on nullable references to access its properties.
- Functions with named, default, and positional arguments, in addition to **varargs**, are a great combination to remember.
- Whenever you work with loops, returns, or jumps, remember to use labeled expressions.
- Extensions are a very helpful feature that allows you to extend a third-party class with new functionalities.
- Operator overloading lets you define your arithmetic functions on your custom classes.

Join our book's Discord space

Join the book's Discord Workspace for Latest updates, Offers, Tech happenings around the world, New Release and Sessions with the Authors:

https://discord.bpbonline.com

Chapter 3
OOP with Kotlin

Introduction

Object-oriented programming (**OOP**) is a programming paradigm based on the concept of *objects*, which can contain fields (attributes or properties) that hold data and procedures (known as **methods**) that use the data to perform dedicated work.

Most OOP languages, including Kotlin, are class-based, meaning that objects are instances of classes, which also determine their types.

Structure

This chapter will cover the following topics:
- Classes and objects
- Inheritance
- Properties
- Interfaces
- Visibility modifiers
- Types of classes

- Delegation
- Type aliases

Objectives

After reading this chapter, you will be able to create some basic real-world applications in Kotlin by following an object-oriented way, and this goal will be possible by following this chapter's sections on object-oriented programming.

You will examine and discover what makes a language object-oriented by learning about the pillars of this concept.

Overview

Kotlin does not only introduce new concepts to the object-oriented programming paradigm but also comes with new practical improvements and features. The OOP concept allows one to solve complex problems by using objects, and it relies on four principles, which are encapsulation, inheritance, abstraction, and polymorphism.

OOP has many advantages, including the following:
- **Re-usability**: It means that we can use some facilities without the need to create them once again by relying on class reuse.
- **Data redundancy**: It means that the same data can be held in two different places using objects.
- **Code maintenance**: Means you can easily maintain code by incorporating new changes to the code.
- **Design benefits**: It gives designers the possibility to design programs in different ways.
- **Easy troubleshooting**: Encapsulation, as an example, is a big help in terms of finding and fixing issues in your code.

Classes and objects

In this section, you will be introduced to object-oriented programming with Kotlin. You will be taught about the building blocks of OOP, which are classes and objects. Next, we will learn about what is a Kotlin class and how to use it to create objects.

Kotlin class

In OOP, a Kotlin *class* is like a template for creating objects. It contains data field descriptions (properties, fields, data members, or attributes); these are usually field types and names that will be associated with state variables at program run time and contain behaviors or methods, which are functions that operate on classes or objects, these methods may alter the state of an object or provide ways for accessing it.

Classes are used to create new objects, and it is a mechanism of organizing information about a type of data so programmers can reuse elements when making multiple instances of that data type.

In the real world, you may need to work with different objects of the same kind but with different properties' values. Let us take an example of a car, there are many car models, but each car has the same properties such as *model, color, speed, category*, and so on.

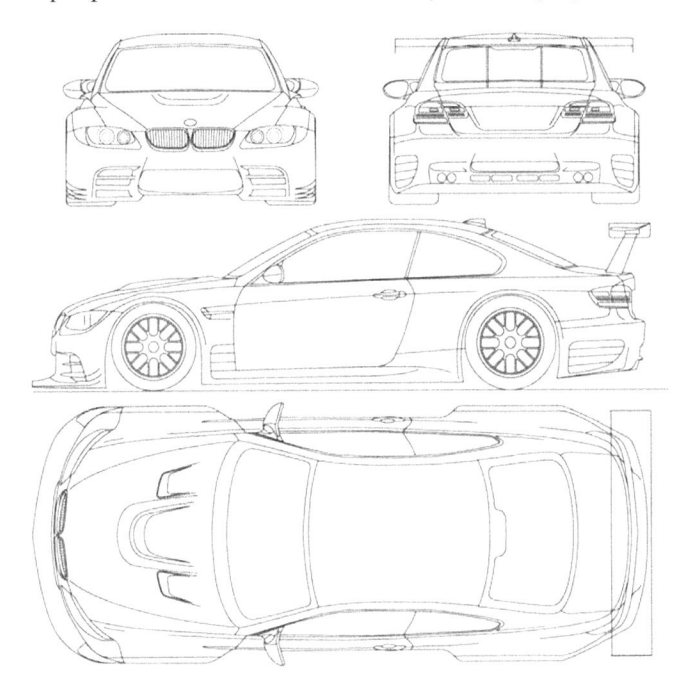

Figure 3.1: *Blueprint of a car*
(source: https://i.pinimg.com/564x/e5/df/62/e5df62d42cdfe225705ea0e95af2f0ca.jpg)

From these blueprints, many factories can build different models; this is the same concept with classes in programming languages:

Figure 3.2: Different car models (source: pinterest.com/)

To define a class in Kotlin, we use the keyword **class** followed by the class name then we declare the properties and methods of the class inside two curly braces.

To define a **Car** class in Kotlin, you may do it using the following code:

```kotlin
class Car {
    var model: String? = null
    var color: String = "Black"
    var speed: Float = 0f
    var category: String? = null
    var running: Boolean = false

    fun run() {
        running = true
    }

    fun accelerate() {
        if (running) speed = speed.plus(1f)
    }
```

```kotlin
    fun stop() {
        running = false
    }

    fun brake() {
        if(speed <= 0f) speed = 0f
        else if (running) speed = speed.minus(1f)
    }

    fun displayCarDetails() {
        println("Car model: $model \nColor: $color \nSpeed: $speed \
        nCategory: $category \nRunning: $running")
    }
}
```

In the preceding **Car** class definition, we have four properties of the car, which are as follows:

- Model
- Color
- Speed
- Category
- Running

And five methods are as follows:

- **run()** to run the car
- **accelerate()**, which increases the car's speed; hence, the car starts moving
- **stop()** method to stop the car
- **brake()** to decrease the car speed
- **displayCarDetails()** to display the car properties

These properties and methods will be common to all objects you will create based on this Car class but with different values.

- **Primary constructor**: In Kotlin, a class can have a primary constructor; it is a part of the class header which can be added after the class name, and it is defined using the keyword **constructor** and with optional parameters.

Example:

```
class Person constructor(var age: Int, var gender: String, var name: String) {
}
```

And if the constructor does not have any annotation or visibility modifier, the **constructor** keyword can be omitted:

```
class Person(var age: Int, var gender: String, var name: String) {
}
```

The properties declared in the constructor using the keyword **var** are mutable, which means that they can be reassigned; if you want these properties to be read-only, you need to use the keyword **val** instead.

```
class Person(val age: Int, val gender: String, val name: String) {
}
```

If a class does not declare any primary or secondary constructor, a primary constructor with no arguments will be generated.

- **Secondary constructor**: A secondary constructor in Kotlin, which can be defined in the body of the class, is declared using the keyword **constructor**:

```
class Manager {
    constructor(name: String, salary: Double, age: Int) {}
}
```

A class in Kotlin can have one or more secondary constructors. If the class has a primary constructor, all secondary constructors need to delegate to the primary constructor. To delegate to another constructor of the same class, we use the keyword **this**, as shown follows:

```
class Employee(var name: String) {
    constructor(name: String, supervisor: Manager):this(name) {}
}
```

Objects

In the object-oriented programming paradigm, the object can be a combination of variables, functions, and data structures; in particular, in class-based variations of the paradigm, it refers to a particular instance of a class.

An object is a real-world entity, and it will contain all properties and methods of the base class from which we create the object. To create an object or an instance of a class, we use the following syntax:

```
var object = ClassName()
```

Or

```
var object = ClassName(arguments)
```

Kotlin does not have a new keyword to create a class instance. In the first syntax, the object will be created with the default values of the class properties, whereas in the second syntax, the object will be an instance of the class with the arguments passed to its corresponding constructor.

Let us see how we create objects in Kotlin. In the following example, we will create a **Car** instance like the following:

```
var bmw = Car()
```

We can access the class properties and methods using the dot (.) operator after the object name and then the name of the property or method. In the following example, we can assign values to the **bmw** object properties and call its methods.

Example:

```
fun main() {
    var bmw = Car()
    bmw.model = "X6"
    bmw.speed = 360f
    bmw.color = "White"
    bmw.category = "4x4"

    bmw.run()
    bmw.displayCarDetails()
    bmw.accelerate()
    bmw.accelerate()

    bmw.displayCarDetails()

}
```

The following will be the output of the preceding code:

```
Car model: X6
Color: White
```

```
Speed: 360.0
Category: 4x4
Running: true
Car model: X6
Color: White
Speed: 362.0
Category: 4x4
Running: true
```

When the class has primary or secondary constructors, we can create instances by passing the arguments corresponding to one constructor as if it were a regular function:

```
val manager = Manager("Adele DOE", 12000.0, 45)
```

Inheritance

Inheritance is one of the building blocks of OOP. It is a mechanism of basing an object or class upon another object or class, retaining a similar implementation. It can also be defined as deriving new classes from other classes, which we call superclass or base class. The derived class is called the **child** class or **subclass**.

In inheritance, a child object acquires all the properties and behaviors of the parent object with some exceptions.

The main purpose of inheritance is to reuse code. For example, the objects **bird**, **fish**, and **reptile** are all animals, so they are all subclasses of the class **Animal**; hence, code that can be common to all these objects can be consolidated into the **Animal** class, and then, all subclasses of this class will inherit this code.

Inheritance in Kotlin

In Kotlin, all classes have a common superclass, which is **Any**, and it is a superclass for any class with no superclass declared. The **Any** class has three methods: **toString()**, **equals()**, and **hashCode()**; these methods are defined for all Kotlin classes and can be overridden with a custom implementation.

Let us see an example of how we can work with inheritance in Kotlin. The following figure is a presentation of how a class **Person** can be inherited:

OOP with Kotlin ◼ 53

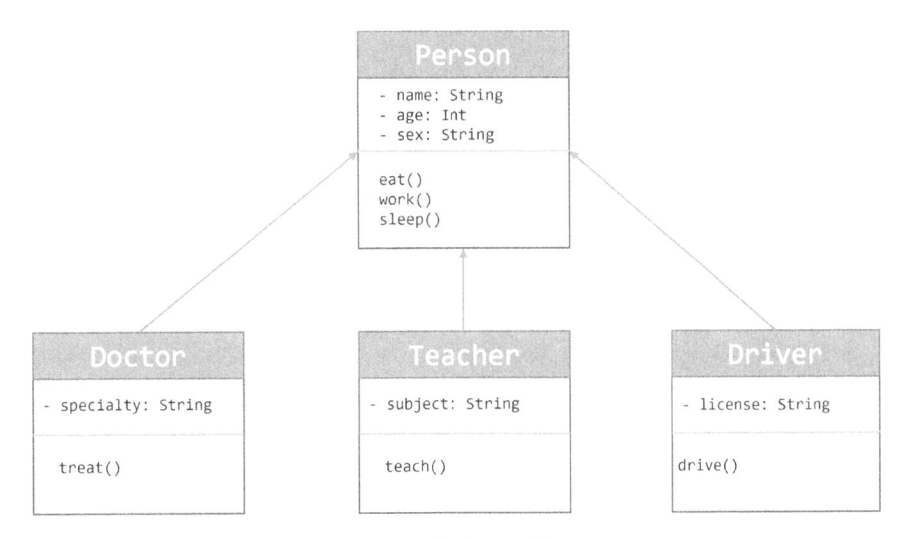

Figure 3.3: Inheritance diagram

This diagram in the preceding figure means that the **Teacher**, **Driver**, and **Doctor** are all **Persons**, so they all inherit the properties and methods of the **Person** class, which is, in this case, the parent class or the superclass; hence, all the properties: **name**, **age**, and **sex**, and all methods: **eat()**, **work()**, and **sleep()** are accessible from **Doctor**, **Teacher** and **Driver** instances/objects.

Let us now see how we can implement this in Kotlin.

In Kotlin, all classes are final by default; you cannot inherit a class until you make it open by adding the keyword **open** before the keyword **class**.

Example:

The **Person** class would be defined as follows:

```
open class Person {
    var name: String? = null
    var age: Int? = null
    var sex: String? = null

    fun work() {
        println("$name is working!")
    }

    fun eat() {
```

```kotlin
        println("$name is eating!")
    }

    fun sleep() {
        println("$name is sleeping!")
    }

    override fun toString(): String {
        return "Name: $name\nAge: $age\nSex: $sex"
    }
}
```

In this example, you might notice an **override** keyword before the **fun** keyword of the function **toString()**. Actually, the **Person** class inherit from the class **Any** by default, as we explained before, and while the class **Any** already has the method **toString()**, you cannot create the same parent method with the same parameters for the inherited class or child class (**Person** class in this example) until you override it by adding the keyword override.

Let us move on and see how we can implement the classes **Doctor**, **Teacher**, and **Driver**, which all inherit from the same superclass **Person** and have their own custom methods and properties.

To make a **Child** class inherit from a **Parent** class, in Kotlin, we do it like the following:

`class Child: Parent() {}`

So, in our example, we would implement it like the following:

```kotlin
    class Teacher: Person() {
        var subject: String? = null

        fun teach() {
            println("I am teaching $subject")
        }
    }

    class Driver: Person() {
        var license: String? = null
```

```kotlin
    fun drive() {
        println("I am driving a car !")
    }
}

class Doctor: Person() {
    var specialty: String? = null

    fun treat() {
        println("I am treating people !")
    }
}
```

Inherited class instances/objects can now access the properties and methods of the parent class.

The following example demonstrates how, by creating objects from child classes (**Doctor**, **Teacher**, and **Driver**), these objects can access the parent class (**Person**) properties and methods:

```kotlin
fun main() {
    val teacher = Teacher()
    teacher.name = "Ameer Khan"
    teacher.age = 45
    teacher.sex = "Male"
    teacher.subject = "Math"
    println("-- Teacher --")
    println(teacher.toString())
    teacher.work()
    teacher.teach()
    teacher.eat()
    teacher.sleep()
    println("-------------")


    val doctor = Doctor()
```

```
        doctor.name = "Jane Smith"
        doctor.age = 40
        doctor.sex = "Female"
        doctor.specialty = "Cardiologist"
        println("-- Doctor --")
        println(doctor.toString())
        doctor.work()
        doctor.treat()
        doctor.eat()
        doctor.sleep()
        println("-------------")

        val driver = Driver()
        driver.name = "Karim Rafi"
        driver.age = 30
        driver.sex = "Male"
        driver.license = "N202203"
        println("-- Driver --")
        println(driver.toString())
        driver.work()
        driver.drive()
        driver.eat()
        driver.sleep()
        println("-------------")

}
```

The output will be the following:

```
-- Teacher --
Name: Ameer Khan
Age: 45
Sex: Male
Ameer Khan is working!
```

```
I am teaching Math
Ameer Khan is eating!
Ameer Khan is sleeping!
------------
-- Doctor --
Name: Jane Smith
Age: 40
Sex: Female
Jane Smith is working!
I am treating people !
Jane Smith is eating!
Jane Smith is sleeping!
------------
-- Driver --
Name: Karim Rafi
Age: 30
Sex: Male
Karim Rafi is working!
I am driving a car !
Karim Rafi is eating!
Karim Rafi is sleeping!
------------
```

Overriding parent class methods

To override a method of the base class, this method should be open, which means you need to add the keyword **open** before the method definition.

Let us take an example of the previous **Doctor** class. To override the **sleep()** method from the base class **Person**, this last one should be declared as **open**; otherwise, the compiler will complain, and you should use the override keyword in the derived class (**Doctor** class) instead as follows:

```
open class Person {
    // properties
    // other methods
```

```kotlin
        open fun sleep() {
            println("$name is sleeping!")
        }
    }
```

And then, the **Doctor** class should be like the following:

```kotlin
    class Doctor: Person() {
        var specialty: String? = null

        fun treat() {
            println("I am treating people !")
        }

        override fun sleep() {
            println("I don't sleep enough")
        }
    }
```

Now, when you run the program, the output should be different for the **Doctor** instances:

```kotlin
    fun main() {
        val doctor = Doctor()
        doctor.name = "Jane Smith"
        doctor.age = 40
        doctor.sex = "Female"
        doctor.specialty = "Cardiologist"

        println("-- Doctor --")
        println(doctor.toString())
        doctor.work()
        doctor.treat()
        doctor.eat()
        doctor.sleep()
    }
```

The following will be the output:

```
-- Doctor --
Name: Jane Smith
Age: 40
Sex: Female
Jane Smith is working!
I am treating people !
Jane Smith is eating!
I don't sleep enough
```

Abstract classes

Suppose you have a class with some functions, and you want each child class must implement these functions to perform their own operations. In this case, you should mark these functions as abstract.

By doing this, you ensure the following:

- No need to provide the body of functions definitions in the abstract class
- The child classes must override these functions and provide their own implementations.

If any function of a class is marked abstract, the class should also be marked abstract. We can declare an **abstract** class, along with some or all its members. An abstract member is not implemented in its class. There is no need to annotate abstract classes or functions as **open**.

Let us see an example of a **Shape** class with one function **calculateArea()**:

```
abstract class Shape {
    abstract fun calculateArea()
}

class Circle: Shape() {
    override fun calculateArea() {
        println("Here I calculate the Circle area.")
    }
}

class Triangle: Shape() {
```

```kotlin
        override fun calculateArea() {
            println("Here I calculate the Triangle area.")
        }
    }

    fun main() {
        val c1 = Circle()
        c1.calculateArea()

        val t1 = Triangle()
        t1.calculateArea()
    }
```

The following will be the output:

```
Here I calculate the Circle area.
Here I calculate the Triangle area.
```

A non-abstract open member can be overridden with an abstract member.

```kotlin
    open class CustomShape {
        open fun draw() {
            // implementation here
        }
    }

    abstract class MyCustomPolygon: CustomShape() {
        abstract override fun draw()
    }
```

Please remember the following points:

- You cannot create an object for **abstract** class.
- All properties and member functions of an **abstract** class are by default non-abstract. So, if you want to override these members in the child class, then you need to use the **open** keyword.
- If you declare a member function as abstract, you do not need to annotate it with an **open** keyword because it is open by default.

Properties

In Kotlin, class properties can be declared either as mutable using the keyword **var** or read-only using the keyword **val**. Properties are like fields in Java but with some differences. Properties have auto-generated getters and setters.

In the previous section, we saw an example of **Person** properties, which are **name**, **age**, and **sex**:

```
open class Person {
    var name: String? = null
    var age: Int? = null
    var sex: String? = null

    /* … */
}
```

To access a property, you use its name like we did in the last example:

```
val adam = Person()
adam.name = "Adam Doe"
adam.age = 45
adam.sex = "Male"
```

Getters and setters

To declare a property in Kotlin, the full syntax is the following:

```
var <propertyName>[: <PropertyType>] [= <property_initializer>]
    [<getter>]
    [<setter>]
```

In this syntax, **property_initializer**, **getter**, and **setter** are optional. The **PropertyType** is not required if it can be inferred from the initializer or from the getter's return type.

```
var authorized = true // has type: Int
```

In the case of read-only properties, the full syntax has two differences: it starts with **val** instead of **var** and does not allow a **setter** method.

```
val demoLicense: String? // type: String, and default getter must be initialized
val defaultOrder = 1 // has type: Int and default getter
```

In Kotlin, getters' and setters' methods do not have to be explicitly defined for a property.

```
var name: String = "Adam Doe"
```

The previous code is the same as the following:

```
var defaultTitle: String = "M"
    get() { //getter
        return field
    }
    set(value) { //setter
        field = value
    }
```

Backing fields

To define a custom logic for the methods **get()** and **set()**, we use the keyword field to access and modify the property's *value*. In Kotlin, fields are only used as parts of properties to hold their values in memory. Fields cannot be declared directly. However, Kotlin provides a backing field to properties automatically when it is needed.

We can define custom getters or setters to perform many numbers of useful operations like input validation, logging, or data transformations. When adding this business logic directly to the property's modifiers (**getters** and **setters**), we ensure that it is always executed when the property is accessed.

Example:

Let us add a custom property to the **Person** class (**hasPermission**):

```
var hasPermission: Boolean = false
    get() {
        if (!field) println("$name need a permission to work.")
        return field
    }
    set(value) {
        if ( value && age!! > 18) {
            field = value
        } else field = false
    }
```

Interfaces

Kotlin interfaces are similar to abstract classes but with some key differences. Kotlin interfaces can be considered as fully abstract classes because all functions and properties of an interface are abstract.

Kotlin interface can be used as a blueprint of a class, where we can define the properties and the functions' headers with their parameters and return types, and when a class is implemented, the interface will define these functions' implementations.

What makes an interface different from an abstract class is that interfaces cannot store a state. In Kotlin, like many other languages, the keyword **interface** is used to declare an interface:

Example:

```
interface DatabaseInterface {
    fun findAll()
    fun deleteALl() {
        // Optional body
    }
}
```

In Kotlin, a class can implement one or many interfaces:

```
class ChildRepository: DatabaseInterface {
    override fun findAll() {
        // implementation here...
    }
}
```

Properties in interfaces

Interfaces can have properties either declared as abstract or provide an implementation for accessors; properties in interfaces cannot have backing fields.

```
interface DemoInterface {
    val myProp: Int // abstract by default

    val myPropWithImplementation: String
        get() = "Kotlin interface"
```

```kotlin
    fun demo() {
        println(myProp)
        println(myPropWithImplementation)
    }
}

class Child: DemoInterface {
    override val myProp: Int = 2022
}
```

Interfaces inheritance

Interfaces in Kotlin can implement other interfaces, and each interface can have its member implementations, properties and functions. Classes implementing such an interface must define only the missing implementations.

```kotlin
    interface Subscriber {
        val subscriptionNumber: String
    }

    interface Person: Subscriber {
        val firstName: String
        val lastName: String
        val idCard: String

        override val subscriptionNumber: String
            get() = "2022$idCard@$lastName"
    }

    data class Visitor(
        // implementing 'subscriptionNumber' is optional
        override val firstName: String,
        override val lastName: String,
        override val idCard: String,
```

```
        val lastVisit: Date
): Person
```

If a class implements more than one interface and two or more interfaces have the same function, the class must implement this function in order to avoid conflicts.

Visibility modifiers

Visibility modifiers are keywords that set the visibility or accessibility of classes, objects, interfaces, properties, constructors, and functions from outside a package. Kotlin has four visibility modifiers: **private**, **protected**, **internal**, and **public**, and public is always the default one if none is specified.

Visibility modifiers can be set to classes, interfaces, objects, functions and constructors, properties, and also their setters and getters.

Packages

Functions, properties, classes, objects, and interfaces can be declared at the *top-level* directly inside a package:

```
// filename is visibility.kt

package chapter_03.visibility_modifiers

fun sayHello() {/* ... */ }
class Demo { /* ... */}
```

Modifier	Description
public	Declarations are visible everywhere
private	Visible inside the file containing the declaration
internal	Visible inside the same module (a set of Kotlin files compiled together)
protected	Not available for packages (used for subclasses)

Table 3.1: *Visibility modifiers*

Examples:

```
package chapter_03.visibility_modifiers

private fun foo() { /*...*/ } // visible inside visibility.kt
```

```
public var bar: Int = 5  // property is visible everywhere
    private set          // setter is visible only in visibility.kt

internal val baz = 6    // visible inside the same module
```

Class and interface visibility modifiers

Inside a class or an interface, visibility modifiers can be applied to properties and functions:

Modifier	Description
`public`	Visible to any client who can see the declaring class
`private`	Visible inside the class only
`protected`	Visible inside the class and its subclasses
`internal`	Visible to any client inside the module that can see the declaring class

Table 3.2: Visibility modifiers inside classes and interfaces

In Kotlin, an outer class does not see private members of its inner classes. When overriding a protected or an internal member and not specifying the visibility explicitly, the overriding member will have the same visibility as the original.

Examples:

```
open class Base {
    private val x = 1
    protected open val y = 2
    internal open val z = 3
    val t = 4   // public by default

    protected class Nested {
        public val p: Int = 5
    }
}

class Derived : Base() {
    // x is not visible
```

```
        // y, z and t are visible
        // Nested and p are visible

        override val y = 5    // 'y' is protected
        override val z = 7    // 'z' is internal
    }

    class Unrelated(b: Base) {
        // b.x, b.y are not visible
        // b.z and b.t are visible (same module)
        // Base.Nested is not visible, and Nested::p is not visible either
    }
```

Types of classes

Classes in Kotlin are used in different ways.

Simple class

As we already have seen, to declare a simple class, we use the keyword class followed by the class name:

```
    // Simple class
    class Simple {
        val prop: Int = 25

        fun detail() {
            println("Simple with prop = $prop")
        }
    }
```

In this example, we created a simple class with one property **prop** and one function **detail()**.

Open class

You already know that classes in Kotlin are final by default, and other classes cannot inherit from the final class. Then, you knew that to make it inheritable, you need to mark your class as **open**, as shown follows:

```kotlin
// Open class
open class Animal(private val alive: Boolean = true) {

    fun isAlive(): Boolean {
        return alive
    }
}

class Tiger(val name: String): Animal() {

    fun roar(): String {
        return "roar-roar"
    }
}
```

Data class

The main purpose of a data class in Kotlin is to hold data, some standard functionalities and some utility functions. These data classes are marked with the keyword **data**, as shown in the following code:

```kotlin
// Data class
data class Patient(val name: String, val age: Int)
```

For classes marked with data keywords, all the following functions will be created for us:

- **toString()**
- **hashCode()/equals()**
- **copy()**: Use the **copy()** function to copy an object, allowing you to alter some of its properties while keeping the rest unchanged

Nested class

A nested class is a class declared inside another class:

```kotlin
// Nested class
class Parent {

    val name = "Parent"
    fun detail() = "I am a $name class"
```

```
    class Nested {
        val name = "Nested"
        fun detail() = "I am a $name class"
    }
}
```

In order to access the nested class, we specify the name of its outer class. So, the show function of the nested class is invoked like `Parent.Nested().show()`. A nested class cannot access the members of the outer class.

Inner class

Inner classes are created with the **inner** keyword. Unlike nested classes, they can access the members of their outer classes:

```
// Inner class
class Outer {
    val name1 = "Outer"
    fun show() = "the name: $name1"

    inner class Inner {

        val name2 = "Inner"
        fun show() = "data: $name2 and $name1"
    }
}
```

After the execution of the following code:

```
fun main() {

    println(Outer().show())
    println(Outer().Inner().show())

}
```

You will get the following output:

`the name: Outer`

`data: Inner and Outer`

Sealed class

A sealed class represents restricted class hierarchies, which make it possible to have full control over inheritance. It is used when a value can have one type from a limited set but cannot have any other type.

A sealed class is abstract and can contain abstract members. It cannot have public constructors (The constructors are private by default). A sealed class can have a subclass, but it must either be in the same file or nested inside the sealed class declaration.

Let us see an example of a sealed **Shape** class with subclasses:

```kotlin
// Sealed class
sealed class Shape
class Circle(var radius: Float) : Shape()
class Square(var width: Int) : Shape()
class Rectangle(var width: Int, var height: Int) : Shape()

fun getArea(e: Shape) =
    when (e) {
       is Circle -> println("Circle area is ${Math.PI * e.radius * e.radius}")
         is Square -> println("Square area is ${e.width * e.width}")
         is Rectangle -> println("Rectangle area is ${e.width * e.height}")
    }

fun main() {

    val circle = Circle(7f)
    val square = Square(5)
    val rectangle = Rectangle(8, 6)

    getArea(circle)
    getArea(square)
    getArea(rectangle)
}
```

The following will be the output:
```
Circle area is 153.93804002589985
```

```
Square area is 25
Rectangle area is 48
```

The `getArea()` function calculates the area for a `shape`; the `else` statement is not needed here since the compiler knows that the list of options is exhaustive.

Delegation

In software engineering, the delegation pattern is an object-oriented design pattern that allows object composition to achieve the same code reuse as inheritance. The Delegation pattern is a good alternative to implementation inheritance, and Kotlin supports it natively, requiring zero boilerplate code.

Example:

In this example, the class `Window` delegates the `area()` call to its internal `Rectangle` object (its delegate).

```
class Rectangle(val width: Int, val height: Int) {
    fun area() = width * height
}

class Window(val shape: Rectangle) {
    // Delegation of area calculation to the internal Rectangle
    fun area() = shape.area()
}
```

With the built-in support of delegation in Kotlin, we can achieve this as follows:

```
interface ClosedShape {
    fun area(): Int
}

class Rectangle(val width: Int, val height: Int) : ClosedShape {
    override fun area() = width * height
}

class Window(private val shape: ClosedShape) : ClosedShape by shape
```

The `by`-clause in the supertype list for `Window` indicates that the shape will be stored internally in objects of `Window`, and the compiler will generate all the methods of `ClosedShape` that forward to shape.

Type aliases

Sometimes, you will work with two or more classes from different packages with the same name, and you have to use them at once. In Kotlin, we can distinguish between them using what we call **TypeAlias**.

TypeAlias in Kotlin means you can give names to existing types. It provides an alternative naming to your existing types. Or, If the type name is too long, you can introduce a different, shorter name and use the new one instead.

The following is the syntax of using type alias in Kotlin:

```
typealias <NewName> = <ExistingType>
```

Examples:

```kotlin
    typealias ClassStudents = Map<String, List<Person>>

    typealias KStringBuilder = kotlin.text.StringBuilder
    typealias JStringBuilder = java.lang.StringBuilder

    fun main() {
        val students: ClassStudents = mapOf(
            "A" to listOf("A1", "A2"),
            "B" to listOf("B1", "B2")
        )

        students.forEach { className, classStudents ->
            println("$className: $classStudents")
        }
    }
```

The following will be output:

A: [A1, A2]

B: [B1, B2]

You can also provide names for function types:

```kotlin
    typealias MyConsumer = (Int, String, Any) -> Unit
```

```kotlin
typealias Predicate<T> = (T) -> Boolean

fun main() {
    val even: Predicate<Int> = { it % 2 == 0 }
    val evenNumbers = (1..10).filter(even)
    println(evenNumbers)
}
```
The following will be the output:
`[2, 4, 6, 8, 10]`

You can have new names for inner classes:
```kotlin
class A {
    inner class C
}

class B {
    inner class C
}

typealias AC = A.C
typealias BC = B.C
```

Conclusion

In this chapter, you learned the basics of the object-oriented programming paradigm in Kotlin; so far, you know how to work with classes and objects, interfaces, inheritance, type aliases, and delegation.

In the upcoming chapter, you will be taught about Generics that complete the previous one and give power to classes and functions.

Points to remember

The following are some points to remember:
- Kotlin is an OOP language.
- A Kotlin class can have a primary constructor and multiple secondary constructors.

- All classes inherit from the class **Any**.
- By default, all classes are final, and classes cannot inherit from a class until you mark it as open (using the keyword **open**).
- Properties in Kotlin have auto-generated getters and setters.
- Type aliasing in Kotlin is used to provide new names to existing types using the keyword **typealias**.
- Delegation has built-in support in Kotlin.

Join our book's Discord space

Join the book's Discord Workspace for Latest updates, Offers, Tech happenings around the world, New Release and Sessions with the Authors:

https://discord.bpbonline.com

CHAPTER 4
Generics

Introduction

In the previous chapter, you have learned about OOP in Kotlin, including classes, object instantiation, interfaces, inheritance, and many other notions like delegation and type aliasing.

Generics, in many programming languages, are used to provide a general implementation of classes and functions; this means that only one implementation will be used for various data types.

Structure

This chapter will cover the following topics:
- Generics
- Variance
- Reified type parameters

Objectives

By the end of this chapter, you will be able to use generics in your programs to be more concise in writing code by getting most of the advantages they offer. You will explore some new concepts that are introduced in Kotlin, such as *reified-type parameters* and *declaration-site variance*.

You will be taught some issues with generics in Java that are resolved in Kotlin in a very concise way.

Overview

Generics let you write code which is applicable to various types with the same underlying behavior; for example, `List<String>` uses the same underlying code as `List<Int>`; using generics, we had to write one piece of code to achieve both results with the same advantages too.

Generics parameters are a great way to provide type safety and avoid explicit type casting. As we will see in the upcoming sections, it ensures compile-time safety by allowing a type or a method to operate on objects of different types.

Generic types are like Java, but Kotlin creators tried to make them more intuitive by introducing some special keywords such as **in**, **out**, and **where** clauses.

Generics

With Generics, you will be able to create types that have *type parameters*. These type parameters will be replaced when you create instances of this generic type by types called type arguments.

Generic classes

The syntax for creating generic classes of generic interfaces is like the following:

```
ClassName_Or_InterfaceName<T>
```

Here, **T** used inside the angle bracket `<>` indicates the **type** parameter. Some naming conventions used to indicate a **type** parameter placeholder:

- E = element
- T = type
- K = key
- V = value
- N = Number

Let us take the following example of a generic class:

```
class GenericType<T>(t: T) {
    var value = t
}
```

When we need to create an instance of this class, we will need to provide type arguments:

```
val genericObj: GenericType<String> = GenericType<String>("Generic type")
```

In this example, the **type** argument is **String**; based on this syntax, you can say that the variable **genericObj** is a *generic type of strings*, similarly to **List<String>**, we could read it *list of strings*.

If the parameter can be inferred, sometimes from the constructor arguments, we can omit the type arguments:

```
val genericObj2 = GenericType("Generic type")
```

Generic type in the preceding example is of type **String**, so the compiler will figure out that **genericObj2** is a **GenericType<String>**.

The same thing here when you need to create a map from the class **Map<String, Double>**:

```
val map = mapOf("A" to 12.0, "B" to 20.5)
```

The type of **map** variable is inferred as **Map<String, Double>**, but if you do not have to initialize your variable, you need to explicitly define the type in the following two equivalent ways:

```
val map2: Map<String, Double> = mapOf()
```

```
val map3 = mapOf<String, Double>()
```

Generic advantages

There are three main advantages of using generics:

- **Type casting is evitable**: No need to typecast the object.
- **Compile time safety**: To avoid run-time errors, generics code is checked at compile time for the parameterized type.
- **Type safety**: Generic does not allow more than one type of object at a time.

Let us take an example of a class **Patient** with a primary constructor that takes a single parameter (of type **Int**). Now, suppose we need to pass different types of data in objects of **Patient** class, for example (**Patient(35)** and **Patient("35")**):

```
class Patient(value: Int) {
    var age:Int = value
    init {
        println(age)
    }
}
```

```
fun main() {
    val patient1: Patient = Patient(35)
    val patient2: Patient = Patient («35») // compile time error
}
```

In this example, passing an argument of type **String** will generate a compile time error as a type mismatch. But, using generics, we can solve this problem by defining a generic class that accepts different types of parameters:

```
// With generics
class Patient<T>(value: T) {
    var age:T = value
    init {
        println(age)
    }
}




fun main() {
    val patient1: Patient<Int> = Patient<Int>(35)
    val patient2: Patient<String> = Patient<String>("60")
}
```

The following will be the output:

35

60

In the preceding example, when the object of the **Patient** class is created using type **Int** as **Patient<Int>(35)** and **Patient<String>("60")**, it replaces the **Patient** class of type **T** with **Int** and **String**, respectively.

Generic functions

A function declaration can also have type parameters. In the case of functions, the **type** parameter is placed before the name of the function. The following is the syntax for creating a generic function in Kotlin:

```
fun <T> methodOrFunctionName(parameter: T)
```

To call a generic function, specify the type arguments at the call site after the name of the function, and if the type arguments can be inferred from the context, they can be omitted:

Example:
```
fun <T> printValue(value: T) {
    println(value)
}

fun main() {
    printValue<Int>(120)
    printValue<Boolean>(true)
    printValue("Hello Kotlin")
}
```

The following will be the output:
```
120
true
Hello Kotlin
```

Generic constraints

We can use generic constraints to restrict the type parameter **T** to the expected types. In Kotlin, we can use the upper bound constraint.

Upper bound constraint

To understand the upper bound constraint, let us take the following example of a generic function that takes a generic element as input and returns a list containing that element:

```
open class BaseClass {
    override fun toString(): String {
        return this.javaClass.simpleName
    }
}

class Derived(val name: String): BaseClass()
class Child(val name: String): BaseClass()
```

```kotlin
class OtherClass(val name: String)


fun <T: BaseClass> returnElementAsList(element: T?): List<T> {
    if (element == null) return emptyList()
    return listOf(element)
}

fun main() {
    val list = returnElementAsList<BaseClass>(Derived("Derived")) // Ok
    val list2 = returnElementAsList<BaseClass>(Child("Child")) // Ok
    val list3 = returnElementAsList<BaseClass>(BaseClass()) // Ok
    val list4 = returnElementAsList<OtherClass>(OtherClass("Other")) //
    Compile time error: Expected BaseClass

    println(list)
    println(list2)
    println(list3)
}
```

The type specified after a colon is the upper bound, **BaseClass**, in this example, indicating that only a subtype of the **BaseClass** is accepted and can be substituted for **T**.

In the preceding example, as **Child** and **Derived** classes are subtypes of **BaseClass**, they all can be substituted for **T**. On the other hand, because **OtherClass** is not a subtype of **BaseClass**, it generates a compile-time error indicating that only a subtype of **BaseClass** is accepted.

The default upper bound—if none was specified—is **Any?**. And only one upper bound can be specified inside the angle brackets. If you need to specify more than one upper bound, then you need to use a separate **where** clause shown as follows:

```kotlin
// Multiple upper bounds
fun <T> returnAnElementAsList(element: T?): List<T>
        where T : BaseClass,
              T : Comparable<T> {
    if (element == null) return emptyList()
```

```
        return listOf(element)
}
```

The passed type must satisfy all conditions of the where clause simultaneously. In the preceding example, the **T** type must implement both **BaseClass** and **Comparable**.

Only one class can be specified as an upper bound because Kotlin does not support multiple inheritance; the other upper bounds can be interfaces.

Type erasure

Just like Java, Kotlin has type erasure, which means at runtime, you cannot query types; the objects instantiated from generic types do not have any information about their real type arguments. The type information will be erased. For example, the instances of **List<String>** and **List<Int?>** are erased to just **List<*>**; at runtime, we can see only a **List**, not a List of strings or anything else.

Type casting to generic type with concrete type arguments, for example, **foo** as **List<String>**, cannot be checked at runtime.

Example:

```
fun <T> genericCollection(list: Collection<T>) {
    if (list is List<Int>) { // this type of check is not possible at runtime
        // ...
    }

    // Projections with star!
    if (list is List<*>) { // if this is a list of any type

        val numberList = list as List<Int> // cast will work at runtime
        val first:Int = numberList.first() // might not work at runtime
    }
}
```

Variance

In Kotlin, Unlike Java, arrays are invariants by default. By extension, a generic type is invariant in Kotlin. It can be managed by the keywords **out** and **in**. Invariance is the property by which a standard generic function/class, already defined for a particular data type, cannot accept or return another datatype. **Any** is a supertype of all the datatypes in Kotlin.

Variance is actually of the following two types:

- Declaration-site variance: using the in and out keywords
- Use-site variance: type projection

Declaration-site variance

In Kotlin, we do not have wildcard types as we have in Java, but instead of these wildcard types, we have other concepts.

out keyword

In Kotlin, we can use the **out** keyword on the generic type, which means we can assign this reference to any of its supertypes. The out value can only be produced by the given class but cannot be consumed.

Example:

```
class Producer<out T>(val value: T) {
    fun produce(): T {
        return value
    }
}


fun main() {
    val producer = Producer("Produced")
    val reference: Producer<Any> = producer
}
```

In the preceding example, we have defined a **Producer** class that can produce a value of type T. Then, we can assign an instance of the **Producer** to the reference that is a supertype of it.

If we did not use the keyword **out** in the preceding example, a compile-time error will be thrown.

in keyword

If we need to assign it to reference of its subtypes, then we can use the **in** keyword on the generic type T. The **in** keyword can be used only on the parameter type that would be consumed and not on the one produced.

Example:

```
class Consumer<in T> {
    fun consume(value: T) {
        println(value.toString())
    }
}

fun main() {
    val consumer: Consumer<Number> = Consumer()
    val reference: Consumer<Int> = consumer
}
```

In this example, we created a **consume()** method that only consumes the value of type **T** and does not produce a value of that type; hence, we can assign a reference of type **Number** to a reference of its subtypes – **Int**.

If we did not use the **in** keyword in the preceding example, a compile-time error will be produced.

Use-site variance: type projection

Let's take the following example of copying data from one list to another:

```
fun <T> copyItems(from: MutableList<T>, to: MutableList<in T>) {
    for (element in from) {
        to.add(element)
    }
}
```

Using the **in** modifier in the preceding example ensures *type-safety* and prohibits copying spiders into a list of ants, even when both lists contain insects, as shown in the following code snippets:

```
open class Insect

class Spider: Insect()
class Ant: Insect()
```

```
fun <T> copyItems(from: MutableList<T>, to: MutableList<in T>) {
    for (element in from) {
        to.add(element)
    }
}


fun main() {
    val spiders = mutableListOf(Spider(), Spider())
    val ants = mutableListOf(Ant())

    val insects = mutableListOf<Insect>()

    copyItems(spiders, insects) // Ok
    copyItems(ants, insects) // Ok

    copyItems(spiders, ants) // compile time error
}
```

The destination list is not a regular **MutableList** but a restricted or projected one, which will only allow certain types based on the in modifier; we call this **Type** projection.

In the following example, copying a list of spiders to a list of insects and list of ants to a list of insects was possible because **MutableList<Insect>** is a subtype of **MutableList<Spider>** and **MutableList<Insect>** is a subtype of **MutableList<Ant>**, respectively.

Reified-type parameters

So, as you know, generics are used to perform operations on a value of any type **T**. Let us take the following function to explain type reification in Kotlin:

```
fun <T> performSomeWork(value: T) {
    println("Working on the value:")
    println(value.toString())
}
```

In this example, calling function **toString()** on the value works as expected. But what about performing some operation on **T** itself?

```kotlin
fun <T> performSomeWork(value: T) {
    println("Working on T: ${T::class.simpleName}") // Error
}
```

Writing the preceding code produces the following compile error:

`Cannot use 'T' as reified type parameter. Use a class in place.`

Let us understand the why behind this error. As you saw in the previous section, because of type erasure, the compiler removes the type arguments from the function call at compile time.

For example, this function calls:

```kotlin
performSomeWork<String>("Learning Kotlin")
```

At runtime, the compiler removes the type argument part **<String>** to become:

```kotlin
performSomeWork("Learning Kotlin")
```

Therefore, we cannot know exactly what is the type **T** inside the function definition at runtime. The Java solution for this issue is to explicitly add an additional argument specifying the type **T** with the **Class** (**KClass** in Kotlin).

```kotlin
fun <T:Any> performSomeWork(value: T, type: KClass<T>) {
    println("Working on T: ${type.simpleName}") // Ok
}
```

In this solution, specifying the upper bound **Any** is mandatory, and the code is a little bit verbose since we need to declare the type as well as call it with other additional arguments:

```kotlin
performSomeWork<String>("Learning Kotlin", String::class)
```

Type reification

In Kotlin, using inline functions (more details in *Chapter 6: Inline Function*) and the reified modifier before the type parameter helps get rid of the type erasure issues as magic.

To have a quick hint about what is an inline function, it is a function that is marked with the **inline** keyword; as a result, the compiler will copy the function body wherever it is called.

Example:

```kotlin
inline fun <reified T> performSomeWork(value: T) {
    println("Working on T: ${T::class.simpleName}") // Ok
}
```

The **reified** keyword in this code snippet enables the type information to be retained at runtime. So, the following function calls:

```
fun main() {
    performSomeWork<String>("Learning Kotlin")
}
```

And:

```
fun main() {
    println("Working on T: ${String::class.simpleName}")
}
```

will produce the same output: "Working on T: String." The **reified** keyword in the first code snippet allows you to work with the type information of T as if it were a concrete class, making it convenient for functions that require runtime access to type information for generic parameters.

In this example, when the compiler copies the inline function body, it also replaces the type parameter T with the actual type argument that is specified or inferred in the function call, **String**, in this example.

Type checking and type casting

Type reification in Kotlin and its main objective is to know exactly what type parameter T represents at runtime using type checking with the **is** keyword.

Let us take the following example:

```
open class Shape {
    override fun toString(): String {
        return this.javaClass.simpleName
    }
}

class Circle : Shape()
class Triangle : Shape()
class Square : Shape()


inline fun <reified T> List<Any>.filterShapes(): List<T> {
```

```
        return this.filter {it is T}.map { it as T }
    }

    fun main() {
        val shapes = listOf<Shape>(Circle(), Triangle(), Circle(), Square())

        val circles = shapes.filterShapes<Circle>()

        println(circles)
    }
```

The following will be the output:

[Circle, Circle]

In the preceding example, the use of reified modifier with the **inline** function **filterShapes()** helps us get rid of the following problems when not using it:

- **Error**: Cannot use "T" as a reified type parameter. Use a class instead.
- **Error**: Cannot check for an instance of erased type: T
- **Warning**: Unchecked cast: Any to T

The preceding example demonstrates the possibility of type filtering in collections using the reified type parameter, which makes it possible by type checking (**{ it is T }**) and type casting (**{ it as T }**), which will not be possible without reification.

Conclusion

So far, you have seen many Kotlin features that might be novel to you, like how it is a very helpful and powerful way of using generics with reified type parameters, using declaration-site variance, and so on. You also have learned many notions and some new Kotlin features that are truly great until now.

In the upcoming chapter, you will learn new features and notions for working with functions and classes, and these notions are *annotations and reflection*.

Points to remember

The following are some points to remember about generics in Kotlin:

- Kotlin's generics can be declared the same way as in Java.
- Type arguments are erased at runtime, so you cannot use type check at runtime.
- Using type reification will allow us to use type parameter **T** at runtime to check its type.
- In Kotlin, you can specify variance for either a generic class as a whole (declaration-site variance) or a specific use of a generic type (use-site variance).
- The star-projection syntax can be used when the exact type arguments are unknown or unimportant.

Join our book's Discord space

Join the book's Discord Workspace for Latest updates, Offers, Tech happenings around the world, New Release and Sessions with the Authors:

https://discord.bpbonline.com

CHAPTER 5
Annotations and Reflection

Introduction

So far, you have learned a lot of features to work on functions and classes, for example, how generics can add more power to classes and functions by making the same code usable in many different cases with different contexts. But, in order to make a call to a specific function, you need to know where it is declared, what the function is, and the class name.

In this chapter, we will go through annotations and reflections and see how this will give you additional power to deal with classes and functions without knowing their names.

Structure

This chapter will cover the following topics:
- Annotations
- Reflections
    o Serialization and deserialization

Objectives

By the end of this chapter, you will learn about annotations and reflection and be able to use and define your custom annotations, and you will be able to use reflection to introspect classes at runtime as well.

Overview

Most frameworks and libraries in Java use annotations, and it is a way to represent metadata. But it is not only Java where we can use and make annotations; Kotlin also uses annotations as well. If you already worked with Java, you probably used annotations a lot when working with different libraries. The same thing goes for Kotlin, but have you ever created your custom annotations? If not, do not worry, we will go through the process of creating our custom annotations, and we will see how to work with them.

Reflection is a powerful technique that allows you to modify the structure of your classes at runtime and permit you to create objects using JSON data, for example.

Annotations

Annotations in Kotlin, like in Java and many other languages, allow you to attach metadata to interfaces, classes, and parameters. The metadata will be accessed at runtime by reflection at the runtime depending on how the annotation is declared.

Usage

In Kotlin, as it is in Java, to apply an annotation to a class, function, or field, you use the annotation name prefixed with the **@** character in front of the correspondent declaration (field, function, and class).

For example, when a function or a property has been deprecated in some libraries, we could use the annotation **Deprecated**, like in the following example:

```
@Deprecated("Use calculate(h,w) in place", ReplaceWith("calculate(h,w)"))
fun calculateSize(height: Double, width: Double): Double {//…}
```

The **@Deprecated** annotation in Kotlin is the same as it is in Java, but with a small enhancement in the first one; Kotlin added the **ReplaceWith** parameter, which allows you to provide an alternative usage of the deprecated behavior to smoothly make a transition to the next library version. For example, when working with IntelliJ IDEA, it should show you a tooltip that the function **calculateSize** is deprecated, and not only that, but it also provides you with a quick fix to perform automatically.

Annotations can accept parameters passed in parentheses like functions, but only of certain types, which are primitives, enums, strings, arrays, annotation classes, and classes references.

To specify the annotation's arguments, you need to do it a little bit differently from the way it is done in Java. The following is how each argument type is specified in Kotlin annotation:

- **Class as argument**: You should put the `::class` after the name of the class like the following:

    @MyCustomAnnotation(MyCustomClass::class)

- **Array as argument**: You need to use the **arrayOf** function as follows:

    @MyCustomAnnotation(roles=arrayOf("ADMIN", "USER"))

- **Another annotation as argument**: To specify another annotation as an argument of your annotation, you only need to remove the `@` sign, like in the previous example of the `@Deprecated` annotation, the `ReplaceWith` is another annotation passed as argument to the `Deprecated` annotation but without the `@` symbol.

To pass any type of argument to your annotation, you need to be sure that these arguments are known at compile time because you cannot pass arbitrary arguments.

So, when you need to pass any property as an annotation argument, you should declare it const to inform the compiler that your property is compile-time constant. These constant properties need to be declared at the top of the file or inside an object block and should be initialized with primitive type or **String** values.

Example:

In the Spring framework, we can schedule the execution of a task using the annotation `@Scheduled` that takes as an argument **fixedRate**, which is the rate of execution of the task in milliseconds; it is done as follows:

```
const val RATE = 10_000L
@Scheduled(fixedRate = RATE)
fun scheduleTask() {
    println("Execute task - ${ System.currentTimeMillis() / 1000}")
}
```

Define custom annotation

To define your custom annotation, all you need is adding the keyword **annotation** before the **class** keyword as follows:

```
annotation class MyCustomAnnotation
```

The annotation itself can have annotations, called meta-annotations, which can be used to specify additional attributes to the annotation.

These meta-annotations are as follows:

- **@Target**: This specifies the possible types of targets the annotation can annotate, such as properties, classes, functions, and expressions; here are the most known targets:
    - **CLASS**: Includes classes, interfaces, annotation classes, and objects.
    - **FUNCTION**: Methods other than constructors.
    - **FIELD**: Field variables and backing fields.
    - **TYPE**: All expressions.

        ```
        @Target(
            AnnotationTarget.CLASS,
            AnnotationTarget.FUNCTION
        )
        annotation class MyCustomAnnotation
        ```

    Multiple targets can be passed as arguments. In the preceding example, the annotation can be bound to functions and classes; otherwise, it will show a compile-time error.

- **@Repeatable**: It specifies if the annotation is allowed to be used multiple times on the same element. This has been introduced in Java 8, so if we need to make an annotation repeatable, we should target a JVM version 1.8 at least.

- **@Retention**: It specifies if the annotation can be stored in the compiled class files and if it is visible during reflection at runtime. It can be taught as a scope of the annotation. There are three types of retention in Kotlin; they have been discussed as follows:
    - **SOURCE**: Same as Java, annotation in this case is only valid in compile time and removed in the binary output.
    - **BINARY**: The annotation will be accessed in the binary output, but we cannot access it via reflection.
    - **RUNTIME**: This is the default option annotation; in this case, it is accessed by reflection and available in the binary output as well.

- **@MustBeDocumented**: Similar to Java's annotation @Documented, it allows the annotation to be generated in the documentation.

These meta-annotations can be used to bind with properties and give powerful and custom behavior to them.

Annotation constructor

We can declare an annotation with a constructor that has parameters:

```
@Target(
    AnnotationTarget.CLASS,
    AnnotationTarget.FUNCTION
)
annotation class MyCustomAnnotation(val name: String)


// Usage
@MyCustomAnnotation( "demo")
class Demo {}
```

As already mentioned, the only parameter types we can pass as arguments are primitive types (**Long**, **Int**, and so on) that correspond to primitive Java types, strings, classes, annotations, Enums, and arrays of these previous types. If we pass another annotation as an argument, we remove the prefix **@** from it, as we saw in the example of **@Deprecated** with the annotation parameter **ReplaceWith**.

As JVM does not support that annotation attribute value be **null**, annotation parameters must be of not nullable types.

In case we need to pass a class as an argument of an annotation, we should use the Kotlin class (**KClass**), which will be automatically converted to a Java class by the Kotlin compiler, making access to its arguments and annotations normal.

Example:

```
import kotlin.reflect.KClass


@Target(AnnotationTarget.CLASS, AnnotationTarget.CONSTRUCTOR)
@Retention(AnnotationRetention.RUNTIME)
annotation class DemoAnn(val param1: KClass<*>, val param2: KClass<out Any>)


// Usage demo
@DemoAnn(String::class, Int::class)
class DemoClass1 {}
```

```kotlin
// Usage demo
@DemoAnn(Int::class, Double::class)
class DemoClass2 {}
```

If you have a class and you need to annotate its primary constructor, you should add the constructor keyword to the declaration of the primary constructor and then add your annotations before it.

Example:

```kotlin
// Demo Annotation
@Target(AnnotationTarget.CONSTRUCTOR, AnnotationTarget.CLASS)
@Retention(AnnotationRetention.RUNTIME)
@MustBeDocumented
annotation class DependencyInjector


// Demo library or a dependency
class MyLibraryTool


// Annotate constructor
class MyDemoClass @DependencyInjector constructor(dep:MyLibraryTool) {}
```

You can also use annotations on lambdas; it will be applied to **invoke()** method of the context where the lambda's body will be generated.

Instantiation

Annotation type in Java is like an interface; therefore, you can create an implementation of it and profit from its use. Kotlin, on the other hand, gives you the possibility to call the annotation class constructor in your code and make use of the resulting instance as well.

```kotlin
annotation class ClassInfo(val type: String)


fun displayInfo(classInfo: ClassInfo): Unit = TODO()


fun main(arguments: Array<String>) {
    displayInfo(ClassInfo("String"))
}
```

Use-site target

In Kotlin, one single annotated declaration can result in many separate declarations in Java. For example, a property declaration in Kotlin will be equivalent to a Java field, a setter, and a getter. Because of that, you might need to target which of these elements will be annotated.

Using the `use-site target`, you can specify the element you need to annotate. It will be used by placing it between the @ symbol and the name of the annotation, separated by a colon from the name like follow:

`@set:Param("default")`

Here, the annotation is **@Param**, and the **use-site** target is **set**.

The possible options for the **use-site** targets available in Kotlin are the following:
- **field**: field generated for a property
- **get**: property getter
- **set**: property setter
- **receiver**: receiver function for an extension property or a function
- **param**: constructor parameter
- **setparam**: property setter parameter
- **delegate**: field holding the delegate instance of a delegated property
- **file**: class that contains top-level properties and functions declared in the file.
- **property**: not visible to Java.

If you need to annotate the receiver parameter as an extension function, the following syntax is used:

`fun @receiver:MyCustomAnnotation(".2f") Double.format() {}`

If no use-site target is specified, the default target will be used is the one specified in the **@Target** annotation of the used annotation, but if there are multiple annotation targets are specified, the first from the following list will be used:
- param
- property
- field

Reflection

Reflection is a way to inspect, examine, and modify the structure of your application at runtime instead of compile-time. It is a very powerful technique that gives you more control over your code.

Reflection allows you to access methods and properties of objects at runtime without the need to know what those properties are in advance. In some cases, you will need to deal with objects of different types, and you will need to access their methods and properties, which you do not have any idea in advance.

The most trivial example of libraries using reflection are JSON libraries, using serialization and deserialization, which can deal with any kind of object.

JVM reflection dependency

In order to reduce the size required by the runtime library used in applications that do not use reflection features, the Kotlin compiler distribution uses a separate runtime component artifact, which is dedicated for that purpose, **kotlin-reflect.jar**.

If you are working on a Gradle or a Maven project, you will need to add the dedicated dependency as follows:

In a Gradle project:

```
dependencies {
    implementation("org.jetbrains.kotlin:kotlin-reflect:VERSION")
}
```

Where **VERSION** is the Kotlin version you are using.

In a Maven project:

```
<dependencies>
  <dependency>
      <groupId>org.jetbrains.kotlin</groupId>
      <artifactId>kotlin-reflect</artifactId>
  </dependency>
</dependencies>
```

If you do not work with Gradle or Maven, you need to add the **kotlin-reflect.jar** library to the **classpath** of your application.

Reference to a Kotlin class

Obtaining the runtime reference to a Kotlin class is a basic reflection feature. To get a statically known Kotlin class reference, we can use the class literal syntax as follows:

```
val myClass = DemoClass1::class
```

The value of **myClass** here is of **KClass** type.

A Kotlin class reference is different from a Java class reference on the JVM. To get the Java class reference, you will need to add the .java property to the **KClass** object as follows:

```
val myJavaClass = DemoClass1::class.java
```

Callable references

You can also work with references to constructors, functions, and properties and call them as function type instances. The supertype of these callable references is **KCallable<out T>**, where **T** is the return value type.

- **Kotlin function references**: For every named function in Kotlin, we can get a functional reference. To obtain this reference, we use the **::** operator. The obtained functional references can be used as function parameters.

    Example of functional reference:

    ```
    fun isEven(x: Int) = x % 2 == 0


    fun main() {
        val numList = listOf(1,2,3,4,5,6,7,8,9)
        println(numList.filter(::isEven))
    }
    ```

    The supertype of a function reference is **KFunction<out R>**, and depending on the parameter count, for example, **KFunction3<T1, T2, T3, R>** is the supertype of functional references for functions with three parameters.

    The **::** operator will be used with overloaded functions if the type is known from its context.

    Otherwise, we can store the function reference in a variable by specifying the type explicitly.

    ```
    fun isEven(s: String) = s.length % 2 == 0


    fun main() {

        val names = listOf("a", "ab", "abc", "abcd", "abcde", "abcdef")
        val isEvenRef: (String) -> Boolean = ::isEven
        println(names.filter(isEvenRef))

    }
    ```

- **Kotlin property references**: The same thing as functional references, we can use `::` operator to obtain the property references. If we deal with class properties, we should specify the class name preceded the `::` operator. The property reference is treated as an object with methods to get its actual value and set a new value.

    Example of property references:

    ```
    class Product(var quantity: Int) {}


    val stock = 1000L

    fun main() {
        val x = ::stock
        println(x.get())
        println(x.name)


        val y = Product::quantity
        println(y.get(Product(25)))
    }
    ```

- **Kotlin constructor references**: Just like properties and methods, we can obtain references to constructors in a similar manner. The reference obtained will be of a function type.

    Example of a constructor reference:

    ```
    // Constructor reference
    val z = ::Product
    println(z.name)
    println(z.parameters)
    ```

    Like function or methods references, constructor reference is a subtype of one of the `KFunction<out T>` depending on the parameters count.

Serialization and deserialization

A JSON library is the most appropriate example of applications where annotations and reflection are used a lot. There are many JSON libraries you can use in your applications to convert your objects into JSON and text representation into objects, such as Gson and Jackson.

In this section, we will go through some basic examples of using annotations and reflection to serialize objects and deserialize JSON back to objects.

Serialization

Serialize an object means to transform it into a text representation, JSON, for example, as key-value pairs. Let us start with declaring a basic function that takes an object as an argument and returns its JSON representation:

```
fun serialize(obj: Any): String = buildString { serializeObject1(obj) }
```

Here, **buildString** lets construct a **String** using a **StringBuilder** by filling its content in a lambda. The function **serializeObject1** will provide that; therefore, we will use a **StringBuilder** extension, and it will serialize the properties of the object.

The **serializeObject1** function will be built without handling annotated elements, and in the second part, we will use a second implementation, **serializeObject2**, that will handle annotations. By serializing an object, primitive types are represented as string value, Boolean, or number, and collections will be represented as JSON arrays, whereas other types are represented as nested objects.

Let us see now how we can use reflection in a real scenario by implementing the **serializeObject1** function:

```
private fun StringBuilder.serializeObject1(obj: Any) {
    obj.javaClass.kotlin.memberProperties.joinTo(this, prefix = "{", postfix = "}") { prop ->
        serializeString(prop.name)
        append(":")
        serializePropertyValue(prop.get(obj))
        return@joinTo ""
    }
}
```

The **joinTo** method takes as a first argument the **StringBuilder**, and then fills its content by appending serialized properties using a lambda function. Here, we have two other **StringBuilder** extensions to help get things done: **serializeString** and **serializePropertyValue**.

```
private fun StringBuilder.serializeString(str: String) {
    append('\"')
    str.forEach { append(it.escape()) }
    append('\"')
}
```

```kotlin
private fun StringBuilder.serializePropertyValue(value: Any?) {
    when (value) {
        null -> append("null")
        is String -> serializeString(value)
        is Number, is Boolean -> append(value.toString())
        is List<*> -> serializeCollection(value)
        else -> serializeObject1(value)
    }
}


private fun StringBuilder.serializeCollection(data: List<Any?>) {
    data.joinTo(this, prefix = "[", postfix = "]") {
        serializePropertyValue(it)
        return@joinTo ""
    }
}
```

The **serializeString** object uses a **Char** extension function to escape special characters:

```kotlin
    private fun Char.escape(): Any = when (this) {
        '\\' -> "\\\\"
        '\"' -> "\\\""
        '\u000C' -> "\\f"
        '\n' -> "\\n"
        '\b' -> "\\b"
        '\t' -> "\\t"
        '\r' -> "\\r"
        else -> this
    }
```

Now, let us take an example of a **Patient** class with nested objects and see how it will behave:

```kotlin
data class Patient(
    val firstName: String,
    val lastName: String,
    val age: Int,
```

```kotlin
        val vip: Boolean? = false,
        val addresses: List<Address> = listOf()
    )

    data class Address(
        val street: String,
        val postalCode: String? = null,
        val city: String? = null
    )

    fun main() {
        val patient = Patient(
            "Adam",
            "Said",
            45,
            addresses = listOf(Address("21st Main Street.", "12000")))
        println(serialize(patient))
    }
```

The following will be the output:

```
{"addresses":[{"city":null, "postalCode":"12000", "street":"21st Main
Street."}], "age":45, "firstName":"Adam", "lastName":"Said", "vip":false}
```

Everything works as expected. Now, let's make the second version with annotation handling, the **serializeObject2**.

First, we create a custom annotation **@JsonProperty**, which will be used to customize the serialization operation, and we will make it as a property target annotation that changes the property name in the JSON representation like the following:

```kotlin
@Target(AnnotationTarget.PROPERTY)
annotation class JsonProperty(val name: String)
```

Using this annotation, we can apply it to the **Patient** properties:

```kotlin
data class Patient(
    @JsonProperty("first_name")
    val firstName: String,
```

```kotlin
        @JsonProperty("last_name")
        val lastName: String,
        val age: Int,
        val vip: Boolean? = false,
        val addresses: List<Address> = listOf()
    )
```

Implementation of the **serializeObject2** function. Here, we use the **findAnnotation<JsonProperty>()** method to get the property annotation.

```kotlin
    private fun StringBuilder.serializeObject2(obj: Any) {
        obj.javaClass.kotlin.memberProperties.joinTo(this, prefix = "{", postfix = "}") { prop ->
            val jsonProperty = prop.findAnnotation<JsonProperty>()
            val propName = jsonProperty?.name ?: prop.name
            serializeString(propName)
            append(":")
            serializePropertyValue(prop.get(obj))
            return@joinTo ""
        }
    }
```

Let us see now how it will handle annotated properties of the **Patient** class:

```kotlin
    fun main() {
        val patient2 = Patient(
            "Mounir",
            "BOUSSETTA",
            35)

        println(serialize(patient2))
    }
```

The following will be the output:

```
{"addresses":[], "age":35, "first_name":"Mounir", "last_name":"BOUSSETTA", "vip":false}
```

Congratulations! You are now able to handle different serialization scenarios by defining your custom annotations and using reflection to handle how the representation will be generated.

Deserialization

Deserialization is a more complex and difficult operation than serialization because it should parse JSON text and use reflection to deal with objects.

In this book, we will not see how to implement deserialization from scratch because this section was intended just to see an application of the chapter subject: annotation and reflection, which we had already seen in the previous section.

Conclusion

In this chapter, you learned about a very interesting topic in programming, which is annotations and reflection. Now, you should be able to understand any source code that uses annotations, and you should be able to define your custom ones in your future projects.

You had also been taught the reflection mechanism and how it is used to serialize objects to JSON.

In the upcoming chapter, we will see a new programming style: functional programming in Kotlin using RxKotlin.

Points to remember

From this chapter, you should remember the following points:
- Annotations are used to modify your code structure.
- Meta-annotations are used to customize your annotations, such as specifying the target, retention mode, and other attributes.
- Reflection lets you access and modify properties and methods of your objects dynamically at runtime.

Join our book's Discord space

Join the book's Discord Workspace for Latest updates, Offers, Tech happenings around the world, New Release and Sessions with the Authors:

https://discord.bpbonline.com

Chapter 6
Functional Programming with Kotlin and RxKotlin

Introduction

So far, you have seen a lot of things, from the basics, then object-oriented programming to annotations and reflections. All you have seen until now belongs to the imperative programming paradigm. Imperative programming is a paradigm where we can use statements to alter or change the state of a given program. It consists of a command given to the computer to change the program's state.

This chapter will go through another different programming paradigm: functional programming. It is a new programming concept where we can build programs by composing and applying functions.

Structure

This chapter will cover the following topics:
- Introduction to reactive programming
- Lambda expressions
- Pure function
- Higher-order functions

- Inline function
- Polymorphic functions
- Functional data structures
- Handling error

Objectives

By the end of this chapter, you will learn about the functional programming paradigm, reactive programming, functional data structures, higher order functions, how error handling is done, and many other concepts.

Overview

Many chip manufacturers knew the physical limit to build processors with higher speeds, which led them to think of multi-core chips. The new hardware solution has been designed to increase concurrency instead of making chips with a faster clock. Hence, programming language designers were obliged to think about a new concept in order to profit the most from the hardware resources so that programs could run concurrently on parallel hardware.

Programming, in its traditional way, relies on altering the program state to perform some work and produce outputs. In the imperative programming paradigm, values are mutable and can be accessed by multiple parts of the program, which makes concurrency a very hard task to accomplish.

Now, the software industry has come up with a new programming paradigm that ensures your program can be parallelized and then makes the most benefits from the available hardware resources. This new programming paradigm is called Functional Programming.

In the functional programming concept, all values are considered immutable, and the program state is not shared. This new concept relies on functions, and these are like first-class citizens. By composing functions, we can make programs easily and clearly.

Introduction to reactive programming

Reactive programming is defined as an asynchronous declarative programming paradigm that is based on the propagation of change and data streams. It has been designed to simplify the building of interactive user interfaces and almost real-time animations. For instance, in the **Model-View-Controller (MVC)** pattern, reactive programming can make the changes in the underlying model reflect easily on the associated view.

Using reactive programming is imperative, considering that the spine of your program is the data stream. These data streams could be events, calls, messages, and errors. Writing reactive code means observing these data streams and triggering some reactions (functions) while values are emitted.

In reactive programming, you can create data streams from almost everything: HTTP requests, click events, messages, notifications, sensor data, and anything that changes over time. This will make our application become asynchronous.

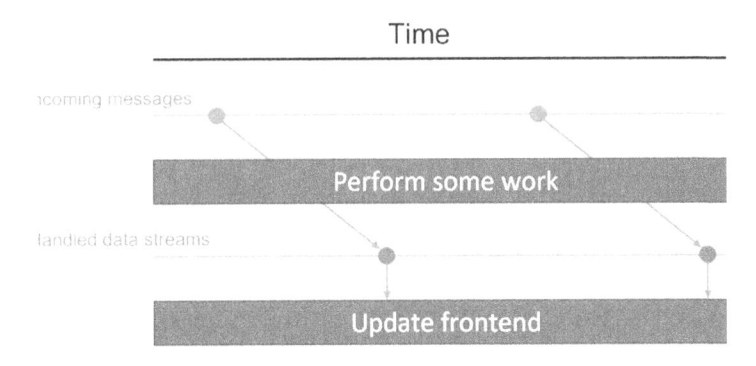

Figure 6.1: Illustration of data streams

A real-world example of reactive behavior is a spreadsheet. Let us suppose you have a column **A** that has numeric data (for example, salaries, monthly income in **$**, and so on) starting from cell **A2** to **A100**, and then you have the cell **A101** with the sum of these data by using the function **=SUM(A2; A100)**. If you change any value in the **A** cells from cell **A2** to **A100**, the changes will automatically affect the result in cell **A101**.

Let us take a look at the following example, where you can understand what it looks like for a program to be not reactive:

```
fun main() {
    var word = "level"
    var palindrome = isPalindrome(word)
        println("The word '$word' is ${if (palindrome) "a" else "not a"} palindrome.")
    word = "stage"
        println("The word '$word' is ${if (palindrome) "a" else "not a"} palindrome.")
}
```

```
fun isPalindrome(str: String): Boolean {
    return str == str.split("").reversed().joinToString("")
}
```

The following will be the output:

```
The word 'level' is a palindrome.
The word 'stage' is a palindrome.
```

This program evaluates a word if it is palindrome or not; a palindrome word is a string that remains the same if we reverse the order of its letters.

If you notice in the output of the program, you will see that even if the variable word is assigned a new value, then the value of **palindrome** is still **true**. If the function **isPalindrome** was made to track changes, then it should automatically output **false**. This behavior is what a reactive program will ensure.

Why adopt a functional reactive programming paradigm?

There should be a lot of benefits to adopting a reactive programming style; otherwise, it is not worth changing our coding method and style to something new.

The following are some benefits we can gain from the functional reactive style:

- **Avoid the callback mechanism**: Earlier, when a specified event occurs, a method gets called and executes some work, and this involves creating interfaces with the callback methods and their implementations with a lot of code. Reactive programming gets rid of all this in a simple, concise, and easy way.
- **One API for everything**: RxKotlin is a reactive programming library that offers an API that can be used to perform almost everything, such as database access, HTTP calls handling, and more.
- **Intuitive error handling mechanism**: Handling errors in a traditional way is a headache; while they are a big concern when used in HTTP call handling, a functional reactive way makes it easier to deal with.
- **Function-based**: The reactive programming coding style involves building functions for each specific operation.
- **Works with threading is easier**: Working with threading in a reactive programming style is easier than a traditional way.
- **Easy to maintain and test**: Working with a reactive programming style makes your code easy to test and maintain.

Reactive Manifesto: reactive principles

Reactive Manifesto (**https://www.reactivemanifesto.org/**) is a document, or you can define it as a norm for people who want to create reactive programming libraries. It defines four principles of being reactive:

1. **Responsive**: Responsiveness in a system means that a problem should be detected quickly and handled rapidly and effectively in a timely manner.
2. **Resilient**: Even if there is a failure, the system should maintain its responsiveness. Resilience is ensured by delegation, isolation, and containment.
3. **Elastic**: Responsiveness should be ensured under variable workload by managing the resources used to deal with inputs effectively and in a cost-efficient manner.
4. **Message-driven**: Reactive systems use asynchronous message passing to make connections between decoupled components; these components provide a way to delegate failures as messages and then establish a boundary between them.

Now, let us see the same example of the palindrome program in a reactive way. In the following example we will use the following maven dependency of RxKotlin:

```xml
<dependency>
    <groupId>io.reactivex.rxjava2</groupId>
    <artifactId>rxkotlin</artifactId>
    <version>2.4.0</version>
</dependency>
```

At the time of writing this book, the latest chapter of RxKotlin was 2.4.0. The previous palindrome program will be written in a reactive style as follow:

```kotlin
fun main() {
    var sub: Subject<String> = PublishSubject.create()

    sub.map { isPalindrome(it) }.subscribe {
        println("The word given is ${if (it) "a" else "not a"} palindrome.")
    }

    sub.onNext("level")
    sub.onNext("stage")
}
```

The following will be the output:

```
The word given is a palindrome.
The word given is not a palindrome.
```

It works! Exactly as expected from a reactive program to do, we have used a **Subject**, **map**, and **subscribe** to track changes. We will cover these in the coming chapters, and this is just to show how it is easy to notify changes in reactive programming.

Lambda expression

Lambda expression, or shortly Lambda, is an anonymous function, and it is a function without a name that we can consider as a value; for example, methods can take lambda expression as an argument, or the lambda expression could be the return of another function.

Declaring a lambda

To declare a lambda expression, we need to follow the following syntax:

```
val lambda: ReturnType = { arguments -> lambdaBody }
```

Where:
- **arguments**: They are the arguments of the lambda expression.
- **lambdaBody**: It is the body of the lambda expression, and it is required.
- **ReturnType**: It is the return type of the lambda expression, and it is the type of the last statement in the lambda body.

Example:

```
fun main() {
    // declare a lambda expression
    val multiply = { a: Int, b: Int -> a * b }
    // call the function and print the result
    println("4 * 5 = ${multiply(4, 5)}")
}
```

The following will be the output:

```
4 * 5 = 20
```

Lambda type declaration

We can explicitly specify the lambda type. This is done by following the syntax **inputTypes -> outputType**, and if the lambda does not return anything, the **outputType** will be Unit.

Example:

```
// Type Declaration
val wordLength: (String) -> Int = {word -> word.length}
val printLong: (Long) -> Unit = { ln -> println(ln) }
val withMixedArgs: (String, Int, Boolean) -> Int = { str, n, isTrue ->
    if (isTrue) str.length else n
}
```

Pure function

A function is pure if it has the following criteria:

- The result produced should depend only on its inputs and not on any external information.
- It should not cause or produce any observable side effects, for example, modifying a parameter passed by reference.

A pure function can be a named function or even a lambda.

Example:

```
// Pure function
fun factorial(n: Int): Int {
    if (n == 0) return 1
    return n* factorial(n-1)
}
```

In this example, the function factorial does not modify the passed variable (**n**) nor refer to an external function or variable.

```
fun isProductAvailable(product: String): Boolean {
    val count = getProductCount(product)
    return count > 0
}
```

The function in the preceding example is not pure because it depends on an external function, which is **getProductCount**.

The following will be the benefits:

- A pure function is easy to test because it does not depend on any external object or function.

- A pure function is good for parallel processing, and you will get more benefits if used in functional programming.

Higher-order functions

Higher-order functions are defined as functions that return functions or take lambdas as arguments. Let us see an example from the *kotlin standard-library*; the function to look at will be **filterTo** higher-order function:

```
public inline fun <T, C : MutableCollection<in T>>Iterable<T>
        .filterTo(destination: C, predicate: (T) -> Boolean): C {
    for (element in this) if (predicate(element))
        destination.add(element)
    return destination
}
```

In the preceding **filterTo** function code, the **predecate** parameter has the function **type (T) -> Boolean**, and it accepts a function that can take an argument of type **T** and return a value of type Boolean. It is called inside a loop over a collection of elements, and if the value is true, the element is added to the destination collection.

To call the **filterTo** function, you will need to pass a function of **type (T) -> Boolean** as an argument or a lambda expression, which is mostly used for higher-order function calls.

Example:

```
fun printEventNumbers() {
    val evenNumbers = mutableListOf<Int>()
    (1..10).filterTo(evenNumbers) { x: Int -> x % 2 == 0 }
    println(evenNumbers)
}
```

Here, we passed the lambda expression **x: Int -> x % 2 == 0** as the function argument to test if a number is even.

When calling a lambda function that takes only one argument, it can be referred to implicitly by using the keyword **it** like in the following alternative example:

```
fun printEventNumbers2() {
    val evenNumbers = mutableListOf<Int>()
    (1..10).filterTo(evenNumbers) { it % 2 == 0 }
```

```
        println(evenNumbers)
    }
```

In the preceding code, the **it % 2 == 0** is equivalent to **x: Int -> x % 2 == 0**.

The *kotlin standard library* has a lot of higher-order functions that we use in almost every code. Among these functions, we can list **filter**, **map**, and **reduce**.

Example using **filter**, **map**, and **reduce** together:

```
    // Calculate the sum of squared even numbers between 1 and 100
    fun sumSquaredEvenNumbers() {
        val sum = (1..100).filter {
            it % 2 == 0
        }.map {
            it*it
        }.reduce { acc, i ->
            acc + i
        }
        println("Sum = $sum")
    }
```

The following will be the output:

Sum = 171700

Inline functions

In *Chapter 4, Generics*, we saw how using *inline functions* with a *reified* modifier before the generic type parameter helps get rid of the type erasure issues. The same problem with higher-order functions; they impose some runtime penalties because of the fact that each function is an object and a function captures a scope of variables (or a *Closure*) defined within its body; therefore, the allocation of memory for function objects will cause certain runtime overhead.

In many cases, the overhead of this kind can be avoided by inlining these functions or the lambda expressions at the call site, which will enhance the performance of higher-order functions.

When inlining a function, the compiler copies the code inside the function body at the calling place and does not allocate any extra memory for this function.

To declare an inline function, we use the inline keyword before the function declaration, illustrated in the following example:

```
inline fun String.removeSlice(
    text: String,
    action: (String) -> Unit
) {
    val startIndex = this.indexOf(text)
    val result = this.removeRange(startIndex, startIndex + text.length)
    action(result)
}

fun main() {
    "email@gmail.com".removeSlice("@gmail") { println(it) }
    "212IPX021".removeSlice("IPX") { println(it) }
}
```

It is not recommended to inline a large function; this will cause the generated code to grow and impact the performance of your application. The **inline** modifier will affect the function itself, and any lambda passed to it; all those are inlined on the call site.

In the following cases, you have to work with **inline** functions:

- When working with higher-order functions
- When your function accepts another function or a lambda expression
- To pass parameters of functional types
- The use of reified type parameters requires using inline

noinline

In many cases, you will not need to inline all passed lambdas to your higher-order function to be inlined as well. In this case, you should mark your function parameters (lambdas) with the **noinline** keyword as follows:

```
inline fun bar(inlined: () -> Unit, noinline notInlined: (String) -> Unit) { }
```

Polymorphic functions

Polymorphic functions here are only generic functions that operate on multiple types of data. For instance, when we intend to use higher-order functions, we will need to deal with many data types it is given.

Declaration and use of *polymorphic functions* were covered in *Chapter 4: Generic* (generic functions). But in this section, we want only to mention that working with higher-order functions requires, in most cases, that functions or lambda expressions passed to them need to be polymorphic (or generic) to ensure dealing with multiple data types.

Example:

```
fun <T> List<T>.printValues(separator:String="\n") {
    this.forEach {
        print(it)
        print(separator)
    }
}

fun main() {
    val doubles = listOf<Double>(1.2, 2.3, 5.5, 7.4, 2.0)
    val names = listOf<String>("Ali", "Samir", "John", "Tania")

    doubles
        .map { it/2 }
        .filter { it > 2.0 }
        .printValues()

    names
        .filter { it.length >= 4 }
        .map { it.toUpperCase() }
        .printValues("__")
}
```

The following will be the output:

2.75
3.7
SAMIR__JOHN__TANIA__

Functional data structures

In this section, we will define and implement our own functional data structure by implementing a **Singly Linked List**. We will get to practice writing and using pure functions.

A functional data structure is meant to use only pure functions. As you previously learned, pure function should not alter the data passed to it or produce any side effect. Therefore, functional data structures are immutable.

Definition and declaration of the singly linked list data structure

A singly linked list is defined as **a specific case of a generic linked list**. Each node in the singly linked list links to only the next node in the sequence; for instance, if we start traversing from a node of the list, we can only move in one direction.

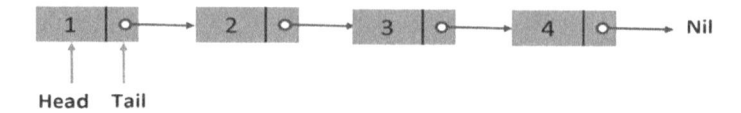

Figure 6.2: Singly linked list

In the singly linked list, each tail points to the next list node.

```
sealed class Node<out T>   (1)


object Nil: Node<Nothing>()   (2)
data class SLL<out T>(val head: T, val tail:Node<T> = Nil): Node<T>()   (3)
```

Here, we declared a sealed class called **Node** of a parameter type **T** **(1)**; using the **sealed** keyword means that the class Node is abstract, so it cannot be instantiated and that the implementation should be done in the same file. Then, we made two implementations of the Node class that it has as data constructs, which are the two possible forms of the Node class in the singly linked list; in line (2), the data constructor **Nil** which represents an empty Node, and a non-empty Node denoted by a data constructor SLL as a reference to singly linked list that takes an initial node, head, and the remaining or the next Node (the **tail**) line (3), the tail default value is **Nil**.

In the preceding declaration, we used a polymorphic definition, which means we can use it with multiple data types. The following are some examples:

```
val node1: Node<Double> = Nil
val node2: Node<Int> = SLL(1)
```

```
val node3: Node<String> = SLL("A", SLL("B"))
```

Now, let us add a **companion** object block to the declaration of the **Node** class where we can define a variadic **helper** function which can be used to create an SLL from a list of items of type **T** (qualified by a keyword **vararg** to make it accept an arbitrary number of parameters of a same type).

```
sealed class Node<out T> {
    companion object {
        fun <T> of(vararg items: T): Node<T> {
            val tail = items.sliceArray(1 until items.size)
            return if (items.isEmpty()) Nil else SLL(items[0], of(*tail))
        }
    }
}
```

Next, we will add two new functions to the companion object of the Node class: sum and product.

The **sum** function will operate on nodes of type **Int**, whereas the product function will be called on nodes of type **Double**:

```
sealed class Node<out T> {
    companion object {
        fun <T> of(vararg items: T): Node<T> {
            val tail = items.sliceArray(1 until items.size)
            return if (items.isEmpty()) Nil else SLL(items[0], of(*tail))
        }

        fun sum(items: Node<Int>): Int {
            return when(items) {
                is Nil -> 0
                is SLL -> items.head + sum(items.tail)
            }
        }

        fun product(items: Node<Double>): Double {
```

```
                return when(items) {
                    is Nil -> 1.0
                    is SLL -> if (items.head == 0.0) 0.0 else items.head *
                    product(items.tail)
                }
            }
        }
    }
```

The following code shows how to use these functions:

```
    val ints = Node.of(1,2,3,4)
    val doubles = Node.of(1.21,2.56,3.14,4.89)

    println(Node.sum(ints))
    println(Node.product(doubles))
```

The following will be the output:

10

47.56240895999999

Let us add some other functions to modify nodes; the function we will implement now is the tail function, which removes the first element of the nodes list:

```
    fun <T> tail(node: Node<T>): Node<T> =
        when(node) {
            is SLL -> node.tail
            is Nil -> throw IllegalStateException(
                        "Nil node doesn't contain a tail.")
        }
```

In the same manner, we will create a function (**setHead**) to replace the first element of a singly linked list with a new value:

```
    fun <T> setHead(node: Node<T>, newHead: T):Node<T> =
        when(node) {
            is Nil -> throw IllegalStateException(
                "Cannot replace a head of Nil node")
```

```
            is SLL -> SLL(newHead, node.tail)
    }
```

Let us go ahead and implement the **dropWhile** function, which removes elements from the *singly linked list* when a predicate is matched. Here, we use a higher-order function:

```
    tailrec fun <T> dropWhile(node: Node<T>, fn: (T) -> Boolean): Node<T> =
        when (node) {
            is SLL -> if (fn(node.head)) dropWhile(node.tail, fn) else node
            is Nil -> node
        }
```

In the preceding code, we used tail recursion by adding the **tailrec** keyword to the function definition. Tail recursion is used by the compiler to rewrite a recursive function in an imperative way, thus enhancing the code performance.

There are a lot of functions we can implement for the singly linked list; if you want, you can use them. The purpose of this section is just to show you how we can use pure functions with higher-order functions in the functional data structures; otherwise, there are many data structures we can implement in the functional style in Kotlin.

Handling errors

Handling exceptions in a traditional way makes the code messy; this is because of using the **try-catch** blocks. In Scala, for example, in its standard library, there is a feature kind of algebraic data type that provides an alternative for handling exceptions rather than using the old try-catch block; this was named **Try**.

The idea behind the **Try** structure is that you need to wrap your function that might throw errors in the **Try**, then the **Try** executes the function and then creates a **Succes** or a **Failure** subtype based on the calling result of the function inside the **Try**.

In Kotlin, we can implement the same handling exception process thanks to the language features it provides.

Let us implement a basic **Try** in Kotlin:

```
    sealed class Try<A> {
        companion object {
            operator fun <A> invoke(fn: () -> A): Try<A> = try {
                Success(fn())
            } catch (e: Exception) {
```

```kotlin
                    Failure(e)
            }
        }

        abstract fun <R> map(transformer: (A) -> R): Try<R>
        abstract fun <R> flatMap(fn: (A) -> Try<R>): Try<R>
    }

    data class Success<A>(val value: A) : Try<A>() {
        override fun <R> map(transformer: (A) -> R): Try<R> =
            Try {  transformer(value) }

        override fun <R> flatMap(fn: (A) -> Try<R>): Try<R> =
            Try {fn(value)}.let {
                when(it) {
                    is Success -> it.value
                    is Failure -> it as Try<R>
                }
            }
    }

    data class Failure<A>(val exception: Exception) : Try<A>() {
        override fun <R> map(transformer: (A) -> R): Try<R> = this as Try<R>
        override fun <R> flatMap(fn: (A) -> Try<R>): Try<R> = this as Try<R>
    }
```

A very basic example of applying the **Try** would be like the following:

```kotlin
    fun main() {
        val res1: Try<Double> = Try {  1.0 / 2 }
        val res2: Try<Double> =
                Try { throw ArithmeticException("Operation not allowed!") }

        println(res1)
        println(res2)
    }
```

This will result in the following output:

`Success(value=0.5)`

`Failure(exception=java.lang.ArithmeticException: Operation not allowed!)`

Now, you see that the result of your operations is encapsulated in a Try; usually, when performing some arithmetic operations, the return result might be a Double, but now it becomes a **Try<Double>**. The **Try** provides, in addition, multiple higher-order functions to perform any kind of transformation on the value it will contain.

This will provide us with a different way of working: we will keep performing our data manipulation without caring about the result, whether it is a **Success** or a **Failure**, until the last moment of our code.

Let us give this a try with a real word application: reading tasks from a CSV file:

```
data class Task(
    val name: String,
    val status: TaskStatus,
    val plannedTime: LocalTime
)

enum class TaskStatus(val status: String) {
    Waiting("Waiting"),
    Completed("Completed"),
    Archived("Archived");

    companion object {
        private val statuses =
            TaskStatus.values().associateBy(TaskStatus::status)
        fun fromString(status: String) = Try { statuses[status]
            ?: throw NoSuchElementException("Status $status not found!") }
    }
}

fun toTask(values: List<String>): Try<Task> {
    val name = values[0]
```

```kotlin
        val plannedTimeTry = Try {
            LocalTime.parse(values[1], DateTimeFormatter.ofPattern("HH:mm"))
        }
        val statusTry = TaskStatus.fromString(values[2])

        return plannedTimeTry.flatMap { plannedTime ->
            statusTry.map { status ->
                Task(name, status, plannedTime)
            }
        }
    }



fun main() {

    val lines = Try {
        File("./tasks.csv").readLines().map { it.split(",") }
    }

    val tasks: Try<List<Try<Task>>> = lines.map { it.map(::toTask) }

    when(tasks) {
        is Success -> println(tasks.value)
        is Failure -> println(tasks.exception)
    }
}
```

Reading a CSV file is a basic and well-chosen real-world example where we can handle all kinds of I/O exceptions. The content of the **tasks.csv** file used in this example is as follows:

```
Go to the market,12:00,Completed
Do homeworks,15:30,""
Feed cats,16:30,Archived
```

The output of the preceding code is as follows:

```
[Success(value=Task(name=Go to the market, status=Completed, plannedTime=12:00)),
Failure(exception=java.util.NoSuchElementException: Status "" not found!),
Success(value=Task(name=Feed cats, status=Archived, plannedTime=16:30))]
```

This would give you a clear idea of how we can use our own data structures to handle errors in a functional way. But if you do not want to make your own handling exception code, you can refer to many Kotlin libraries that handle this very well, for example, the **Arrow** library.

Conclusion

So far, you have been taught about functional programming paradigms, and you also saw how we can refer to some Kotlin libraries like RxKotlin to go reactive. You also learned about lambda expressions, pure functions, and higher-order functions and how each is related to the other. You also got some introductions to data structure in a functional way and how to handle exceptions in functional programming by creating your own data structure for error handling.

In the upcoming chapter, we will learn about another topic in the reactive programming paradigm: *Observables and observers*.

Points to remember

The following are some points to remember about the functional programming in Kotlin:

- The lambda expression is an anonymous function and is used the most in functional programming.
- Pure functions are easy to maintain and test.
- **Higher-order functions (HOF)** are functions that return a function or accept a lambda expression as a parameter.
- Inline functions are declared with the keyword **inline**, and they are meant to enhance the performance and memory allocation of a program.
- Handling exceptions in functional programming is more elegant and easier to deal with.

Join our book's Discord space

Join the book's Discord Workspace for Latest updates, Offers, Tech happenings around the world, New Release and Sessions with the Authors:

https://discord.bpbonline.com

Chapter 7
Observables, Observers, and Subjects

Introduction

In the previous chapter, we explored the concept of functional programming in Kotlin. In this chapter, we will continue our journey into Kotlin programming by introducing the concepts of observables, observers, and subjects.

Observables, observers, and subjects are important concepts in the reactive programming paradigm, which aims to simplify the creation of asynchronous and event-based programs.

Structure

In this chapter, we will cover the following topics:

- How do observables work?
- Observable factory methods
- Subjects

Objectives

By the end of this chapter, you will understand the concepts of observables, observers, and subjects in the context of reactive programming. Learn how to create observables and observers in Kotlin using the RxKotlin library. Explore the various factory methods and operators the RxKotlin library provides for working with observables. Understand the different types of Subjects available in the RxKotlin library and how they can be used. Learn how to use observables, observers, and subjects to create asynchronous and event-based programs in Kotlin.

Overview

Reactive programming is a programming paradigm that aims to simplify the creation of asynchronous and event-based programs. It does this by using observables, which represent streams of data or events, and observers, which consume items emitted by observables.

In reactive programming, an observable can emit a sequence of items and then complete or error out. An observer can perform some action on each item and be notified of when the observable completes or errors out. This allows for a clean separation of concerns between the producer of data (the observable) and the consumer (the observer).

In Kotlin, the RxKotlin library provides a variety of factory methods for creating observables, as well as a wide range of operators for transforming and combining observables. It also provides several types of subjects and special observables that can act as observers.

Reactive programming can be used to simplify the creation of asynchronous and event-based programs in Kotlin and make it easier to manage and manipulate data streams. It is particularly useful for handling data streams in a non-blocking, thread-safe manner and can help avoid the need for complicated asynchronous code.

How do observables work?

Observables are a fundamental concept in reactive programming, which aims to simplify the creation of asynchronous and event-based programs. An observable class represents a stream of data or events, and it can emit a sequence of items and then complete or error out. An observable can be considered a producer of items and observers as consumers of those items.

Observables are created using factory methods provided by the RxKotlin library. These factory methods allow us to specify the data or events that the observable will emit. Once an observable is created, it can be subscribed to by an observer, consuming the items emitted by the observable.

A real-world example of how do observables works is as follows:

A weather forecasting service is one example of how observables can be used to model real-world situations. Imagine that you have subscribed to a weather forecasting service that sends you updates about the weather in your area.

In this scenario, the weather forecasting service can be considered an observable that emits weather updates. Each time the service receives new weather data, it can emit a weather update to its observers (in this case, you). The weather update could be a simple message or a more complex data object containing detailed information about the weather.

As an observer, you are interested in receiving and using these weather updates to plan your day. You might have a list of activities you want to do based on the weather, such as hiking if it is sunny or staying indoors if it is raining.

Whenever the weather forecasting service emits a new weather update, you can consume it and use it to update your list of activities. You might also have some code that sends you notifications or alerts based on the weather, such as a notification to bring an umbrella if it is going to rain.

In this example, the weather forecasting service is the observable, and you are the observer. The weather updates emitted by the observable are consumed by the observer and used to plan your day and receive notifications.

Observable factory methods

In Kotlin, observables are created using factory methods provided by the RxKotlin library. These factory methods allow us to specify the data or events that the observable will emit. Once an observable is created, it can be subscribed to by an observer, consuming the items emitted by the observable.

The following is an example of creating an observable that emits a range of integers and subscribing to it with an observer that prints each item to the console:

```
fun main() {
    val observable: Observable<Int> = Observable.range(1, 10)
    val observer: Observer<Int> = object : Observer<Int> {
        override fun onSubscribe(d: Disposable) {
            // This method is called when the Observer subscribes to the Observable
            println("An observer has been subscribed")
        }

        override fun onNext(value: Int) {
            println("Received value: $value")
        }
```

```
        override fun onComplete() {
            println("Observable completed")
        }

        override fun onError(e: Throwable) {
            println("Observable encountered an error: $e")
        }
    }
    observable.subscribe(observer)
}
```

The following will be the output:

```
An observer has been subscribed
Received value: 1
Received value: 2
Received value: 3
Received value: 4
Received value: 5
Received value: 6
Received value: 7
Received value: 8
Received value: 9
Received value: 10
Observable completed
```

In the preceding example, we created an observable (**observable**) and an observer (**observer**) and then subscribed the observer to the observable. The observable is created using the **range** factory method provided by the RxKotlin library, which creates an observable that emits a range of integers. In this case, the observable will emit the values 1–10.

The observer is created using an object expression that implements the observer interface. The **onSubscribe** method is called when the observer subscribes to the observable, and the other methods (**onNext**, **onComplete**, and **onError**) are called as the observable emits items, completes, or encounters an error. In this case, the observer simply prints a message to the console when each event occurs.

Finally, the observer is subscribed to the observable using the subscribe method. This causes the observable to emit items that the observer will consume. In this example, the observer will receive the values 1 through 10 as they are emitted by the observable, and then the observable will complete.

We can also use operators provided by the RxKotlin library to transform the items emitted by an observable. For example, we can use the **filter** operator to filter even numbers and the **map** operator to apply a transformation function to each item (*double it here*):

```
//2. Observable with filter and map operators
observable
    .filter { it % 2 == 0 }
    .map { it * 2 }
    .subscribe(observer)
```

The following will be the output:

```
An observer has been subscribed
Received value: 4
Received value: 8
Received value: 12
Received value: 16
Received value: 20
Observable completed
```

In this example, the observer will receive the even numbers between 1 and 10 multiplied by 2 as they are emitted by the observable. Observables can also be combined using operators such as **zip**, which combines the emissions of multiple observables into a single observable.

Example:

```
fun main() {
    val observable1: Observable<Int> = Observable.range(1, 4)
    val observable2: Observable<String> = Observable.just("A", "B", "C", "D")

    val observer: Observer<Pair<Int, String>> = object : Observer<Pair<Int, String>> {
        override fun onSubscribe(d: Disposable) {
            println("An observer has been subscribed")
        }
```

```
            override fun onNext(value: Pair<Int, String>) {
                println("Received value: $value")
            }

            override fun onComplete() {
                println("Observable completed")
            }

            override fun onError(e: Throwable) {
                println("Observable encountered an error: $e")
            }
        }

        Observable.zip(observable1, observable2) { a, b ->
            Pair(a, b)
        }.subscribe(observer)
    }
```

In this example, the observer will receive the values **(1, "A"), (2, "B"), (3, "C")**, and **(4, "D")** as they are emitted by the combined observable.

The following is the output of the code execution:

```
An observer has been subscribed
Received value: (1, A)
Received value: (2, B)
Received value: (3, C)
Received value: (4, D)
Observable completed
```

These are just a few examples of how observables can be used in Kotlin with the RxKotlin library. Many more operators and features are available for working with observables, including error handling, scheduling, and more.

Subjects

A subject is a special type of observable that can also act as an observer, meaning it can both emit and consume items emitted by another observable. Subjects are useful for bridging the gap between observables and observers and for multicasting events to multiple observers.

Several types of subjects are provided by the RxKotlin library, each with its own behavior and use cases. Let us see the example in the following subsections.

BehaviorSubject

This type of Subject stores the last emitted item and will emit it to any new observers who subscribe to it. If the Subject has not yet emitted any items, it will emit a default value to new observers. The following is an example of using a **BehaviorSubject** in Kotlin:

```
fun main() {
    val subject: BehaviorSubject<Int> = BehaviorSubject.create()

    subject.onNext(1)
    subject.onNext(2)
    subject.onNext(3)

    val observer1: Observer<Int> = object : Observer<Int> {
        override fun onSubscribe(d: Disposable) {
            println("Observer 1 has a new subscription")
        }

        override fun onNext(value: Int) {
            println("observer 1 received value: $value")
        }

        override fun onComplete() {
            println("Observable completed")
        }

        override fun onError(e: Throwable) {
            println("Observable encountered an error: $e")
        }
```

```kotlin
        }

        subject.subscribe(observer1)

        val observer2: Observer<Int> = object : Observer<Int> {
            override fun onSubscribe(d: Disposable) {
                println("Observer 2 has a new subscription")
            }

            override fun onNext(value: Int) {
                println("observer 2 received value: $value")
            }

            override fun onComplete() {
                println("Observable completed")
            }

            override fun onError(e: Throwable) {
                println("Observable encountered an error: $e")
            }
        }

        subject.subscribe(observer2)

}
```

The following will be the output:

```
Observer 1 has a new subscription
observer 1 received value: 3
Observer 2 has a new subscription
observer 2 received value: 3
```

In this example, the **BehaviorSubject** receives the values 1, 2, and 3 from its producer. When **observer1** and **observer2** are subscribed to the **BehaviorSubject**, they will each receive the last emitted value, **3**.

PublishSubject

This type of Subject does not store any items and will only emit items to observers who have subscribed to it after the items are emitted.

The following is an example of using a **PublishSubject** in Kotlin:

```
fun main() {
    val subject: PublishSubject<Int> = PublishSubject.create()

    subject.onNext(1)
    subject.onNext(2)
    subject.onNext(3)

    val observer1: Observer<Int> = object : Observer<Int> {
        override fun onSubscribe(d: Disposable) {
            println("Observer 1 has a new subscription")
        }

        override fun onNext(value: Int) {
            println("observer 1 received value: $value")
        }

        override fun onComplete() {
            println("Observable completed")
        }

        override fun onError(e: Throwable) {
            println("Observable encountered an error: $e")
        }
    }
```

```kotlin
        subject.subscribe(observer1)

        subject.onNext(4)
        subject.onNext(5)

        val observer2: Observer<Int> = object : Observer<Int> {
            override fun onSubscribe(d: Disposable) {
                println("Observer 2 has a new subscription")
            }

            override fun onNext(value: Int) {
                println("observer 2 received value: $value")
            }

            override fun onComplete() {
                println("Observable completed")
            }

            override fun onError(e: Throwable) {
                println("Observable encountered an error: $e")
            }
        }

        subject.subscribe(observer2)

    }
```

The following will be the output:

```
Observer 1 has a new subscription
observer 1 received value: 4
observer 1 received value: 5
Observer 2 has a new subscription
```

In this example, the **PublishSubject** receives the values 1, 2, and 3 from its producer. When **observer1** subscribes to the **PublishSubject**, it will not receive any of these values because it subscribed after they were emitted. However, when the **PublishSubject** receives values 4 and 5 after **observer1** subscribed, it will receive the values 4 and 5. However, **observer2** still does not receive the emitted values because it just subscribes after the values were emitted and not before.

ReplaySubject

It is another type of Subject provided by the RxKotlin library. It allows you to specify how many items should be replayed to new observers or a time window in which items should be replayed.

The following is an example of using a **ReplaySubject** in Kotlin:

```kotlin
fun main() {
    val subject: ReplaySubject<Int> = ReplaySubject.create()

    subject.onNext(1)
    subject.onNext(2)
    subject.onNext(3)

    val observer1: Observer<Int> = object : Observer<Int> {
        override fun onSubscribe(d: Disposable) {
            println("Observer 1 has a new subscription")
        }

        override fun onNext(value: Int) {
            println("observer 1 received value: $value")
        }

        override fun onComplete() {
            println("Observable completed")
        }

        override fun onError(e: Throwable) {
            println("Observable encountered an error: $e")
        }
```

```kotlin
        }

        subject.subscribe(observer1)

        val observer2: Observer<Int> = object : Observer<Int> {
            override fun onSubscribe(d: Disposable) {
                println("Observer 2 has a new subscription")
            }

            override fun onNext(value: Int) {
                println("observer 2 received value: $value")
            }

            override fun onComplete() {
                println("Observable completed")
            }

            override fun onError(e: Throwable) {
                println("Observable encountered an error: $e")
            }
        }

        subject.subscribe(observer2)

}
```

The following will be the output:

```
Observer 1 has a new subscription
observer 1 received value: 1
observer 1 received value: 2
observer 1 received value: 3
Observer 2 has a new subscription
observer 2 received value: 1
observer 2 received value: 2
observer 2 received value: 3
```

In this example, the **ReplaySubject** receives the values 1, 2, and 3 from its producer. When **Observer 1** and **Observer 2** are subscribed to the **ReplaySubject**, they will each receive the values 1, 2, and 3 because the **ReplaySubject** will replay all the items to new Observers by default.

You can also customize the behavior of the **ReplaySubject** by specifying how many items should be replayed or by specifying a time window in which items should be replayed. For example:

```
val subject: ReplaySubject<Int> = ReplaySubject.createWithSize(2)

subject.onNext(1)
subject.onNext(2)
subject.onNext(3)
```

The following will be the output:

```
Observer 1 has a new subscription
observer 1 received value: 2
observer 1 received value: 3
Observer 2 has a new subscription
observer 2 received value: 2
observer 2 received value: 3
```

In this example, the **ReplaySubject** is configured to replay the last two items to new Observers. When **Observer 1** and **Observer 2** are subscribed to the **ReplaySubject**, they will each receive the values 2 and 3 because these are the last two items emitted by the **ReplaySubject**.

You can also specify a time window in which items should be replayed using the **createWithTime** factory method to replay items emitted within the last configured time to new Observers. When **observer1** and **observer2** are subscribed to the **ReplaySubject**, they will each receive only the values emitted within the last configured time-bound.

Conclusion

In conclusion, observables, observers, and subjects are important concepts in the reactive programming paradigm and are widely used in Kotlin programming with the Rxkotlin library. Observables represent streams of data or events and can be created using factory methods provided by the library. Observers consume items emitted by observables and can perform some action on each item and be notified of when the observable completes or errors out. Subjects are special observables that can also act as observers and are useful for bridging the gap between observables and observers and for multicasting events to multiple observers.

These concepts form the foundation of the reactive programming paradigm and are used to simplify the creation of asynchronous and event-based programs in Kotlin. They allow for a clean separation of concerns between the producer of data (the observable) and the consumer (the observer). They can help to avoid the need for complicated asynchronous code. By using observables, observers, and subjects, Kotlin programmers can more easily manage and manipulate data streams non-blocking, thread-safe.

Points to remember

Some key points to remember about observables, observers, and subjects in Kotlin are as follows:

- Observables represent data streams or events and can be created using factory methods provided by the RxKotlin library.
- Observers consume items emitted by observables and can perform some action on each item and be notified of when the observable completes or errors out.
- Subjects are special observables that can also act as observers and are useful for bridging the gap between observables and observers and for multicasting events to multiple observers.
- The RxKotlin library provides a variety of operators for transforming and combining observables, as well as several types of Subjects with different behaviors.
- Reactive programming can simplify the creation of asynchronous and event-based programs in Kotlin. It can make it easier to manage and manipulate data streams in a non-blocking, thread-safe manner.

Chapter 8
Flowables and Backpressure

Introduction

In the previous chapter, we learned about observables, observers, and subjects, important concepts in the reactive programming paradigm. These concepts allow developers to represent asynchronous data streams and react to changes in the data over time.

In this chapter, we will continue our exploration of reactive programming by focusing on Flowables and observables in Kotlin. Kotlin is a modern, statically typed programming language that is concise, expressive, and designed to be safer and more readable than Java. It is fully interoperable with Java and is widely used for building Android and server-side applications.

Structure

In this chapter, we will cover the following topics:
- Flowables and observables
- Flowable from observable
- Backpressure
- Flowable with backpressure

Objectives

By the end of this chapter, you will gain a comprehensive understanding of key concepts in reactive programming with Kotlin. This includes an introduction to flowables and observables and their role in this paradigm. You'll learn how to convert an observable into a Flowable using the toFlowable operator. Furthermore, the chapter will explain the crucial concept of backpressure and its importance in ensuring efficient data processing within a Flowable. You'll see practical examples of using the onBackpressureBuffer operator to implement backpressure strategies, such as dropping excess items, buffering items, and controlling the emission rate, providing you with valuable tools for managing data flow effectively.

Overview

Flowables and observables are types of data streams that are used in reactive programming. They allow developers to represent asynchronous data streams and react to changes in the data over time. Flowables are a type of data stream designed to handle large volumes of data, known as **backpressure**. They allow developers to control the rate at which data is emitted and processed, ensuring that it can be processed efficiently and without overloading the system. On the contrary, observations are a simpler type of data stream that does not have built-in support for backpressure. They are often used for smaller data volumes or cases where backpressure is unnecessary.

Flowables and observables

Flowables are a type of data stream, part of the reactive stream specification. They emit events over time and are particularly useful for handling large amounts of data, such as data from a database or a network connection. Flowables have built-in support for backpressure, allowing them to handle situations where the producer emits data faster than the consumer can handle it.

Using flowables in Kotlin: To use flowables in Kotlin, you must include the following reactive-streams library in your project:

```
<dependency>
    <groupId>org.jetbrains.kotlinx</groupId>
    <artifactId>kotlinx-coroutines-rx2</artifactId>
    <version>1.6.4</version>
</dependency>
```

You can then create a flowable by using the **flow** function and specifying the data that you want to **emit**. For example, the following code creates a flowable that emits a range of numbers and then consumes the data emitted by the flowable using the **collect** operator to print the values emitted to the console:

```
import kotlinx.coroutines.flow.*

suspend fun main() {
    val numbersFlowable = flow {
        for (i in 1..10) {
            emit(i)
        }
    }

    numbersFlowable.collect {
        println(it)
    }
}
```

The following will be the output:

```
1
2
3
4
5
6
7
8
9
10
```

Difference between observables and flowables

Observables and flowables are data streams that can emit a sequence of events over time. However, there are some key differences between these two, and these differences are given as follows:

- Observables are part of the RxJava library, whereas Flowables are part of the reactive stream's specification.

- Observables do not have built-in support for backpressure, whereas Flowables do. Backpressure is a mechanism that helps to control the flow of data in a stream by allowing the consumer to slow down the producer.
- Observables are implemented using the observable and observer interfaces, part of the RxJava library. Flowables, on the contrary, are implemented using coroutines, a lightweight and efficient way to manage concurrency in Kotlin.
- Observables are more commonly used in Java applications, whereas Flowables are more suitable for Kotlin applications requiring reactive and concurrent behavior.

Flowables are a more modern and efficient alternative to observables, generally preferred for building reactive and concurrent applications. However, observables may still be useful in certain situations, such as when working with existing RxJava code or when backpressure is not a concern.

When to use flowables and not observables?

For example, suppose you are building a mobile application that retrieves data from a remote server and displays it to the user. If the server sends a large amount of data, you might want to use a flowable to handle the data stream and apply backpressure to ensure the data is processed efficiently. This would allow you to avoid overloading the device's resources and ensure the user experience is smooth and responsive.

Flowables are a good choice whenever you need to handle large amounts of data reactively and concurrently and are particularly useful when backpressure is a concern.

Flowable from observable

If you have an observable data source and want to use the backpressure capabilities of flowable, you can convert the observable into a flowable using the **toFlowable** operator. For example, the following code converts an observable into a flowable:

```
import io.reactivex.rxjava3.core.BackpressureStrategy
import io.reactivex.rxjava3.core.Observable
import kotlinx.coroutines.flow.buffer
import kotlinx.coroutines.flow.filter
import kotlinx.coroutines.reactive.asFlow

suspend fun main() {
    val numbersObservable = Observable.range(1, 10)
```

```
        val numbersFlowable = numbersObservable.
        toFlowable(BackpressureStrategy.BUFFER)

        numbersFlowable.asFlow()
            .buffer(2)
            .filter { it % 2 == 0 }
            .collect { println(it) } // consume the flowable and print items to
            the console
    }
```

The following will be the output:

6

12

18

24

30

This code creates an observable that emits a range of numbers from 1 to 10. We then use the **toFlowable** operator to convert the observable into a flowable and specify the **BackpressureStrategy.BUFFER** strategy. This strategy tells the flowable to buffer items until the consumer is ready to process them. It can be useful for handling situations where the producer emits data faster than the consumer.

Next, we use the **asFlow** operator to convert the flowable into a Kotlin flow. This allows us to use the various operators of the **kotlinx.coroutines** provide and **flow** library to transform and filter the data stream.

We then use the **buffer** operator to group the items emitted by the flowable into pairs and the filter operator to filter out items that are not even. Finally, we use the **collect** operator to consume the flowable and print the items to the console.

Overall, this code demonstrates how to use the **toFlowable** operator to convert an observable into a flowable in Kotlin and how to use the **asFlow** operator to convert the flowable into a Kotlin flow. It also shows how to use the **buffer** and **filter** operators to transform and filter the data stream.

Backpressure

As mentioned earlier, backpressure is a mechanism that helps to control the flow of data in a stream. It is particularly useful when the producer emits data faster than the consumer can handle it, as it allows the consumer to slow down the producer and prevent the stream from overflowing.

Several strategies can be used to apply backpressure to a flowable. These include dropping excess items, buffering items until the consumer is ready to process them, and limiting the rate at which the producer emits items.

Flowable with backpressure

Several strategies can be used to apply backpressure to a stream, including the following:

- **Dropping excess items**: This strategy involves discarding items that the consumer cannot process in a timely manner. This can be useful when the consumer is overwhelmed and needs to reduce the amount of data it is processing.

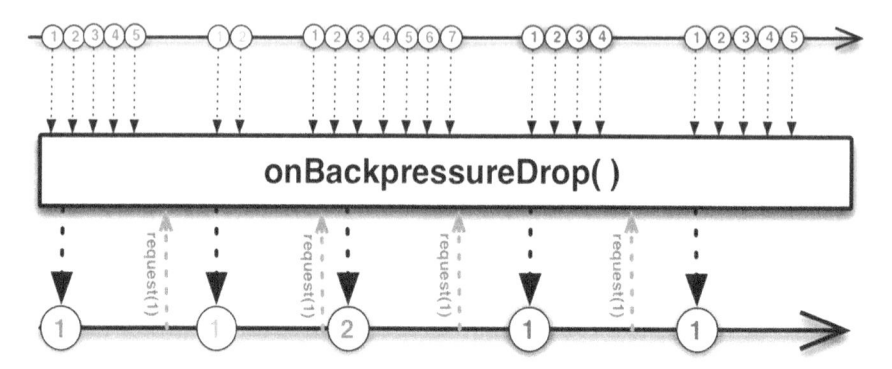

Figure 8.1: Dropping excess items illustration
(source: https://reactivex.io/documentation/operators/backpressure.html)

When dealing with backpressure in reactive programming, **onBackPressureDrop** is like a pressure relief valve that discards excess items when the downstream subscriber is unable to keep up. It ensures that the upstream source does not overwhelm the downstream consumer by simply dropping the excess items that cannot be processed immediately.

- **Buffering items**: This strategy involves storing excess items in a buffer until the consumer is ready to process them. This can be useful when the consumer is temporarily unable to process items but will be able to catch up later.

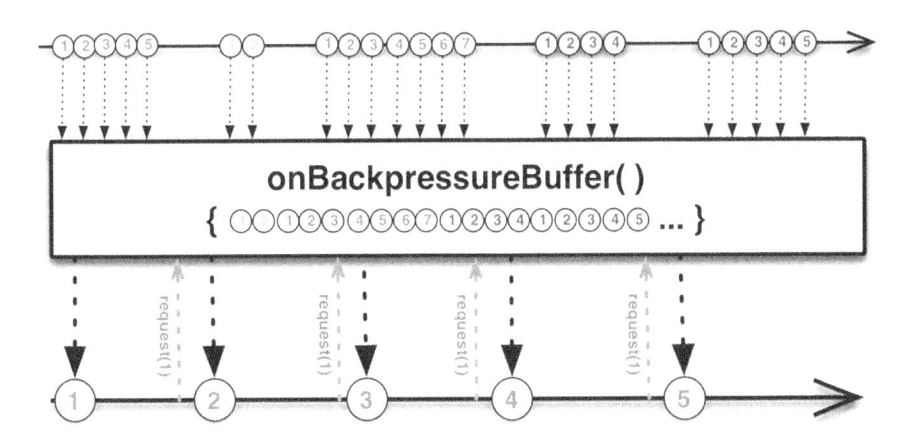

Figure 8.2: *Buffering items illustration*
(source: **https://reactivex.io/documentation/operators/backpressure.html**)

Imagine you have a reactive stream where the producer emits items at a faster rate than the consumer can process. In such a scenario, **onBackpressureBuffer** acts like a buffer that temporarily stores the excess items, allowing the downstream subscriber to consume them at its own pace. It ensures that no items are lost, buffering them until they can be processed.

- **Limiting the emission rate**: This strategy involves slowing down the rate at which the producer emits items so the consumer can keep up. This can be useful when the consumer cannot process items as fast as the producer emits them.

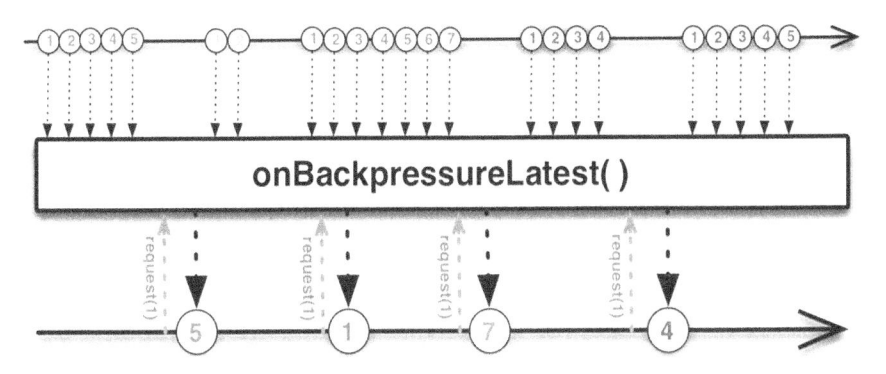

Figure 8.3: *Limiting the rate of emission*
(source: https://reactivex.io/documentation/operators/backpressure.html)

Sometimes, when the downstream consumer cannot keep up with the upstream producer, you may want to receive only the latest item emitted by the producer and drop the previous ones. This is where **onBackpressureLatest** comes into play. It allows the downstream subscriber to receive only the most recent item emitted by the producer, discarding any previously emitted but unprocessed items. It ensures that the consumer always operates on the most up-to-date data.

Overall, backpressure is an important mechanism for controlling data flow in a stream and ensuring it is processed efficiently. Using the appropriate backpressure strategy, you can ensure that your reactive and concurrent applications perform optimally and deliver a smooth and responsive user experience.

The followng are some examples of using backpressure with Flowables in Kotlin:

Example 1: Dropping excess items

```
import kotlinx.coroutines.flow.flow
import kotlinx.coroutines.reactive.collect
import kotlinx.coroutines.rx2.asFlowable

suspend fun main() {
    val numbersFlowable = flow {
        for (i in 1..10) {
            emit(i)
        }
    }

    numbersFlowable.asFlowable()
        .onBackpressureDrop { println("Dropping item: $it") }
        .buffer(2)
        .map { it.sum() }
        .filter { it % 2 == 0 }
        .collect { println(it) }
}
```

In this example, we create a flowable that emits a range of numbers from 1 to 10. We then use the **onBackpressureDrop** operator to specify that the flowable should drop excess items if the consumer cannot process them. This operator takes a lambda function that is called for each dropped item.

Next, we use the **buffer** operator to group the items emitted by the flowable into pairs. Finally, we use a **filter** to get even numbers and the **collect** operator to consume the flowable and print the items to the console.

This code demonstrates the **onBackpressureDrop** operator's application of the dropping backpressure strategy to a flowable.

Example 2: Buffering items

```
import kotlinx.coroutines.flow.flow

import kotlinx.coroutines.reactive.collect

import kotlinx.coroutines.rx2.asFlowable


suspend fun main() {
    val numbersFlowable = flow {
        for (i in 1..10) {
            emit(i)
        }
    }

    numbersFlowable.asFlowable()
        .buffer(3)
        .onBackpressureBuffer(3)
        .collect { println(it) }

}
```

The following will be the output:

[1, 2, 3]

[4, 5, 6]

[7, 8, 9]

[10]

In this code, we create a flowable that emits a range of numbers from 1 to 10. We then use the **asFlowable** operator to convert the flowable into one compatible with the RxJava library. This allows us to use the various operators provided by the RxJava library to transform and filter the data stream.

We then use the **buffer** operator to group the items emitted by the flowable into groups of 3. Next, we use the **onBackpressureBuffer** operator to specify that the flowable should buffer excess items until the consumer is ready to process them. This operator takes an argument specifying the maximum size of the buffer, in this case, 3.

Finally, we use the **collect** operator to consume the flowable and print the items to the console.

This code demonstrates how to use the **asFlowable** operator to convert a Kotlin flowable into a flowable that is compatible with the RxJava library and how to use the **onBackpressureBuffer** operator to apply the **buffering** backpressure strategy to a flowable. It also shows how to use the **buffer** operator to group items emitted by the flowable into a specific size.

Example 3: Limiting the rate of emission

```
import io.reactivex.rxjava3.core.Flowable
import kotlinx.coroutines.reactive.collect
import java.util.concurrent.TimeUnit

suspend fun main() {
    Flowable.interval(100, TimeUnit.MILLISECONDS)
        .onBackpressureLatest()
        .map {
            Thread.sleep(1000)
            it
        }
        .buffer(10)
        .collect { println(it) }


}
```

The following will be the output:

[0, 1, 2, 3, 4, 5, 6, 7, 8, 9]
[10, 11, 12, 13, 14, 15, 16, 17, 18, 19]
[20, 21, 22, 23, 24, 25, 26, 27, 28, 29]
[30, 31, 32, 33, 34, 35, 36, 37, 38, 39]
[40, 41, 42, 43, 44, 45, 46, 47, 48, 49]
[50, 51, 52, 53, 54, 55, 56, 57, 58, 59]

...

In this code, we use the **Flowable.interval** operator to create a flowable that emits a sequence of long values at a fixed rate of 100 milliseconds. This operator takes two arguments: the initial delay before the first value is emitted and the time unit in which the delay is specified.

We then use the **onBackpressureLatest** operator to specify that the flowable should emit items at the rate the consumer can process them. This operator discards all but the most recent item if the consumer cannot keep up with the emission rate.

Next, we use the **map** operator to transform the items emitted by the flowable by sleeping for one second before emitting each item. This operator takes a lambda function that specifies the transformation applied to each item.

Finally, we use the **buffer** operator to group the items emitted by the flowable into groups of 10, and the **collect** operator consumes the flowable and prints the items to the console.

This code demonstrates how to use the **Flowable.interval** operator to create a flowable that emits a sequence of values at a fixed rate and how to use the **onBackpressureLatest** operator to apply the *limiting the rate of emission* backpressure strategy to a flowable. It also shows how to use the map and buffer operators to transform and group the items emitted by the flowable.

Conclusion

In this chapter, we explored the concepts of flowables and observables and how they enable reactive programming. We learned about converting observables to flowables and the importance of handling backpressure in reactive streams to ensure efficient and reliable data processing. We discussed various strategies such as **onBackPressureDrop**, **onBackpressureBuffer**, and **onBackpressureLatest** to handle backpressure effectively.

In the upcoming chapter, we will dive into the world of data transformers and async operators. We will discover powerful operators that allow us to transform and manipulate the data flowing through our reactive streams. In addition, we will explore asynchronous operators that enable us to handle concurrency and parallelism in our reactive applications, making them more efficient and responsive.

Points to remember

The following are some points to remember about Flowables and Backpressure in Kotlin:
- Flowables are a type of data stream that is part of the Reactive Streams specification and have built-in support for backpressure.
- To use flowables in Kotlin, you will need to include the **kotlinx-coroutines-rx2** library in your project and use the **flow** function to create a flowable.
- You can consume the data emitted by a flowable using the **collect** operator.

- If you have an observable data source, you can convert it into a flowable one using the **toFlowable** operator.
- Backpressure is a mechanism that helps to control the flow of data in a stream by allowing the consumer to slow down the producer.
- Several strategies can be used to apply backpressure to a flowable, including dropping excess items, buffering items, and limiting the rate at which items are emitted.

Join our book's Discord space

Join the book's Discord Workspace for Latest updates, Offers, Tech happenings around the world, New Release and Sessions with the Authors:

https://discord.bpbonline.com

CHAPTER 9
Data Transformers and Async Operators

Introduction

In the previous chapter, we covered the concept of Flowable and its role in handling backpressure in data streams. As a continuation of that, in this chapter, we will cover the concepts of data transformers and async operators.

Data transformers are a set of operators that allow you to transform the elements of a stream by applying a function to each element. This allows you to change the data's structure, format, or type in a stream.

Async operators are a set of operators that allow you to perform asynchronous operations on a stream of data. They help to ensure that data flows smoothly through the system, even when dealing with asynchronous operations.

Data transformers and async operators provide powerful tools for handling data streams in a reactive programming paradigm. They allow developers to manipulate and control data flow in a stream, ensuring it is handled properly and efficiently.

Structure

In this chapter, we will cover the following topics:
- Rx-operator
- Filtering operators
- Transforming operators
- Reducing operators
- Processors
- Grouping operators
- Mapping operators
- Error handling
- Example

Objectives

By the end of this chapter, you will be able to Introduce the concept of Rx operators and their role in working with data streams in a reactive programming paradigm. Discuss using Flowable and data transformers and async operators to handle backpressure and ensure smooth data flow. Introduce the concept of filtering and its role in selecting specific elements from a stream. Explain the concept of grouping and its role in organizing data into related groups. Discuss the use of mapping and its role in transforming the elements of a stream. Introduce the concept of error handling and its role in ensuring that data flows are robust and reliable. Provide examples and explanations of the various Rx operators and how they can be combined to create more complex data flows and handle more complex scenarios.

This chapter aims to provide a comprehensive understanding of the various Rx operators and how they can be used to work with streams of data in a reactive programming paradigm. Understanding these operators and their use will help developers create powerful, efficient, and responsive data flows that can handle real-world scenarios.

Overview

Rx operators are tools provided by the ReactiveX library to work with data streams in a reactive programming paradigm. They allow developers to handle backpressure, filter, group, map, and handle errors in the data. Flowable is a special type of observable that handles backpressure, and it is recommended to use it when working with large data sets or infinite streams. Data transformers and async operators provide a way to handle backpressure and ensure that data flows smoothly through the system. Filtering and mapping operators filter and transform the data, respectively. Grouping operators are used to organize data into related groups. Error handling operators provide a way to handle errors and ensure the data flow is robust and reliable. With the right understanding and implementation, Rx operators can help you create powerful, efficient, and responsive data flows that can handle real-world scenarios.

Rx-operators

ReactiveX (**Rx**) is a general library for programming with asynchronous data streams. It provides a set of operators for manipulating and transforming data streams concisely and expressively. These Rx-operators are the building blocks for creating powerful and flexible data flows. In this chapter, we will take a closer look at Rx operators and how they can be used to transform data streams.

An important concept in Rx is a stream, a sequence of elements that can be emitted over time. Streams can be considered an asynchronous version of a list, where the elements are not available all at once but arrive over time. Rx-operators provide a way to manipulate and transform these streams in various ways.

Rx-operators also provide a way to handle errors and exceptions that may occur during stream processing. The `catch` operator allows for catching errors and exceptions and can be used to provide a fallback value or to retry the operation.

Rx-operators provide a powerful and expressive way to manipulate and transform data streams. They can be used for various tasks, such as filtering, transforming, reducing, grouping, and handling errors. Whether you are working with sensor data streams, user interactions, or any other asynchronous data, Rx-operators can help you create powerful and flexible data flows that can adapt to changing requirements and scale to handle large amounts of data.

Filtering operators

Filtering is a common operation when working with data streams, and Rx-operators provide a variety of ways to filter elements from a stream. The basic operator for filtering is the `filter` operator, which allows for selecting specific elements from a stream based on certain criteria. The filter operator takes as a parameter a function that returns a `Boolean`, indicating whether an element should be included in the resulting stream.

For example, let us say we have a stream of integers, and we want to filter out only even numbers from the stream, and we can use the filter operator as follows:

```
fun main() {
    val stream:Observable<Int> = Observable.fromArray(1,2,3,4,5,6,7,8,9,10)
    val evenNumbers: Observable<Int> = stream.filter { x -> x % 2 == 0 }
```

```kotlin
        evenNumbers.subscribe(::println)
}
```

In this example, the filter operator filters out only **even** numbers from the stream. The resulting stream, **evenNumbers**, will contain only the elements **2, 4, 6, 8**, and **10**. For another example, let us say we have a stream of string, and we want to filter out only strings that contain the letter **a**, and we can use the filter operator as follows:

```kotlin
fun main() {
    val stream: Observable<String> = Observable.fromArray("Kiwi",
    "Banana", "Lemon", "Orange")
  val containsA: Observable<String> = stream.filter { str -> str.contains("a")}
    containsA.subscribe(::println)
}
```

In this example, the **filter** operator is used to filter out only strings that contain the letter **a**. The resulting stream, **containsA**, will contain only the elements **Banana** and **Orange**.

Rx-operators also provide a variety of other filtering operators, such as **take**, **takeLast**, **takeUntil**, **takeWhile**, **skip**, **skipLast**, **skipUntil**, and **skipWhile**, which can be used to filter elements from a stream in different ways.

The **take** operator, for example, allows you to take only a specific number of elements from a stream. The following example demonstrates how to use the **take** operator to take only the first three elements from a stream of integers:

```kotlin
fun main() {
 val stream: Observable<Int> = Observable.fromArray(2000,2005,2010,2015,2020)
    val firstThreeYears: Observable<Int> = stream.take(3)
    firstThreeYears.subscribe(::println)
}
```

In this example, the **take** operator is used to take only the first three elements from the stream. The resulting stream, **firstThreeYears**, will contain only the years **2000**, **2005**, and **2010**.

The **takeWhile** operator, on the other hand, allows you to take elements from a stream while a certain condition is **true**. The following example demonstrates how to use the **takeWhile** operator to take elements from a stream of integers while the element is less than or equal to 3:

```kotlin
fun main() {
    val stream: Observable<Int> = Observable.fromArray(1,2,3,4,5,6)
    val lessOrEqualThree: Observable<Int> = stream.takeWhile { x -> x <= 3 }
```

```
        lessOrEqualThree.subscribe(::println)
}
```

In this example, the **takeWhile** operator is used to take elements from the stream while the element is less than or equal to 3. The resulting stream, **lessOrEqualThree**, will contain only the elements **1**, **2**, and **3**.

The **skip** operator allows you to skip a certain number of elements from a stream. The following example demonstrates how to use the **skip** operator to skip the first four elements from a stream of integers:

```
fun main() {
        val stream: Observable<Int> = Observable.fromArray(1, 2, 3, 4, 5, 6,
        7, 8, 9, 10)
        val skipFour: Observable<Int> = stream.skip(4)
        skipFour.subscribe(::println)
}
```

In this example, the **skip** operator is used to skip the first four elements from the stream. The resulting stream, **skipFour**, will contain the elements **5**, **6**, **7**, **8**, **9**, and **10**.

The **skipWhile** operator allows you to skip elements from a stream while a certain condition is **true**. The following example demonstrates how to use the **skipWhile** operator to skip elements from a stream of integers while the element is less than or equal to 4:

```
fun main() {
        val stream: Observable<Int> = Observable.fromArray(1,2,3,4,5,6,7,8,9)
        val greaterThanFour: Observable<Int> = stream.skipWhile { x -> x <= 4 }
        greaterThanFour.subscribe(::println)
}
```

In this example, the **skipWhile** operator is used to skip elements from the stream while the element is less than or equal to 4. The resulting stream, **greaterThanFour**, will contain the elements **5, 6, 7, 8,** and **9**.

There are many advanced use cases for filtering in Rx-operators. Some examples include the following:

- **distinct**: This operator filters out duplicate elements from a stream. For example, you can use the **distinct** operator to filter out duplicate strings from a stream of names. We can use the **distinct** operator as follows:

    ```
    fun main() {
    ```

```kotlin
    val stream: Observable<String> = Observable.fromArray("Ali",
    "John", "Sarah", "Ali", "John", "Mike")
    val distinctNames: Observable<String> = stream.distinct()
    distinctNames.subscribe(::println)
}
```

In this example, the **distinct** operator is used to filter out duplicate names from the stream. The resulting stream, **distinctNames**, will contain only the elements **"Ali"**, **"John"**, **"Sarah"**, and **"Mike"**.

- **distinctUntilChanged**: This operator filters out consecutive duplicate elements from a stream. For example, let us say we have a stream of numbers and we want to filter out consecutive duplicate numbers, and we can use the **distinctUntilChanged** operator as follows:

```kotlin
fun main() {
    val stream: Observable<Int> = Observable.fromArray(1, 2, 2, 3,
    3, 3, 4, 4, 5, 6, 6)
    val distinctUntilChanged: Observable<Int> = stream.
    distinctUntilChanged()
    distinctUntilChanged.subscribe(::println)
}
```

In this example, the **distinctUntilChanged** operator is used to filter out consecutive duplicate numbers from the stream. The resulting stream, **distinctUntilChanged**, will contain only the elements **1**, **2**, **3**, **4**, **5**, and **6**.

- **elementAt**: This operator allows you to select a specific element from a stream by its index. For example, let us say we have a stream of numbers and we want to select the fourth element from the stream, and we can use the **elementAt** operator as follows:

```kotlin
fun main() {
    val stream: Observable<Int> = Observable.fromArray(1, 2, 3, 4, 5)
        val fourthElement: Observable<Int> = stream.elementAt(3).
toObservable()
    fourthElement.subscribe(::println)
}
```

In this example, the **elementAt** operator is used to select the fourth element from the stream by passing the index 3 to the operator. The resulting value, **fourthElement**, will be **3**.

- **first**: This operator allows you to select the first element from a stream that meets certain criteria. For example, let us say we have a stream of numbers, and we want to select the first even number from the stream, and we can use the **first** operator as follows:

```
fun main() {
    val stream: Observable<Int> = Observable.fromArray(1, 2, 3, 4, 5)
    val firstEven: Observable<Int> = stream.filter { x -> x % 2 == 0
    }.first(0).toObservable()
    firstEven.subscribe(::println)
}
```

In this example, the **first** operator is used in combination with the **filter** operator to select the first even number from the stream. The **filter** operator is used to filter out only even numbers from the stream, and the **first** operator is used to select the first element from the filtered stream. The resulting value, **firstEven**, will be **2**. If no even number is found, the value passed to the **first** operator will be returned instead, here the value 0.

- **last**: This operator allows you to select the last element from a stream that meets certain criteria. For example, let us say we have a stream of numbers, and we want to select the last odd number from the stream; we can use the **last** operator as follows:

```
fun main() {
    val stream: Observable<Int> = Observable.fromArray(2, 3, 4, 5, 6, 7, 8)
    val lastOdd: Observable<Int> = stream.filter { x -> x % 2 == 1
    }.last(0).toObservable()
    lastOdd.subscribe(::println)
}
```

In this example, the **last** operator is used in combination with the **filter** operator to select the last odd number from the stream. The **filter** operator is used to filter out only odd numbers from the stream, and the **last** operator is used to select the last element from the filtered stream. The resulting value, **lastOdd**, will be **7**. If no even number is found, the value passed to the **last** operator will be returned instead, here the value 0.

- **throttleFirst**: This operator allows you to filter out elements from a stream that arrive too frequently. For example, let us say we have a stream of mouse clicks and we want to filter out elements that arrive at a rate faster than one click per second, and we can use the **throttleFirst** operator as follows:

```kotlin
data class MouseEvent(val x: Int, val y: Int)

fun main() {
    val mouseClicks: Observable<MouseEvent> =
        Observable.fromIterable(mapOf(230 to 100, 350 to 452, 780 to 21)
            .map { MouseEvent(it.key, it.value) })
    val filteredClicks: Observable<MouseEvent> = mouseClicks.throttleFirst(1, TimeUnit.SECONDS)
    filteredClicks.subscribe(::println)
}
```

In this example, the **throttleFirst** operator is used to filter out mouse clicks that arrive at a rate faster than one click per second. The resulting stream, **filteredClicks**, will contain only one mouse click every second. The resulting value, **filteredClicks**, will be **MouseEvent(x=230, y=100)**.

- **debounce**: This operator allows you to filter out elements from a stream that are emitted too frequently by waiting for a certain period after the last emission before emitting the next. For example, let us say we have a stream of search queries, and we want to filter out queries that are emitted too frequently by waiting for 300 milliseconds before emitting the next; we can use the **debounce** operator as follows:

```kotlin
fun main() {
    val searchQueries = Observable.create<String> { emitter ->
        // Simulating user typing in search field
        emitter.onNext("React")
        Thread.sleep(100)
        emitter.onNext("React Native")
        Thread.sleep(300)
        emitter.onNext("React Native Dev")
        Thread.sleep(500)
        emitter.onNext("React Native Development")
        Thread.sleep(300)
        emitter.onNext("React Native Development with Redux")
        Thread.sleep(200)
        emitter.onComplete()
```

```
        }

                val filteredQueries = searchQueries.debounce(300, TimeUnit.
MILLISECONDS)
        filteredQueries.subscribe { query -> println("Search query: $query")
}
    }
```

In this example, the **debounce** operator is used with a time window of 300 milliseconds, which means that any query that is emitted within 300 milliseconds of the previous query will be ignored. The resulting stream, **filteredQueries**, will only contain the queries that are entered after a period of at least 300 milliseconds has passed between them.

In this example, we should have the following output:

`Search query: React Native Dev`

`Search query: React Native Development with Redux`

As we can see, the **debounce** operator filters out the first two queries that are entered too quickly and only passes through the last two queries that are entered after a period of at least 300 milliseconds has passed between them.

It is important to note that the **debounce** operator works with the time passed between emissions. If you have a long time between emissions, the **debounce** operator will emit the last received event. Conversely, if the time between emissions is shorter than the specified time window, it will ignore the event.

These are just a few examples of the many advanced filtering use cases available with Rx-operators. The key is to understand the problem you are trying to solve and to choose the right operator for the task. It is also important to note that these operators can be combined with other Rx-operators to create more complex and powerful data flows.

Transforming operators

Transforming operators are a powerful feature of Rx-operators that allow you to transform the elements of a stream in various ways. These operators provide a way to manipulate the data in a stream and include operations such as mapping, flat-mapping, scanning, and grouping.

- **map**: One of the most basic transforming operators is the **map** operator. This operator allows you to apply a function to each element of a stream and transform it into a new value. For example, let us say we have a stream of integers, and we want to square each integer; we can use the **map** operator as follows:

```
fun main() {
    val integerStream: Observable<Int> = Observable.fromArray(1,2,3,4,5,6)
        val squaredNumbers = integerStream.map { x -> x * x }
        squaredNumbers.forEach(::println)
}
```

In this example, the map operator is used to apply the function x -> x*x to each element of the stream of integers, resulting in a new stream of squared integers. The resulting stream, **squaredNumbers**, will contain the elements 1, 4, 9, 16, 25, and 36.

- **flatMap**: Another useful operator is the **flatMap** operator. This operator allows you to apply a function to each element of a stream, transform it into a new stream, and then merge all the resulting streams into a single stream. For example, let us say we have a stream of lists of integers, and we want to flatten the lists into a single stream of integers; we can use the **flatMap** operator as follows:

```
fun main() {
    val integerStreamList: Observable<List<Int>> =
        Observable.fromArray(listOf(1, 2), listOf(3, 4, 5), listOf(6))
    val flat = integerStreamList.flatMap { list ->
        Observable.fromIterable(list)
    }
    flat.forEach(::println)
}
```

In this example, the **flatMap** operator is used to apply the function of creating an observable of integers from each list and then merge all the resulting observables into a single stream of integers. The resulting stream, **flat**, will contain the elements 1, 2, 3, 4, 5, and 6.

- **scan**: This operator allows you to perform an operation on each element of a stream, accumulate the result, and emit this result as a new stream. For example, let us say we have a stream of integers, and we want to sum them up; we can use the **scan** operator as follows:

```
fun main() {
    val integerStream: Observable<Int> = Observable.fromArray(1,2,3,4,5,6)
        val sum = integerStream.scan { x, y -> x + y }
        sum.forEach(::println)
}
```

In this example, the scan operator is used to apply the function of summing up each element with the previous accumulated value, resulting in a new stream that holds the sum of all elements seen so far in the stream. The resulting stream, **sum**, will contain the elements 1, 3, 6, 10, 15, and 21.

These are just a few examples of the many transforming operators available with Rx-operators. The key is to understand the problem you are trying to solve and to choose the right operator for the task. It is also important to note that these operators can be combined with other Rx-operators to create more complex and powerful data flows.

Reducing operators

Reducing operators are a powerful feature of Rx-operators that allow you to reduce a stream of data to a single value or a smaller stream of data. These operators provide a way to aggregate the data in a stream and include operations such as reduce, count, min, max, and average.

- **reduce**: This operator allows you to apply a function to each element of a stream, accumulate the result, and emit this result as a single value. For example, let us say we have a stream of integers, and we want to sum them up; we can use the **reduce** operator as follows:

    ```
    fun main() {
        val numbers: Observable<Int> = Observable.fromArray(1, 2, 3, 4, 5)
        val sum: Int = numbers.reduce(0) { x, y -> x + y }.blockingGet()
        println("Sum: $sum")
    }
    ```

    In this example, the **reduce** operator is used to apply the function of summing up each element with the previous accumulated value, resulting in a single value that holds the sum of all elements in the stream. The resulting value, **sum**, will be **15**.

- **count**: This operator allows you to count the number of elements in a stream. For example, let us say we have a stream of integers, and we want to count the number of elements in the stream; we can use the **count** operator as follows:

    ```
    fun main() {
        val numbers: Observable<Int> = Observable.fromArray(1, 2, 3, 4, 5)
        val count: Long = numbers.count().blockingGet()
        println("Count: $count")
    }
    ```

In this example, the count operator is used to count the number of elements in the stream of integers. The resulting value, **count**, will be **5**.

- **min and max**: The **min** and **max** operators are also very useful; they allow you to find the minimum and maximum element in the stream, respectively. For example, let us say we have a stream of integers, and we want to find the minimum and maximum element in the stream; we can use the **min** and **max** operators as follows:

```
fun main() {
    val numbers: Observable<Int> = Observable.fromArray(1, 2, 3, 4, 5)
    val min = numbers.blockingStream().min { o1, o2 -> o1.compareTo(o2) }
    val max = numbers.blockingStream().max { o1, o2 -> o1.compareTo(o2) }
    println("Min=${min.get()}, Max=${max.get()}")
}
```

In this example, the min and max operators are used to find the minimum and maximum elements in the stream of integers. The resulting values, **min** and **max** will be **1** and **5,** respectively.

- **average**: The RxJava library does not provide an **average** operator out of the box. However, you can use the reduce operator to accumulate the sum of the integers and the **count** operator to count the number of integers, then divide the sum by the count to get the average. The following is an example of how to do this:

```
fun main() {
    val numbers = Observable.fromArray(1, 2, 3, 4, 5, 6, 7, 8, 9, 10)
    val average = numbers
        .reduce(0) { acc, next -> acc + next }
        .zipWith(numbers.count()) { sum, count -> sum.toDouble() / count }
        .toObservable()
    average.subscribe { println(it) }
}
```

In this example, we are creating an observable of a list of integers. Then, we use the **reduce** operator to accumulate the sum of the integers and the **count** operator to count the number of integers. The **reduce** operator applies a function to each item emitted by an observable and emits the final value; in this case, we are accumulating the sum of the integers. The **count** operator returns the number of items emitted by an observable.

Finally, we use the **zipWith** operator to combine the sum and the count and divide the sum by the count to get the average. The **zipWith** operator combines the emissions of multiple observables together via a specified function and emits single items for each combination based on the results of this function.

The resulting stream, average, will emit a single item, which is the average of the integers in the list.

These are just a few examples of the many reducing operators available with Rx-operators. The key is to understand the problem you are trying to solve and to choose the right operator for the task. It is also important to note that these operators can be combined with other Rx-operators to create more complex and powerful data flows.

Processors

Processors are a special type of observable that also implements the subscriber interface, allowing them to both emit and receive data. This makes them useful for creating advanced data flows and implementing various types of backpressure strategies.

One of the most basic processors is the **PublishProcessor**. This processor allows you to publish data to multiple subscribers, similar to a subject. For example, let us say we have a stream of integers, and we want to publish them to multiple subscribers; we can use the **PublishProcessor** as follows:

```
fun main() {
    val numbers: PublishProcessor<Int> = PublishProcessor.create()
    numbers.subscribe { x -> println("Subscriber 1: $x") }
    numbers.subscribe { x -> println("Subscriber 2: $x") }
    numbers.onNext(1)
    numbers.onNext(2)
}
```

In this example, the **PublishProcessor** is used to publish the integers 1 and 2 to two subscribers. Each subscriber will print the received integer, resulting in the following output:

Subscriber 1: 1

Subscriber 2: 1

Subscriber 1: 2

Subscriber 2: 2

Another useful processor is the **ReplayProcessor**. This processor allows you to replay a certain number of items from the stream to new subscribers. For example, let us say we have a stream of integers, and we want to replay the last two items of the stream to new subscribers; we can use the **ReplayProcessor** as follows:

```
fun main() {
    val numbers: ReplayProcessor<Int> = ReplayProcessor.createWithSize(2)
    numbers.onNext(1)
    numbers.onNext(2)
    numbers.onNext(3)
    numbers.subscribe { x -> println("Subscriber 1: $x") }
    numbers.subscribe { x -> println("Subscriber 2: $x") }
}
```

In this example, the **ReplayProcessor** is used to replay the last two integers, 2 and 3, to two new subscribers. Each subscriber will print the received integers, resulting in the following output:

Subscriber 1: 2

Subscriber 1: 3

Subscriber 2: 2

Subscriber 2: 3

Another useful processor is the **BehaviorProcessor**. This processor allows you to keep the latest value emitted to the stream and replay it to new subscribers. For example, let us say we have a stream of integers, and we want to keep the latest value emitted and replay it to new subscribers; we can use the **BehaviorProcessor** as follows:

```
fun main() {
    val numbers: BehaviorProcessor<Int> = BehaviorProcessor.createDefault(0)
    numbers.onNext(1)
    numbers.onNext(2)
    numbers.subscribe { x -> println("Subscriber 1: $x") }
    numbers.onNext(3)
    numbers.subscribe { x -> println("Subscriber 2: $x") }
}
```

In this example, the **BehaviorProcessor** is used to keep the latest value emitted, which is 3, and replay it to two new subscribers. The first subscriber will print the received integers 1 and 2, and the second subscriber will print 3, resulting in the following output:

Subscriber 1: 2

Subscriber 1: 3

Subscriber 2: 3

These are just a few examples of the many processors available with Rx-operators. The key is to understand the problem you are trying to solve and to choose the right processor for the task. It is also important to note that these processors can be combined with other Rx-operators to create more complex and powerful data flows. Processors are a special type of observable that also implements the subscriber interface, allowing them to both emit and receive data. They provide a way to handle backpressure, replay, and caching data and offer more flexibility in creating advanced data flows.

Grouping operators

Grouping is a powerful feature of Rx-operators that allows you to group the elements of a stream based on a certain key. This allows you to organize and process the data in a stream in more efficient ways.

The **groupBy** operator is used to group elements of a stream by a certain key and emit the grouped elements as separate streams. For example, let us say we have a stream of integers, and we want to group them into even and odd numbers; we can use the **groupBy** operator as follows:

```
fun main() {
    val numbers: Observable<Int> = Observable.fromArray(1, 2, 3, 4, 5)
    val grouped: Observable<GroupedObservable<Boolean, Int>> =
                                    numbers.groupBy { x -> x % 2 == 0 }

    grouped.subscribe { group ->
        group.subscribe { x ->
            println(if (group.key == true) "Even: $x" else "Odd: $x")
        }
    }
}
```

In this example, the **groupBy** operator is used to group the elements of the stream into two separate streams based on the key of whether the number is even or odd. The resulting stream, grouped, will contain two **GroupedObservable**, one for even numbers and one for odd numbers. Each **GroupedObservable** will contain the corresponding elements from the original stream. The resulting output will be as follows:

Odd: 1

Even: 2

Odd: 3

Even: 4

Odd: 5

Another example of using the **groupBy** operator is when we have a stream of objects, and we want to group them based on a certain property. For example, let us say we have a stream of **Person** objects, and we want to group them by their **age**; we can use the **groupBy** operator as follows:

```kotlin
data class Person(val name: String, val age: Int)

fun main() {
    val people: Observable<Person> = Observable.fromArray(
        Person("John", 25),
        Person("Jane", 35),
        Person("Sarah", 25)
    )
    val grouped: Observable<GroupedObservable<Int, Person>> =
        people.groupBy { person -> person.age }
    grouped.subscribe { group ->
        group.subscribe { person ->
            println("G-${group.key}: ${person.name}")
        }
    }
}
```

In this example, the **groupBy** operator is used to group the elements of the stream of **Person** objects based on the person's age. The resulting stream, **grouped**, will contain two **GroupedObservable**, one for age **25** and one for age **35**. Each **GroupedObservable** will contain the corresponding **Person** objects from the original stream. The resulting output will be as follows:

G-25: John

G-35: Jane

G-25: Sarah

Grouping can also be used in combination with other operators such as reduce, count, min, max, and average to perform aggregate operations on the grouped data. In the previous example, we can use the **reduce** operator to sum up the ages of people in each group:

```
grouped.subscribe { group ->
    group.reduce(0) { age, p ->
        return@reduce age + p.age
    }.subscribe { ageSum: Int ->
        println(group.key.toString() + ": " + ageSum)
    }
}
```

Using the **reduce** operator, we can sum up the ages of people in each group, and the final output will be as follows:

35: 35

25: 50

It is worth noting that the **groupBy** operator returns a cold observable, meaning that it will not start emitting items until a subscriber subscribes to it. This can be useful in situations where you only want to perform operations on a specific group of items.

Grouping is a powerful feature of Rx-operators that allows you to group the elements of a stream based on a certain key. The **groupBy** operator is used to group elements of a stream by a certain key and emit the grouped elements as separate streams. This allows you to organize and process the data in a stream in more efficient ways and perform aggregate operations on the grouped data. Additionally, grouping can be used in combination with other operators to achieve more complex data processing.

Mapping operators

Mapping is a powerful feature of Rx-operators that allows you to transform the elements of a stream by applying a function to each element. This allows you to change the structure, format, or type of the data in a stream.

The **map** operator is used to apply a function to each element of a stream and emit the resulting elements. We have already seen an example in the *Transforming operators* section.

Another example of using the **map** operator is when we have a stream of objects and we want to extract a specific property from each object. For example, let us say we have a stream of **Person** objects, and we want to extract the name property from each object; we can use the **map** operator as follows:

```kotlin
fun main() {
    val people: Observable<Person> = Observable.fromArray(
        Person("Jane", 25),
        Person("John", 35),
        Person("Sarah", 25)
    )

    val names = people.map { p -> p.name }
    names.subscribe { println(it) }
}
```

In this example, the **map** operator is used to extract the name property from each **Person** object in the stream. The resulting stream **names** will contain the names of the people in the original stream. The resulting output will be as follows:

Jane

John

Sarah

It is worth noting that the **map** operator returns a new stream and does not modify the original stream. This can be useful in situations where you want to work with a modified version of the original data without changing the original data itself. Mapping is a powerful feature of Rx-operators that allows you to transform the elements of a stream by applying a function to each element. The **map** operator is used to apply a function to each element of a stream and emit the resulting elements. This allows you to change the structure, format, or type of the data in a stream. Mapping can be used to extract specific properties from objects, perform calculations, or convert the elements of a stream to a different format or type. In addition, mapping can be used in combination with other operators to achieve more complex data processing. It is important to note that the **map** operator returns a new stream and does not modify the original stream. This can be useful in situations where you want to work with a modified version of the data without changing the original data itself.

Error handling

Error handling is an essential aspect of working with streams of data in Rx-operators. Errors can occur at any stage in a data flow, and it is important to have a strategy in place to handle them properly.

One of the most basic error-handling operators is the **onErrorReturn** operator. This operator allows you to specify a default value that will be emitted in case of an error. For example, let us say we have a stream of integers, and we want to return **-1** in case of an error; we can use the **onErrorReturn** operator as follows:

```
fun main() {
    val numbers: Observable<Int> =
        Observable.fromArray(1, 2, 3, 4, 5)
            .concatWith(Observable.error(Exception()))
    val safeNumbers: Observable<Int> = numbers.onErrorReturn { -1 }
    safeNumbers.subscribe(::println) { error -> println("Error: $error") }
}
```

In this example, the **onErrorReturn** operator is used to specify that *-1* should be emitted in case of an error. The resulting stream, **safeNumbers**, will contain the original integers, and **-1** will be emitted when an error occurs. The resulting output will be as follows:

```
1
2
3
4
5
-1
```

Another useful error-handling operator is the **onErrorResumeNext** operator. This operator allows you to specify a backup stream that will be used in case of an error. For example, let us say we have a stream of integers, and we want to switch to a stream of default integers in case of an error; we can use the **onErrorResumeNext** operator as follows:

```
fun main() {
    val numbers: Observable<Int> =
        Observable.fromArray(1, 2, 3, 4, 5)
            .concatWith(Observable.error(Exception()))
    val defaultNumbers: Observable<Int> = Observable.fromArray(-1, -2, -3)
    val safeNumbers: Observable<Int> = numbers.onErrorResumeNext {
        defaultNumbers }
    safeNumbers.subscribe(::println) { error -> println("Error: $error") }
}
```

In this example, the **onErrorResumeNext** operator is used to switch to the **defaultNumbers** stream in case of an error. The resulting stream, **safeNumbers**, will contain the original integers and the default integers when an error occurs. The resulting output will be as follows:

1

2

3

4

5

-1

-2

-3

It is worth noting that you can use different strategies to retry, such as using a counter to limit the number of retries or using different delays for each retry.

Error handling is an essential aspect of working with streams of data in Rx-operators. Errors can occur at any stage in a data flow, and it is important to have a strategy in place to handle them properly. Error handling operators such as **onErrorReturn** and **onErrorResumeNext** provide a way to handle errors by specifying a default value or a backup stream, respectively.

Example

The following is an example that covers the use of Flowable, data transformers and async operators, filtering, grouping, mapping, and error handling:

```
fun main() {
    val numbers: Flowable<Int> = Flowable.fromIterable(1..10)
        .onBackpressureBuffer()
        .doOnNext { x ->
            if (x == 4) throw Exception("Error: Number 4 is not allowed")
        }

    numbers
        .filter { x -> x % 2 == 0 }
        .groupBy { x -> x > 3 }
        .flatMap { group -> group.map { x -> x * 2 }.onErrorReturn { error -> -1 } }
```

```
        .subscribe(
            { x -> println("Result: $x") }
        ) { error -> println("Error: $error") }

}
```

In this example, we are using a Flowable that emits integers from 1 to 10, and using the **onBackpressureBuffer** operator, we are handling backpressure. Then, using the **doOnNext** operator, we are simulating an error when the value is 4. After that, we use the **filter** operator to only emit even numbers, then use the **groupBy** operator to group the numbers based on whether they are greater than 3 or not. Finally, we are using the **flatMap** operator to map the numbers to their double values and the **onErrorReturn** operator to return –1 in case of an error. The final result will be as follows:

`Result: 4`

`Result: -1`

This example is a simple demonstration of how various Rx-operators can be used together to create a more complex data flow, handle errors, and handle backpressure. In real-world scenarios, you would need to consider more complex cases and edge cases, but the concept remains the same.

Conclusion

In conclusion, Rx-operators are a powerful tool for working with streams of data in a reactive programming paradigm. The operators provide a way to handle backpressure, filter, group, map, and handle errors in the data. By combining these operators, one can create complex data flows that are efficient, robust, and responsive. It is important to remember that proper error-handling strategies should be implemented to ensure that data flows are reliable and handle any exceptional situations. With the right understanding and implementation, Rx-operators can help you create powerful, efficient, and responsive data flows that can handle real-world scenarios.

Points to remember

The following are some key points to remember when working with Rx-operators:
- Flowable is a special type of observable that handles backpressure, and it is recommended to use it when working with large data sets or infinite streams.
- Data transformers and async operators provide a way to handle backpressure and ensure that data flows smoothly through the system.

- Filtering and mapping operators are used to filter and transform the data, respectively.
- Grouping operators are used to organize data into related groups.
- Error handling operators provide a way to handle errors and ensure that the data flow is robust and reliable.
- Proper error-handling strategies should be implemented to ensure that data flows are robust and reliable.
- Rx-operators can be combined to create more complex data flows and handle more complex scenarios.
- Remember that the key to using Rx-operators effectively is to understand their behavior and how they can be combined to solve different problems.

Join our book's Discord space

Join the book's Discord Workspace for Latest updates, Offers, Tech happenings around the world, New Release and Sessions with the Authors:

https://discord.bpbonline.com

Chapter 10
Concurrency and Parallel Processing

Introduction

In today's world, efficient and fast data processing is crucial. Concurrency and parallel processing are two important concepts that can help achieve this goal. Concurrency is the ability of a system to handle multiple tasks simultaneously, whereas parallel processing is the ability of a system to execute multiple tasks simultaneously.

In this chapter, we will delve into the concepts of concurrency and parallel processing in the context of reactive programming and explore how they can be used to improve the performance of our systems.

Structure

In this chapter, we will cover the following topics:

- Concurrency
- Schedulers
- Schedulers with `subscribeOn` and `observeOn`

Objectives

By the end of this chapter, readers will have a basic understanding of concurrency, schedulers, and their usage in **RxKotlin**. They will be able to use them to achieve concurrency and parallel processing in their systems.

Readers will gain the ability to understand the concepts of concurrency and how it can be applied to their systems. They will also learn about schedulers and their role in concurrency and parallel processing.

Furthermore, readers will gain an understanding of the usage of schedulers with the `subscribeOn` and `observeOn` operators in **RxKotlin**. They will learn how to use schedulers effectively to achieve concurrency and parallel processing in their code.

Finally, readers will be equipped with knowledge about best practices for using schedulers in **RxKotlin**, ensuring they can make optimal use of this powerful tool.

Overview

This chapter will cover the concepts of concurrency, schedulers, and their usage in RxKotlin. We will start by understanding the basics of concurrency and how it can be applied in our systems. Then, we will delve into the world of schedulers, which are responsible for scheduling the execution of our tasks. We will learn how to use schedulers with the `subscribeOn` and `observeOn` operators in **RxKotlin** to achieve concurrency and parallel processing.

Concurrency

Concurrency is the ability of a system to handle multiple tasks simultaneously. In a concurrent system, multiple tasks can be in progress at the same time, but they may not necessarily be executed at the same time. Concurrency is important because it allows a system to use its resources, such as CPU and memory, improving performance and responsiveness.

One of the main advantages of concurrency is that it allows a system to handle multiple tasks simultaneously instead of waiting for one task to complete before starting another. This can greatly improve the performance and responsiveness of a system. For example, in a Web server, concurrency allows the server to handle multiple requests simultaneously instead of waiting for one request to complete before starting another. This can greatly improve the performance and responsiveness of the Web server.

Another advantage of concurrency is that it allows a system to use its resources, such as CPU and memory.

In a concurrent system, multiple tasks can be executed simultaneously, leading to better CPU and memory utilization. This can greatly improve the performance of a system. However, concurrency also comes with some challenges. One of the main challenges of concurrency is dealing with shared resources. When multiple tasks execute simultaneously, they may need to access and modify shared resources, such as data structures and variables. This can lead to issues such as race conditions and deadlocks, which can cause errors and crashes in a system.

One way to address these challenges is by using synchronization mechanisms such as locks, semaphores, and monitors. These mechanisms control access to shared resources and prevent issues like race conditions and deadlocks. The following are some illustrations of these mechanisms:

- **Deadlocks**: A deadlock is a situation where two or more threads are blocked, waiting for each other to release a needed resource. Let us consider a simple scenario to help beginners understand. Suppose we have two threads, A and B, that both want to use a shared resource; let us say it is a file. Now, imagine thread A manages to grab hold of the file and starts working with it. However, thread A also wants to acquire another resource that thread B is currently using. Because thread B is trying to acquire the file but cannot because thread A has it, thread B gets stuck and has to wait until thread A releases the file. In this situation, we have what is called a deadlock. It is a state where both threads are waiting for each other, preventing any progress and potentially causing the program to freeze or hang. To avoid deadlocks, we can use synchronization mechanisms such as lock order to establish a specific order in which locks should be acquired. If a thread tries to acquire a lock in the wrong order, it will be blocked until the correct lock is acquired.

- **Semaphores**: A semaphore is a synchronization mechanism that controls access to a shared resource using a counter. The counter is initially set to a specific value, representing the available resources. Each time a thread wants to access the resource, it decrements the counter, and each time it releases the resource, it increments the counter. A thread will be blocked if the counter is zero and there are no available resources. Semaphores can be useful to control access to a shared resource and avoid race conditions and overuse of resources.

- **Monitors**: A monitor is a synchronization mechanism that allows multiple threads to access a shared resource, but only one can access it simultaneously. Monitors are implemented using a lock and a condition variable. A thread can acquire the lock and enter the monitor, and while it holds the lock, no other thread can enter the monitor. When the thread releases the lock, another thread can acquire it and enter the monitor. Monitors can be useful to control access to a shared resource and guarantee that only one thread can access it at a time, avoiding race conditions and ensuring the consistency of the shared resource.

Another way is to use Lock-free data structures, which are data structures that allow multiple threads to access and update them without the need for locks and the risk of race conditions or deadlocks. Some examples of lock-free data structures include the following:

- **Non-blocking Queue**: A non-blocking queue allows multiple threads to push and pop elements simultaneously without needing locks. This can be achieved using **Compare-and-Swap** (**CAS**) and double-checked locking techniques.
- **Non-blocking Stack**: A non-blocking stack is a stack that allows multiple threads to push and pop elements simultaneously without the need for locks. This can be achieved using techniques such as CAS and double-checked locking.
- **Non-blocking HashMap**: A HashMap allows multiple threads to insert, update, and delete elements simultaneously without locking. This can be achieved using lock-free linked lists, CAS, and fine-grained locking techniques.
- **Non-blocking linked list**: A non-blocking linked list t allows multiple threads to insert and delete elements simultaneously without needing locks. This can be achieved using CAS techniques and fine-grained locking.

These are just a few examples of lock-free data structures, and there are many other types of lock-free data structures available, and each one has advantages and disadvantages depending on the use case and the system's requirements. We can achieve high performance and scalability in concurrent systems by using lock-free data structures.

Common pitfalls and best practices for concurrency include the following:

- **Deadlocks**: As mentioned earlier, a deadlock occurs when two or more threads are blocked, waiting for each other to release a needed resource. It is best practice to establish a specific order in which locks should be acquired and to release locks as soon as possible to avoid deadlocks. In addition, it is a good idea to use lock-free data structures and algorithms whenever possible.
- **Race conditions**: A race condition occurs when multiple threads access and modify a shared resource simultaneously, leading to inconsistent or unexpected results. To avoid race conditions, it is to use synchronization mechanisms such as locks and semaphores to control access to shared resources. Also, it is good to use atomic variables, lock-free data structures, and algorithms whenever possible.
- **Starvation**: It occurs when a thread cannot acquire a resource it needs because another thread has acquired it and is not releasing it. To avoid starvation, it is best to use fairness policies when acquiring locks so that all threads have an equal chance to acquire the resource.
- **Priority inversion**: Priority inversion occurs when a high-priority thread is blocked by a low-priority thread that holds a resource that the high-priority thread needs. To avoid priority inversion, it is best to use priority inheritance or priority ceiling protocols when

acquiring locks so that the priority of a thread is temporarily raised when it acquires a resource that a high-priority thread needs.

- **Not releasing resources**: Not releasing resources occurs when a thread acquires a resource and does not release it, causing other threads to be blocked. To avoid not releasing resources, it is best to release resources as soon as they are no longer needed and to use the try-finally or try-with-resources block to ensure that resources are always released.

Schedulers

In the context of reactive programming, schedulers are used to control the execution of asynchronous tasks and to manage resources efficiently. Schedulers are a fundamental concept in reactive programming, as they allow you to specify where and when a given piece of code should be executed.

One common use case for schedulers is to control the execution of a data stream. For example, imagine you have an observable stream of data that emits many items. If you subscribe to this stream on the same thread it is being emitted on, it can cause your application to become unresponsive. To avoid this, you can use a scheduler to control the execution of the stream. For example, you can use the **subscribeOn** operator to specify that the stream should be emitted on a background thread and the **observeOn** operator to specify that the stream should be consumed on the main thread.

Another use case for schedulers is to control the execution of a computation. For example, imagine you have a computation that performs a complex calculation on large data. If you perform this computation on the main thread, it can cause your application to become unresponsive. To avoid this, you can use a scheduler to perform the computation on a background thread. For example, you can use the **subscribeOn** operator to specify that the computation should be performed on a background thread.

Schedulers in reactive programming and those in *Coroutines* are two different concepts, even though they serve a similar purpose in managing concurrency and parallel processing. In reactive programming, schedulers are part of the *RxKotlin* library and control the thread on which the items are emitted and received. They manage concurrency and parallel processing within the context of reactive programming. On the contrary, schedulers in *Coroutines* are part of the Kotlin Coroutines library and are used to manage concurrency and parallel processing within the context of *Coroutines*.

While both reactive programming and coroutines are used for concurrent and parallel programming, they have different characteristics and use cases. Reactive programming focuses on handling asynchronous data streams and event-based programming, whereas Coroutines focuses on lightweight concurrency, emphasizing suspension, and cancellation. Each library has its scheduler implementation, and it is important to understand the distinctions between the two when deciding which library to use for a given task.

In general, schedulers are a powerful tool for controlling the concurrent execution of tasks in Reactive Programming. By using schedulers, you can ensure that your application is using resources efficiently, avoiding potential issues such as blocking the main thread, and by using **subscribeOn** and **observeOn** operators, you can control where the computation or stream is executed and consumed.

Schedulers with subscribeOn and observeOn

As mentioned earlier, In RxKotlin, schedulers are used to control the execution of asynchronous tasks and to manage resources efficiently. The **subscribeOn** and **observeOn** operators specify the scheduler on which a given code should be executed.

The **subscribeOn** operator is used to specify the scheduler on which an observable should emit its items. Let us say you have a bunch of things to handle in your code, and you want to make sure they happen on a separate thread instead of the main one. This way, the main thread will not get stuck or slowed down.

To achieve this, you can use something called an "observable" that emits these things one by one. Now, you want to make sure these emissions happen on a background thread so you do not block the main thread.

To make it happen, you can use a special operator called **subscribeOn**. By using this operator and specifying the **Schedulers.io()** scheduler, you are telling your code to emit those things on a background thread instead of the main one. This ensures smooth execution without slowing down the main thread.

```
fun main() {
    val dataSource: Observable<Int> = Observable.fromIterable(1..10 step 2)

    val dataObservable = dataSource
        .subscribeOn(Schedulers.io())

    dataObservable
        .blockingSubscribe { data ->
            processData(data)
        }
}
```

```
    fun processData(data: Int) {
        println("Processing data: $data on thread ${Thread.currentThread().name}")
    }
```

The following will be the output:

Processing data: 1 on thread main
Processing data: 3 on thread main
Processing data: 5 on thread main
Processing data: 7 on thread main
Processing data: 9 on thread main

In this example, an observable is created that emits odd integers from 1 to 10. The **subscribeOn** operator specifies that this observable should emit its items on the **Schedulers.io()** scheduler, a background thread intended for performing I/O-bound work. The **subscribe** function is used to subscribe to the observable and pass the emitted items to the **processData** function, which will receive the emitted items.

You need to add a mechanism to wait for the completion of the **dataObservable** execution. You can use the **blockingSubscribe** function instead of the **subscribe** function. **blockingSubscribe** will block the current thread until the observable completes. You can see that the **processData** function will process the data and print out the result with the thread name; it will run on the **Schedulers.io()** thread.

In this example, the **processData** function will be called for each item emitted by the **dataSource** observable on the same **Schedulers.io()** thread.

The **observeOn** operator is used to specify the scheduler on which an observer should receive the items emitted by an observable. For example, imagine you have an observable that emits many items and want to ensure that the items are received on the main thread to update the UI. You can use the **observeOn** operator to specify that the items should be received on the **Schedulers.computation()** scheduler:

```
    fun main() {
        val dataSource = 1..10 step 2

        val dataObservable = Observable.create<Int> {
            for (data in dataSource) {
                it.onNext(data)
```

```
            }
            it.onComplete()
        }


        dataObservable
            .subscribeOn(Schedulers.io())
            .observeOn(Schedulers.computation())
            .blockingSubscribe { data ->
                updateUI(data)
            }
    }


    fun updateUI(data: Int) {
        println("New data has come: $data on thread ${Thread.currentThread().name}")
    }
```

The following will be the output:

```
New data has come: 1 on thread main
New data has come: 3 on thread main
New data has come: 5 on thread main
New data has come: 7 on thread main
New data has come: 9 on thread main
```

The **subscribeOn** function is used to specify the scheduler on which the source observable will emit the items. In this case, the source observable will emit the items on the IO scheduler.

The **observeOn** function is used to specify the scheduler on which the observer will receive the items emitted by the source observable. In this case, the observer will receive the items on the computation scheduler.

dataObservable.observeOn(Schedulers.computation())

To further enhance the performance of the code, we can use the **observeOn** function along with the **Schedulers.computation()** scheduler. By applying this combination, we can control where the processing of our data occurs, allowing for efficient computation of appropriate resources.

Finally, the **blockingSubscribe** function subscribes to the observable and blocks the current thread until the observable completes. The function **updateUI(data: Int)** will be called for each item emitted by the observable.

The **updateUI** function will print the received data along with the current thread name, and this is just an example to illustrate the concept of schedulers. In a real-world scenario, this function will be used to update the UI.

In general, the **subscribeOn** and **observeOn** operators are powerful tools for controlling the concurrent execution of tasks in RxKotlin. By using these operators, you can ensure that your application uses resources efficiently and avoids potential issues such as blocking the main thread. It is worth noticing that multiple **subscribeOn** or **observeOn** calls on the same observable chain will only take effect on the first call; the rest will be ignored.

Note that in these examples, we use schedulers from the **io.reactivex.rxjava3.schedulers** package, which provides a variety of schedulers that can be used for different purposes. Some examples include **Schedulers.io()** for *I/O-bound* work, **Schedulers.computation()** for CPU-bound work, and **Schedulers.newThread()** for creating new threads.

Conclusion

In this chapter, we have explored the concept of schedulers in the context of reactive programming in Kotlin. We have discussed the importance of schedulers in managing concurrency and parallel processing. We have also looked at the **subscribeOn** and **observeOn** functions, which specify the schedulers on which the source observable will emit items and the observer will receive items, respectively.

In summary, schedulers play an important role in managing concurrency and parallel processing in Reactive Programming, and the **subscribeOn** and **observeOn** functions provide an easy way to specify the schedulers on which the source observable will emit items and the observer will receive items. This is a fundamental concept when working with *RxKotlin* in reactive application development, and it is important to have a good understanding of it to develop robust and efficient applications.

Points to remember

The following are the key takeaways from the chapter:
- Schedulers are used to manage concurrency and parallel processing in reactive programming.
- **subscribeOn** and **observeOn** specify the schedulers on which the source observable will emit items and the observer will receive items, respectively.

- Schedulers can control the thread on which the items are emitted and received, allowing for more efficient concurrency and parallel processing management.
- It is important to understand schedulers well when working with RxKotlin in server-side development.
- BlockingSubscribe is a way to make sure that all the items are received and processed before the main thread exits.
- The `schedulers.io()` is used for I/O-bound work, and `schedulers.computation()` is used for CPU-bound work.
- In this chapter, schedulers are part of the RxKotlin library, and it is not the same as the Kotlin coroutines schedulers.

Join our book's Discord space

Join the book's Discord Workspace for Latest updates, Offers, Tech happenings around the world, New Release and Sessions with the Authors:

https://discord.bpbonline.com

CHAPTER 11
Testing Reactive Applications

Introduction

You are aware that reactive programming is a modern approach to work with concurrency and asynchrony in software development. To ensure that reactive applications work as intended, it is important to test them thoroughly. This chapter will provide an overview of testing libraries and techniques that are available to test reactive applications in Kotlin.

Structure

In this chapter, we will cover the following topics:
- Importance of unit testing
- Junit tests
- RxKotlin testing
- TestSubscriber
- TestScheduler
- TestObserver

Objectives

By the end of this chapter, readers will have acquired the skills and knowledge necessary to effectively perform application testing within a reactive context. This chapter serves to offer a comprehensive introduction to testing reactive applications in Kotlin. It emphasizes the significance of unit testing as a fundamental practice in ensuring the reliability and quality of reactive applications. Moreover, the chapter elaborates on a range of tools and techniques essential for conducting tests in the realm of reactive applications, including JUnit tests, RxKotlin testing, and the utilization of tools such as TestSubscriber, TestScheduler, and TestObserver. These insights and resources will empower readers to carry out thorough and reliable testing processes, thereby enhancing the robustness and performance of their reactive Kotlin applications.

Overview

Testing reactive applications in Kotlin requires a different approach than testing traditional applications. Reactive applications are asynchronous and often handle concurrency, which can make them more difficult to test. However, there are several testing tools and techniques that can be used to make testing reactive applications easier.

Importance of unit testing

Unit testing is an essential part of software development. It is especially important when building reactive applications. A reactive application is a type of software that is designed to respond to events in real-time. These events can come from a variety of sources, such as user input, network traffic, or database updates. Reactive applications are designed to be highly responsive and scalable, but they also require careful testing to ensure that they perform as expected. In this section, we will explore the importance of unit testing reactive applications and discuss some real-world scenarios.

- **Ensuring correct behavior**: The primary goal of the unit testing is to ensure that the application behaves as expected. This is especially important for reactive applications because of the complexity involved in responding to real-time events. A unit test can help you verify your application handles events correctly, and that produces the expected outputs. For example, you might write a test to verify that your application correctly handles the user clicking a button or that it correctly fetches data from a database when a specific event occurs.
- **Finding bugs early**: Unit tests are designed to catch bugs early in the development process. By writing tests before you write the actual implementation, you can catch

bugs before they become harder to fix. This helps you to catch issues early and prevents them from becoming bigger problems later on. In addition, running unit tests on a regular basis can help you catch new bugs as soon as they are introduced, making it easier to fix them.

- **Improving code quality**: Unit testing can also help to improve the overall quality of your code. By writing tests, you are forced to think about how your code works and what it should do. This can help you to write cleaner, more readable code that is easier to maintain. In addition, by running unit tests regularly, you can ensure that your code continues to work as expected, even as you make changes to it.

- **Facilitating continuous integration and deployment**: Unit testing is also essential for facilitating continuous integration and deployment. Continuous integration is the practice of integrating code changes into a shared repository several times a day. This helps to catch integration problems early before they become more difficult to fix. Unit tests can be run as part of the continuous integration process, allowing you to catch any issues before they are deployed to production.

- **Improving testability:** Finally, unit testing can help to improve the testability of your code. When you write tests, you are forced to think about how your code can be tested, which can lead you to write code that is easier to test. In addition, by writing tests, you are documenting how your code works and what it should do, which can make it easier for other developers to understand and maintain your code in the future.

To conclude, unit testing is essential to ensure that reactive applications work as expected. By writing tests, you can catch bugs early, improve code quality, facilitate continuous integration and deployment, and improve the testability of your code. By taking the time to write comprehensive unit tests, you can ensure that your reactive applications are reliable, scalable, and responsive, even as they grow and evolve over time.

JUnit tests

JUnit is a popular testing framework for Java applications, widely used for writing unit tests for reactive applications in Kotlin as well. JUnit provides a simple and straightforward way to write and run tests, making it a great choice for developers who are new to testing or who need to write tests quickly. In this section, we will explore JUnit tests in more detail and provide some examples of using JUnit to test reactive applications in Kotlin.

Setting up Junit

To get started with JUnit, you need to include the JUnit library in your project. This can usually be done by adding a dependency to your project. For example, in Maven, you can add the following to your **pom.xml** file:

```xml
<dependency>
    <groupId>junit</groupId>
    <artifactId>junit</artifactId>
    <version>4.13.2</version>
</dependency>
```

Writing your first JUnit test

Once you have set up JUnit, you can start writing tests. To write a JUnit test, you need to create a class that extends the **junit.framework.TestCase** class. You can then write test methods in this class that verify that your code behaves as expected. For example, the following code shows a simple JUnit test that verifies a **String** variable is not null:

```kotlin
import junit.framework.TestCase.assertNotNull
import org.junit.Test

class MyFirstTest {

    @Test
    fun testStringIsNotNull() {
        val s = "Kotlin is real!"
        assertNotNull(s)
    }
}
```

Using assertions

JUnit provides a number of assertions that you can use to verify that your code behaves as expected. For example, you can use the **assertEquals** method to verify that two values are equal or the **assertTrue** method to verify that a condition is true. In the preceding example, we used the **assertNotNull** method to verify that a **String** variable is not null.

The following example uses the previously-mentioned assertions to test some **Math** operations:

```kotlin
class MathUtil {
    fun add(a: Int, b: Int): Int {
        return a+b
    }
```

```kotlin
    fun subtract(a: Int, b: Int): Int {
        return a-b
    }
}

class MathUtilTest {
    @Test
    fun testAdd() {
        val mathUtil = MathUtil()

        // Test that 2 + 3 = 5
        assertEquals(5, mathUtil.add(2, 3))

        // Test that adding a negative number of works
        assertEquals(2, mathUtil.add(5, -3))

        // Test that adding zero works
        assertEquals(7, mathUtil.add(7, 0))

        // Test that the result is negative
        assertTrue(mathUtil.subtract(3, 4) < 0)

        // Test that adding a large number doesn't cause overflow
        assertEquals(2147483646, mathUtil.add(2147483645, 1))

        // Test that the result is not null
        assertNotNull(mathUtil.add(1, 2))
    }
}
```

Ensuring correct behavior is one of the key objectives of JUnit testing. This means that tests should not only verify that the code runs without errors but also that it produces the expected output.

The following are some examples of tests that ensure correct behavior:

- **Testing for expected results:** A simple way to test for expected results is to use the **assertEquals()** method, which verifies if the expected value matches the actual value. For example, let us say we have a method that adds two numbers together:

    ```
    import junit.framework.TestCase.assertEquals
    import org.junit.Test

    fun add(a: Int, b: Int): Int {
        return a + b
    }

    class TestAddNumbers {
        @Test
        fun testAdd() {
            val result = add(2, 3)
            assertEquals(5, result)
        }

    }
    ```

    This test ensures that the **add()** method returns the expected result for the given inputs.

- **Testing edge cases:** Edge cases are inputs at the extreme ends of the possible input range for a method. Testing edge cases can uncover unexpected behavior and help ensure that the method behaves correctly in all scenarios. For example, let us say we have a method that calculates the factorial of a number:

    ```
    import org.junit.Assert.assertEquals
    import org.junit.Assert.assertThrows
    import org.junit.Test

    fun factorial(n: Int): Int {
        if (n < 0) {
            throw IllegalArgumentException("n must be >= 0")
        }
        var result = 1
    ```

```
        for (i in 2..n) {
            result *= i
        }
        return result
    }

    class TestFactorial {
        @Test
        fun testFactorial() {
            assertEquals(1, factorial(0))
            assertEquals(1, factorial(1))
            assertEquals(120, factorial(5))
        assertThrows(IllegalArgumentException::class.java) { factorial(-1)
}
        }

    }
```

This test verifies that the method returns the correct result for a variety of inputs, including the edge case of **n** = **0**. It also verifies that the method throws the expected exception when **n** is negative.

- **Testing for exceptions:** It's important to verify that methods that are supposed to throw exceptions indeed do so and that the specific expected exception is thrown accurately. For example, let us say we have a method that divides two numbers:

```
    import org.junit.Assert.assertEquals
    import org.junit.Assert.assertThrows
    import org.junit.Test

    fun divide(p: Int, q: Int): Int {
        if (q == 0) {
            throw IllegalArgumentException("Cannot divide by zero")
        }
        return p / q
    }
```

```
class TestDivision {
    @Test
    fun testDivide() {
        assertEquals(3, divide(15, 5))
        assertThrows(IllegalArgumentException::class.java) {
        divide(5, 0) }
    }

}
```

This test verifies that the method returns the expected result when dividing two numbers and that the correct exception is thrown when attempting to divide by zero. By using these and other techniques to ensure correct behavior, we can write effective JUnit tests that verify the functionality of our code and help ensure that it works correctly in all scenarios.

- **Multithreading tests**: Suppose we have a simple class called **Counter** that increments a value using the method **increment()**. We want to ensure that the **increment()** method is thread-safe, meaning that multiple threads can call it simultaneously without issues. To test this, we can write a multithreading test using JUnit.

  The following is an example of a JUnit test that creates multiple threads to increment the counter:

```
import org.junit.Assert.assertEquals
import org.junit.Test

class Counter {
    var value: Int = 0

    fun increment() {
        value++
    }
}

class CounterTest {
    @Test
```

```kotlin
fun `increment() should be thread-safe`() {
    val counter = Counter()

    // Create 10 threads to increment the counter
    val threads = (1..10).map {
        Thread {
            for (i in 1..100) {
                counter.increment()
            }
        }
    }

    // Start all the threads
    threads.forEach { it.start() }

    // Wait for all the threads to complete
    threads.forEach { it.join() }

    // Check that the counter was incremented 1000 times (10 threads x 100 increments)
    assertEquals(1000, counter.value)
}
```

In this test, we first create a **Counter** instance. We then create 10 threads that will each call the **increment()** method 100 times. Using **join()**, we start the threads and wait for them to complete. Finally, we checked that the counter was incremented 1,000 times.

This test ensures that the **increment()** method is thread-safe, meaning that multiple threads can call it simultaneously without causing any issues. If the **increment()** method was not thread-safe, we would expect the test to fail due to race conditions.

This is a simple example, but multithreading tests can be useful in more complex scenarios where you must ensure that your code is thread-safe and does not have any race conditions.

Writing tests for reactive applications

When testing reactive applications, you can use JUnit to verify that events are emitted and processed correctly. For example, you might write a test to verify that a **Subject** emits events to its subscribers or that a **Flowable** processes events in the correct order. To write these tests, you can use the JUnit framework to set up and verify the state of your application and then use the reactive libraries (such as RxKotlin or Reactor) to observe and verify the events that are emitted.

- **Example 1: Testing a subject**

    The following code shows an example of how you might write a JUnit test to verify that a **Subject** in RxKotlin emits events to its subscribers:

    ```
    import io.reactivex.subjects.BehaviorSubject
    import junit.framework.TestCase.assertEquals
    import org.junit.Test

    class MySubjectTest {

        @Test
        fun testSubjectEmitsEvents() {
            val subject = BehaviorSubject.create<Int>()

            subject.subscribe { value ->
                assertEquals(1, value)
            }

            subject.onNext(1)
        }
    }
    ```

- **Example 2: Testing a flowable**

    The following code shows an example of how you might write a JUnit test to verify that a **Flowable** in RxKotlin processes events in the correct order:

    ```
    import io.reactivex.Flowable
    import org.junit.Test
    ```

```kotlin
class MyFlowableTest {

    @Test
    fun testFlowableProcessesEvents() {
        val flowable = Flowable.fromArray(1, 2, 3)
        flowable.test()
            .assertResult(1, 2, 3)
    }
}
```

In this example, we create a **Flowable** from an array of integers and then use the **test** method to subscribe to the **Flowable** and verify its results. The **assertResult** method is used to verify that the events emitted by the **Flowable** are equal to the expected values.

JUnit is a powerful and easy-to-use testing framework that makes it simple to write and run tests for reactive applications in Kotlin. Whether you are new to testing or an experienced developer, JUnit is a great choice for testing your reactive applications in Kotlin.

RxKotlin testing

RxKotlin is a library for reactive programming in Kotlin. It provides a number of tools and techniques for testing reactive applications in Kotlin. RxKotlin tests can be written using JUnit and can be used to test individual components of a reactive application, including observables, operators, and subjects.

The following are some examples of RxKotlin tests for observables, operators, and subjects:

Observables

The following example tests an **Observable** that emits a single value:

```kotlin
import io.reactivex.rxjava3.core.Observable
import io.reactivex.rxjava3.observers.TestObserver
import org.junit.Test

class TestObservable {
    @Test
    fun `should emit a single value`() {
```

```kotlin
        val observable = Observable.just("Ping")
        val testObserver = TestObserver<String>()
        observable.subscribe(testObserver)

        // Check that the expected value was emitted, and the Observable completed
        testObserver.assertValue("Ping")
        testObserver.assertComplete()
    }
}
```

In this test, we create an **Observable** that emits a single value **Ping**. We then create a **TestObserver** and subscribe it to the **Observable** (you can refer to the **TestObserver** section later in this chapter to get more details about it). We then check that the expected value was emitted and the **Observable** successfully.

Operators

The following is a test of an operator that filters the emissions of an **Observable**:

```kotlin
import io.reactivex.rxjava3.core.Observable
import io.reactivex.rxjava3.observers.TestObserver
import org.junit.Test

class TestOperator {
    @Test
    fun `should filter even numbers`() {
        val observable = Observable.just(1, 2, 3, 4, 5, 6)
        val testObserver = TestObserver<Int>()

        observable.filter { it % 2 == 0 }
            .subscribe(testObserver)

        // Check that the expected values were emitted in the correct order
        testObserver.assertValues(2, 4, 6)
        testObserver.assertComplete()
    }
}
```

In this test, we create an **Observable** that emits the values 1, 2, 3, 4, 5, and 6. We then apply a filter operator that only emits even numbers. We create a **TestObserver** and subscribe it to the filtered **Observable**. We then checked that the expected values were emitted in the correct order, and the **Observable** was completed successfully.

Subjects

The following example test a Subject that acts as both an Observable and an Observer:

```
class TestSubjects {
    @Test
    fun `should emit values to subscribers`() {
        val subject = PublishSubject.create<String>()
        val testObserver1 = TestObserver<String>()
        val testObserver2 = TestObserver<String>()

        subject.subscribe(testObserver1)
        subject.onNext("Hello")

        subject.subscribe(testObserver2)
        subject.onNext("World")
        subject.onComplete()

        // Check that the expected values were emitted in the correct
        order to each subscriber
        testObserver1.assertValues("Hello", "World")
        testObserver1.assertComplete()

        testObserver2.assertValue("World")
        testObserver2.assertComplete()
    }
}
```

In this test, we create a **PublishSubject** that emits **String** values. We create two **TestObservers** and subscribe them to the Subject at different times. We then emit two values, **Hello** and **World**, to the Subject. We then check that the expected values were emitted in the correct order to each subscriber and that each subscriber completed successfully.

Overall, these examples demonstrate how you can use RxKotlin to test Observables, operators, and Subjects and ensure that they behave correctly.

TestSubscriber

TestSubscriber is a class provided by RxKotlin that allows us to test the emissions of a Flowable. **TestSubscriber** is a type of Subscriber that records all the events emitted by a Flowable, including any errors that occur, and makes it easy to write assertions about these events in our tests.

To create a **TestSubscriber**, we can simply create a new instance of the class and subscribe it to a Flowable. For example:

```
import io.reactivex.rxjava3.core.Flowable
import io.reactivex.rxjava3.subscribers.TestSubscriber
import org.junit.Test

class MyTestSubscriber {
    @Test
    fun testWithSubscriber() {
        val flowable = Flowable.just("Ping")
        val testSubscriber = TestSubscriber<String>()

        flowable.subscribe(testSubscriber)

        // Write assertions about the emitted events
        testSubscriber.assertValue("Ping")
        testSubscriber.assertComplete()
        testSubscriber.assertNoErrors()
    }
}
```

In this example, we create a **TestSubscriber** that expects the **Flowable** to emit a single value **Ping**. We then subscribe the **TestSubscriber** to the Flowable and write assertions using the **assertValue**, **assertComplete**, and **assertNoErrors** methods provided by **TestSubscriber**.

TestScheduler

TestScheduler is a class provided by RxKotlin that allows us to control the timing of events in our tests. **TestScheduler** is used to simulate the passage of time so we can test how our code reacts to different timings and schedules.

To create a **TestScheduler**, we can simply create a new instance of the class. For example:

```
import io.reactivex.rxjava3.core.Flowable
import io.reactivex.rxjava3.schedulers.TestScheduler
import io.reactivex.rxjava3.subscribers.TestSubscriber
import org.junit.Test
import java.util.concurrent.TimeUnit

class MyTestScheduler {
    @Test
    fun `should emit values with a custom scheduler`() {
        val testScheduler = TestScheduler()
        val flowable = Flowable.intervalRange(0, 3, 0, 1000, TimeUnit.MILLISECONDS, testScheduler)
        val testSubscriber = TestSubscriber<Long>()

        flowable.subscribe(testSubscriber)

        testScheduler.advanceTimeBy(1500, TimeUnit.MILLISECONDS)

        // Write assertions about the emitted events
        testSubscriber.assertValues(0, 1)
        testSubscriber.assertNotComplete()

        testScheduler.advanceTimeBy(1000, TimeUnit.MILLISECONDS)

        // Write assertions about the emitted events
        testSubscriber.assertValues(0,1,2)
        testSubscriber.assertComplete()
    }

}
```

In this example, we create a **TestScheduler** and use it to control the timing of a **Flowable** that emits values every second. We use the **advanceTimeBy** method to simulate the passage of time and check the emitted events after 1.5 seconds, then 2.5 seconds, and use **assertValues**, **assertNotComplete()**, and **assertComplete()** methods to check that everything is working as expected.

TestScheduler provides various methods that allow us to control the timing of events in our tests. Some of the commonly used methods are as follows:

- **advanceTimeBy(time:Long, unit:TimeUnit)**: Advances the virtual clock by the specified amount of time.
- **triggerActions()**: Triggers any pending actions that were scheduled to run at or before the current virtual time.
- **scheduleDirect(action:()-> Unit)**: Schedules an action to run at the current virtual time.

TestScheduler is a powerful tool that allows us to simulate the passage of time in our tests. By using the various methods provided by **TestScheduler**, we can control the timing of events and ensure that our code behaves correctly under different schedules and timings.

TestObserver

TestObserver, as you noticed earlier in this chapter, is a class provided by the RxKotlin library for testing reactive code. It provides a convenient way to test the emissions, errors, and completion events of an Observable. **TestObserver** is similar to **TestSubscriber** but has some added functionality.

To use **TestObserver**, we first create an instance of it and then subscribe to the **Observable** we want to test. We can then use the methods provided by **TestObserver** to test the emissions, errors, and completion events.

The following is an example where we will use some **TestObserver** methods to test the values emitted by an **Observable**:

```
import io.reactivex.rxjava3.core.Observable
import io.reactivex.rxjava3.observers.TestObserver
import org.junit.Test

class MyTestObserver {

    @Test
    fun `test observable with TestObserver`() {
```

```
        val testObserver = TestObserver<Int>()
        val observable = Observable.fromIterable(1..5)
            .map { it * 2 }

        observable.subscribe(testObserver)

        testObserver
            .assertValues(2, 4, 6, 8, 10)
            .assertNoErrors()
            .assertComplete()
            .assertValueCount(5)
            .assertValueAt(2, 6)
    }

}
```

In this example, we are creating an **Observable** that emits integers from a list and then multiplies each emitted integer by 2 using the **map** operator. We then subscribe to this **Observable** using a **TestObserver** instance and proceed to call several of its methods to verify the behavior of the observable.

The following are the methods we used to test the behavior of our observable:

- The **assertValues** method is used to assert that the observable emits the expected sequence of values. It takes a **vararg** parameter that specifies the expected values in the order in which they are emitted.

  In our example, we are using the **assertValues** method to assert that the observable emits the sequence of values (in this case, 2, 4, 6, 8, and 10). If any of the values emitted by the observable do not match what is expected, the test will fail.

- The **assertNoErrors** method is used to assert that the observable does not emit any errors. If any error is emitted by the observable, the test will fail.

  In our example, we are using the **assertNoErrors** method to assert that the observable does not emit any errors.

- The **assertComplete** method is used to assert that the observable completes successfully. If the observable is not complete or completed with an error, the test will fail.

  In our example, we are using the **assertComplete** method to assert that the observable completes successfully.

- The `assertValueCount` method is used to assert the number of values emitted by the observable. If the number of emitted values does not match the expected value count, the test will fail.

  In our example, we are using the `assertValueCount` method to assert that the observable emits exactly five values.

- The `assertValueAt` method is used to assert that a specific value was emitted at a specific position in the stream. It takes two parameters—the index of the position to check and the expected value.

Conclusion

Testing reactive applications in Kotlin is a crucial aspect of developing high-quality, performant, and scalable software. Reactive programming can be challenging to test due to its asynchronous and non-blocking nature, which is why specialized testing frameworks and tools like JUnit and RxKotlin are essential.

It is important to remember that testing is an ongoing process and should be done throughout the development cycle to ensure the quality of the software. With the right tools and techniques, developers can write reliable, high-quality code that is well-tested and performs well in production.

Overall, testing is an essential component of building reactive applications in Kotlin, and it is important to invest time and effort into testing to ensure that the application meets the needs of the end-users.

Points to remember

The following are some points to remember:

- Unit testing is crucial in reactive programming to ensure that the application behaves correctly and to catch bugs early in the development cycle.
- JUnit is a popular framework for writing and running unit tests in Kotlin.
- RxKotlin is a library that provides abstractions for reactive programming in Kotlin, making it easy to write reactive code.
- The `TestSubscriber`, `TestScheduler`, and `TestObserver` are classes provided by RxKotlin for testing reactive code.
- When testing reactive applications, it is important to test for correct behavior and handle multithreading effectively.

Chapter 12
Spring Reactive for Kotlin

Introduction

Building reactive applications has become increasingly important in today's fast-paced world, where users demand highly performant and scalable applications that can handle large amounts of data.

So far, we have seen many things that enable us to dig into various **Java Virtual Machine (JVM)** based frameworks that support Kotlin language to build our applications as fast as possible. The most popular choice for this purpose is the Spring Framework. But there are other frameworks like Ktor maintained by JetBrains.

In this chapter, we will explore how to leverage the power of Spring Boot to build reactive applications using Kotlin. We will start with an introduction to Spring Boot and its key features that make it a popular choice for building reactive applications.

Structure

In this chapter, we will cover the following topics:
- Introduction to Spring Boot
- Gradle

- Getting started with Spring Boot
- Flux and Mono
- Spring Data reactive

Objectives

In this chapter, readers will attain several key skills. They will first grasp the fundamental concepts of Spring Boot, including its core features that make it a highly favored choice for developing reactive applications. Furthermore, they will gain knowledge about creating a basic Spring Boot application using the Kotlin programming language and establish a conducive development environment for their projects.

The chapter will also guide readers through the utilization of Gradle for dependency management and building reactive applications with Spring Boot and Kotlin. It will delve into the essential components of reactive programming in Spring Boot, namely Flux and Mono, demonstrating how to leverage them to craft efficient and scalable reactive code. Additionally, readers will learn how to implement Spring Data Reactive, enabling data access in a reactive manner and facilitating the creation of a seamless reactive data access layer seamlessly integrated into their Spring Boot applications.

Overview

Spring Boot is a popular framework for building JVM-based applications, and Kotlin, as we already know, is a modern programming language that has gained popularity in recent years due to its concise syntax and powerful features. Together, they provide a powerful combination for building efficient and scalable applications.

Gradle, on the other hand, is a build automation tool that is often used with Spring Boot and Kotlin. It provides a flexible and powerful way to manage dependencies and build applications. With Gradle, developers can easily manage dependencies and plugins, customize the build process, and automate tasks.

When building a Spring Boot application with Kotlin and Gradle, developers can take advantage of a number of powerful features, including automatic configuration, embedded servers, and a range of pre-built components and libraries. They can also leverage Kotlin's concise syntax and powerful features, such as null safety and extension functions, to write clean and efficient code.

To get started with building a Spring Boot application in Kotlin with Gradle, developers typically start by setting up a basic project structure and configuring their build system. They then add dependencies for Spring Boot, Kotlin, and any other libraries or frameworks they plan to use.

Introduction to Spring Boot

In this section, we will cover several key aspects of Spring Boot and its relevance in building reactive applications. To provide you with a solid foundation, let us start with an overview of Spring Boot, understanding its significance in modern software development.

Overview of Spring framework

The Spring framework has a rich history that dates back to 2002 when it was first developed by *Rod Johnson*. The framework was designed to simplify Java development by providing a comprehensive set of tools for building enterprise applications. Spring became popular quickly, thanks to its focus on simplifying application development and its support for a wide range of use cases.

Over time, however, Spring began to suffer from some of the same challenges that other popular Java frameworks faced. Specifically, as the framework grew in complexity and scope, it became more challenging for developers to configure and use it effectively. In response to this challenge, the Spring team began to explore new ways of simplifying application development using Spring.

This effort led to the development of Spring Boot, which was first released in 2014. Spring Boot quickly became popular with developers because of its ease of use, flexibility, and powerful features. In particular, Spring Boot's auto-configuration feature, which allows developers to automatically configure their applications based on a set of defaults and best practices, has been a major driving force for its success. In addition, Spring Boot's support for containerization and microservices architectures has made it a popular choice for building cloud-native applications.

Today, Spring Boot is widely regarded as one of the most popular and powerful frameworks for building enterprise applications in many JVM-based languages, including Java, Kotlin, and Groovy. Its success is because of its ability to simplify the development process and help developers get started quickly. As organizations continue to adopt cloud-native architectures and embrace reactive programming, Spring Boot is likely to remain a popular choice for building modern, scalable, and reactive applications.

Spring Boot is now adopted by many organizations and has reported a range of success stories. For example, *Netflix* has used Spring Boot to build its video streaming platform, and the company has reported that the framework has helped them to reduce development time and increase productivity. Other companies such as *Alibaba*, *Target*, and *PayPal* have also reported success using Spring Boot.

Key features of Spring Boot

Spring Boot's design to simplify the process of building and deploying applications is due to a wide range of powerful features and tools. The following are the key features of Spring Boot that make it a popular choice among developers as well as organizations:

- **Auto-configuration:** Spring Boot's auto-configuration feature allows developers to automatically configure their applications based on a set of defaults and best practices. This feature saves developers a significant amount of time and effort and makes it easier to get started with Spring.

    With auto-configuration, Spring Boot automatically configures various aspects of an application, such as database connections, logging, and Web servers, based on the dependencies that are included in the project.

- **Embedded server:** Spring Boot includes an embedded server that allows developers to run their applications without having to deploy them to an external server. This feature simplifies the deployment process and makes it easier to develop and test applications locally.

    Spring Boot includes several embedded servers, such as Tomcat, Jetty, and Undertow, which can be used to run Web applications.

- **Microservices support:** Spring Boot is designed to support microservices architectures, which allow developers to break down applications into smaller, more manageable components. This approach makes it easier to develop and deploy complex applications.

    Spring Boot includes several features that support microservices, such as support for RESTful Web services, service discovery, and load balancing.

- **Spring Data:** Spring Boot includes support for Spring Data, which provides a comprehensive set of tools for working with databases and other data sources. This feature makes it easier to build data-driven applications in Spring.

    Spring Data provides a unified API for working with various data sources, such as relational databases, NoSQL databases, and in-memory data stores.

- **Security:** Spring Boot includes a powerful security framework that makes it easy to add authentication and authorization to applications. This feature ensures that applications are secure and protected against unauthorized access.

    Spring Security provides a wide range of features for securing Web applications, such as support for various authentication mechanisms, authorization rules, and secure communication protocols.

- **Actuator:** Spring Boot includes an actuator that provides detailed information about the health and performance of applications. This feature makes it easier to monitor and troubleshoot applications.

The actuator provides various endpoints that can be used to monitor an application's health, such as health, metrics, and trace endpoints.

- **Integration with popular tools:** Spring Boot integrates seamlessly with a wide range of popular tools, including Gradle, Maven, and IntelliJ IDEA. This feature makes it easy to incorporate Spring Boot into existing development workflows.

    Spring Boot also includes several plugins for popular build tools, such as the Spring Boot Gradle plugin and the Spring Boot Maven plugin.

- **Easy testing:** Spring Boot makes it easy to write and run tests for applications, thanks to its support for testing frameworks like JUnit and Mockito.

    Spring Boot includes several testing utilities, such as `TestRestTemplate` and `MockMvc`, which can be used to test Web applications. Spring Boot also includes support for testing Spring applications in isolation, using the `@SpringBootTest` annotation.

- **Containerization:** Spring Boot is designed to support containerization, which makes it easy to deploy applications in container environments like Docker.

    Spring Boot includes several features that support containerization, such as support for external configuration files, environment variables, and container-specific properties.

- **Community support:** Spring Boot has a large and active community of developers who contribute to the framework and provide support and guidance to other developers. This community provides a wealth of knowledge and resources that can help developers build applications more easily.

    The Spring community includes various resources, such as forums, documentation, tutorials, and open-source projects, that can help developers learn and use Spring Boot more effectively.

Support of reactive programming

One of the key features of Spring Boot is its support for reactive programming, which allows developers to build applications that are responsive, resilient, and elastic. Reactive programming is a programming paradigm that is focused on handling streams of data and events in a non-blocking and asynchronous way.

Spring Boot's support for reactive programming is built on top of the Reactor project, which is a reactive library for the JVM. Its support includes several key features, such as support for reactive Web applications, reactive data access, and reactive messaging. This allows developers to build applications that can handle a large number of concurrent requests and scale seamlessly as demand increases. Reactive programming also makes it easier to build fault-tolerant and resilient applications that can handle failures gracefully and recover quickly.

The following are some points where Spring Boot support for reactive programming shines:

- **High-performance:** Reactive applications built with Spring Boot are highly performant due to their non-blocking and asynchronous nature. Spring Boot's support for reactive programming allows developers to build applications that can handle a large number of concurrent requests without blocking. For example, the Reactor project provides a set of high-performance reactive libraries that can be used to build reactive applications.

- **Scalability:** Reactive applications built with Spring Boot are highly scalable, as they can be easily scaled up or down to meet changing demands. Spring Boot's support for reactive programming allows developers to build applications that can handle a large number of requests without sacrificing performance. For example, Spring Cloud provides a set of tools for building and managing microservices, which can be easily scaled as needed.

- **Resilience:** Reactive applications built with Spring Boot are resilient as they can handle failures and recover quickly. Spring Boot's support for reactive programming makes it easier to build fault-tolerant and resilient applications that can handle failures gracefully and recover quickly. For example, Hystrix and Resilience4J libraries provide a set of tools for building fault-tolerant and resilient applications.

- **Flexibility:** Reactive applications built with Spring Boot are highly flexible, as they can be easily integrated with a range of technologies and frameworks. Spring Boot's support for reactive programming allows developers to easily integrate reactive components with existing Spring applications. For example, Spring Cloud Stream provides a set of tools for building reactive stream processing applications.

- **Reactive data access:** Spring Boot provides support for reactive data access, which allows applications to access data in a reactive manner. Spring Data provides support for reactive data access with the Spring Data Reactive module, which allows applications to interact with data sources like databases and message brokers in a reactive way.

- **Reactive Web support:** Spring Boot provides support for reactive Web frameworks like Spring WebFlux, which allows applications to handle Web requests in a reactive manner. Spring WebFlux provides support for non-blocking I/O and reactive programming, which makes it easier to build high-performance and scalable Web applications. For example, the Netty project provides a set of high-performance networking libraries that can be used with Spring WebFlux to build reactive Web applications.

Overall, Spring Boot's support for reactive programming provides developers with the tools and frameworks needed to build modern, scalable, and high-performance applications on the JVM. With Spring Boot's support for reactive programming, developers can take advantage of the benefits of reactive programming without having to deal with the complexity of low-level reactive APIs.

Gradle

Gradle is a powerful build tool that helps you to automate building, testing, and deploying your application. It uses a build script, usually written in a language like Groovy or Kotlin, to define the tasks and dependencies that make up your build process.

Gradle is highly customizable, making it a great choice for any software development project, regardless of its size or complexity. In this section, we will walk through the basic steps of using Gradle to build a simple Kotlin application:

1. **Installing Gradle:** Before we can use Gradle, we need to install it. You can download the latest version of Gradle from the official website: **https://gradle.org/install/**. Or use your default system package manager like Chocolaty for Windows users and Homebrew for Mac users, as mentioned on the Gradle installation page.

   Before installing Gradle, you have to make sure that Java is already installed and globally available; you can test by running the command **$ java -version**.

   Once you have downloaded and installed Gradle, you should be able to run the **gradle** command from your terminal as follows:

   ```
   PS C:\Users\mouni> gradle -version

   ------------------------------------------------------------
   Gradle 7.6
   ------------------------------------------------------------

   Build time:   2022-11-25 13:35:10 UTC
   Revision:     daece9dbc5b79370cc8e4fd6fe4b2cd400e150a8

   Kotlin:       1.7.10
   Groovy:       3.0.13
   Ant:          Apache Ant(TM) version 1.10.11 compiled on July 10 2021
   JVM:          17.0.1 (Oracle Corporation 17.0.1+12-39)
   OS:           Windows 10 10.0 amd64
   ```

2. **Creating a Kotlin application with Gradle:** The first step in using Gradle is to create a new project. To do this, we will use the **gradle init** command. Go to the directory where you want to create your Kotlin project. Then, run the following command:

```
PS C:\Users\mouni\chapter_12\gradle_demo> gradle init --type kotlin-
application
```

You will be prompted to choose between Groovy and Kotlin for the build script DSL like follows:

```
Starting a Gradle Daemon (subsequent builds will be faster)

Select build script DSL:
  1: Groovy
  2: Kotlin
Enter selection (default: Kotlin) [1..2] 2
```

Here, we choose Kotlin by typing the number **2** or hitting *Enter* because Kotlin is the default choice.

This will create a new Gradle project for Kotlin application with a basic directory structure and a build script. Refer to *Figure 12.1*:

```
gradle_demo
├── .gradle
├── app
│   └── src
│       ├── main
│       │   ├── kotlin
│       │   │   └── com.demo
│       │   │       └── App.kt
│       │   └── resources
│       └── test
│           ├── kotlin
│           │   └── com.demo
│           │       └── AppTest
│           └── resources
│   └── build.gradle.kts
├── gradle
├── .gitattributes
├── .gitignore
├── gradlew
├── gradlew.bat
└── settings.gradle.kts
```

Figure 12.1: Generated Gradle structure for Kotlin application

It generates by default a **Hello World** application written in Kotlin code:

```
/*
 * This Kotlin source file was generated by the Gradle 'init' task.
```

```
     */
    package com.demo

    class App {
        val greeting: String
            get() {
                return "Hello World!"
            }
    }

    fun main() {
        println(App().greeting)
    }
```

3. **Understanding the Gradle build script:** The build script is the heart of any Gradle project. It defines the tasks and dependencies that make up your build process. Let us take a closer look at the build script generated by the **gradle init** command:

    ```
    plugins {                                                        (1)
        // Apply the kotlin-jvm Plugin to add support for Kotlin.
        kotlin("jvm") version "1.7.10"

        // Apply the application plugin to add support for building a CLI
        application in Java.
        application                                                  (2)
    }

    repositories {                                                   (3)
        // Use Maven Central for resolving dependencies.
        mavenCentral()
    }

    dependencies {                                                   (4)
        // Use the Kotlin JUnit 5 integration.
    ```

```
        testImplementation("org.jetbrains.kotlin:kotlin-test-junit5")


        // Use the JUnit 5 integration.
        testImplementation("org.junit.jupiter:junit-jupiter-engine:5.9.1")


        // This dependency is used by the application.
        implementation("com.google.guava:guava:31.1-jre")
    }


    application {                                                          (5)
        // Define the main class for the application.
        mainClass.set("com.demo.AppKt")
    }


    tasks.named<Test>("test") {                                            (6)
        // Use JUnit Platform for unit tests.
        useJUnitPlatform()
    }
```

The first section of the build script defines the **plugins** that we will be using. In this case, we are using the **kotlin-jvm** plugin **(1)**, which adds support for building Kotlin applications. Then, apply the **application** plugin **(2)** to add support for building a CLI application in Kotlin.

The second section **(3)**, which is the **repositories** section, tells Gradle where to look for external dependencies. In this case, we are using the **mavenCentral** repository, which is a popular repository for Java libraries.

The third section **(4)** defines the dependencies for the project:

- **kotlin-test-junit5:** Kotlin JUnit 5 integration.
- **junit-jupiter-engine:** JUnit 5 integration.
- **guava:** Guava dependency used by the application.

In this section, you can add all the dependencies (libraries) you will use in your project, for example, database drivers, e-mail libraries, or any external Java library.

In the fourth section (5), you specify the main class for your application.

In the last section, you configure the **test** task by using the JUnit Platform for running tests.

4. **Building and running the project:** Now that we have our project set up and our build script configured, we can build our project using Gradle. To build the project, you will need to run the following command:

   PS C:\Users\mouni\chapter_12\gradle_demo> gradle build

   BUILD SUCCESSFUL in 4s

   8 actionable tasks: 8 executed

   This will compile our Kotlin code, run any tests that we have defined, and create a JAR file that contains our application.

Once we have built our application, we can run it using Gradle. To run the application, run the following command:

PS C:\Users\mouni\chapter_12\gradle_demo> gradle run

Starting a Gradle Daemon, 1 incompatible and 1 stopped Daemons could not be reused,   use --status for details

> Task :app:run
Hello World!

BUILD SUCCESSFUL in 10s

2 actionable tasks: 2 executed

This will execute the **main** method in our Kotlin code (**App.kt**) and run the application.

Now, you have created a new Gradle project for Kotlin, written a simple Kotlin application, and understood how Gradle works. You can continue to add new source files, dependencies, and tasks to your Gradle build script to customize your project as needed.

Getting started with Spring Boot

Spring Boot can be used to build Web applications using the n-tier architecture. In fact, Spring Boot is designed to support the development of applications that are well-structured and modular, making it an excellent fit for the n-tier architecture.

Spring Boot and the n-tier architecture

N-tier architecture is a software architecture pattern that divides an application into multiple layers or tiers, with each tier having a specific responsibility and communicating with the other tiers through well-defined interfaces.

The following are some examples of n-tier architectures and where each example fits best:

- **Three-tier architecture:** This architecture consists of three layers, namely, the presentation layer, the business logic layer, and the data access layer. The presentation layer handles the user interface and user input, the business logic layer handles the application logic and data validation, and the data access layer handles the storage and retrieval of data from a database. Three-tier architecture is suitable for small to medium-sized applications that have a simple data flow.
- **Four-tier architecture:** This architecture adds a middleware layer between the presentation layer and the business logic layer. The middleware layer handles tasks such as authentication, caching, and load balancing. Four-tier architecture is suitable for large applications that have high traffic and require additional scalability and security.

The main idea behind n-tier architecture is to separate the concerns of an application, making it easier to develop, test, maintain, and scale. N-tier architecture is commonly used in Web applications, where the tiers can be distributed across multiple servers or data centers, improving performance and availability.

Spring Boot provides a lot of features that can help with building the different tiers of an n-tier architecture. For example, Spring Boot's Web support provides a flexible and powerful mechanism for implementing the presentation tier. It includes support for handling HTTP requests, generating HTML views, and integrating with client-side JavaScript frameworks.

Spring Boot also includes support for building the business logic tier. It provides a range of tools for working with databases, including support for popular SQL and NoSQL databases. Spring Boot also provides an integrated approach for defining and managing the data access layer, which is often implemented using the Spring Data project.

In addition, Spring Boot includes support for building the middleware layer, which is often used to provide additional functionality such as security, caching, and load balancing. Spring Boot includes support for implementing middleware services using Spring Cloud, which provides tools for building microservices and distributed systems.

Let us take a closer look at each layer and see how they work together to form our n-tier Spring Boot application:

- **Presentation layer:** The presentation layer in our Spring Boot application will consist of RESTful endpoints that are exposed to the outside world. These endpoints will receive HTTP requests and return JSON responses. To implement this layer, we will use Spring Web, which provides annotations such as `@RestController` and `@RequestMapping` to define RESTful endpoints.
- **Business logic layer:** The business logic layer in our Spring Boot application will consist of services that implement business rules and perform data processing. To implement this layer, we will use Spring Service, which provides annotations such as `@Service` to define service classes.
- **Data access layer:** The data access layer in our Spring Boot application will consist of repositories that access data from the database. To implement this layer, we will use Spring Data, which provides annotations such as `@Repository` to define repository interfaces.

The following is a high-level diagram of our n-tier Spring Boot application; see *Figure 12.2*:

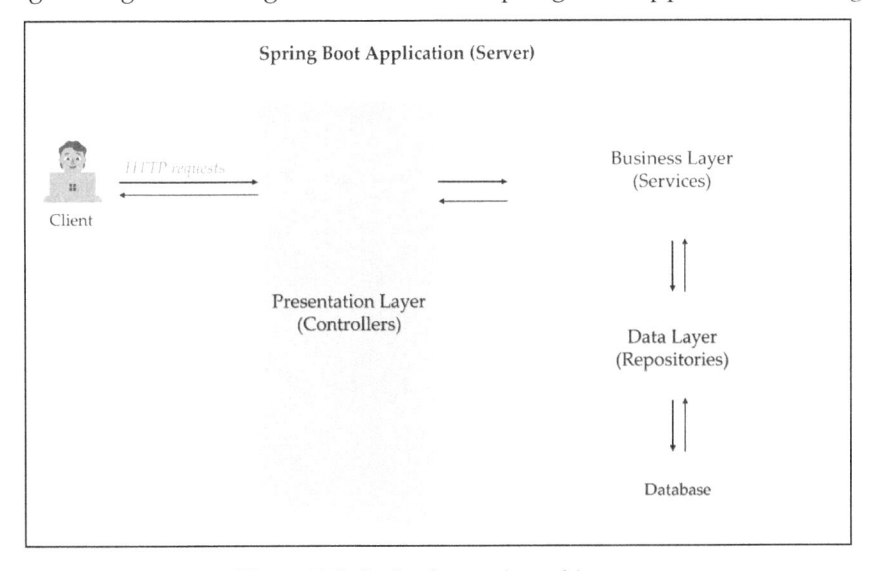

Figure 12.2: Spring boot n-tier architecture

Creating a basic Spring Boot application

In this section, we will walk through the steps for getting started with Spring Boot using Kotlin and Gradle by creating a simple user Web application:

1. **Setting up the project:** The first step is to create a new Spring Boot project. You can do this easily using a tool like *Spring Initializr* or by creating a new project in your IDE (such as *IntelliJ IDEA*) and selecting the Spring Boot and Kotlin options.

Building Kotlin Applications

If you choose to use Gradle as your build system, you will need to add the Spring Boot and Kotlin dependencies to your **build.gradle** file. The following is an example:

```
import org.jetbrains.kotlin.gradle.tasks.KotlinCompile

plugins {
    id("org.springframework.boot") version "3.0.3"
    id("io.spring.dependency-management") version "1.1.0"
    kotlin("jvm") version "1.7.22"
    kotlin("plugin.spring") version "1.7.22"
}

group = "com.mboussetta"
version = "0.0.1-SNAPSHOT"
java.sourceCompatibility = JavaVersion.VERSION_17

repositories {
    mavenCentral()
}

dependencies {
    implementation("org.springframework.boot:spring-boot-starter-web")
    implementation("com.fasterxml.jackson.module:jackson-module-kotlin")
    implementation("org.jetbrains.kotlin:kotlin-reflect")
    testImplementation("org.springframework.boot:spring-boot-starter-test")
}

tasks.withType<KotlinCompile> {
    kotlinOptions {
        freeCompilerArgs = listOf("-Xjsr305=strict")
        jvmTarget = "17"
    }
}
```

```
tasks.withType<Test> {
    useJUnitPlatform()
}
```

This sets up your project with the necessary Spring Boot and Kotlin dependencies, as well as the dependencies needed for building and testing your application. Until this moment of writing this section, the current version of Spring Boot is 3.0.3.

2. **Write the application main class:** In Spring Boot, the main class is responsible for bootstrapping the application and starting up the Web server. The following is the main class of our application in Kotlin:

```
@SpringBootApplication
class SpringDemoApplication


fun main(args: Array<String>) {
    runApplication<SpringDemoApplication>(*args)
}
```

This class uses the **@SpringBootApplication** annotation, which is a combination of three other annotations: **@Configuration**, **@EnableAutoConfiguration**, and **@ComponentScan**. This preferred annotation tells Spring to scan this package and any sub-packages for components (such as controllers) to configure and auto-configure the application. The **@SpringBootApplication** annotation is used to indicate the main class of a Spring Boot application.

The following are some reasons why it is preferred over the individual annotations:

- **@Configuration:** This annotation is used to mark a class as a configuration class, which defines beans and their dependencies. The **@SpringBootApplication** annotation implicitly marks the main class as a configuration class, allowing you to define your beans and their dependencies in one place.

- **@EnableAutoConfiguration:** This annotation is used to configure the Spring application context with sensible defaults and automatically configure the required infrastructure for your application based on its **classpath**. With **@SpringBootApplication**, this annotation is included by default, which means you do not need to add it separately.

- **@ComponentScan:** This annotation is used to scan the package and its sub-packages for components such as controllers, services, and repositories. By default, **@SpringBootApplication** scans the package and its sub-packages for components, eliminating the need to specify a separate **@ComponentScan** annotation.

- **@SpringBootApplication:** Using `@SpringBootApplication` instead of the individual annotations provides a cleaner and more concise way to configure and auto-configure a Spring Boot application. It is also easier to read and understand, as it makes it clear that the main class is both a configuration class and a component scanning configuration. In addition, by including `@EnableAutoConfiguration` by default, it ensures that sensible defaults are set up automatically without requiring additional configuration.

In summary, `@SpringBootApplication` is a convenient annotation that simplifies the configuration of a Spring Boot application by combining three commonly used annotations into one. It is recommended to use `@SpringBootApplication` in all new Spring Boot applications.

The `main` function calls `runApplication` to start up the Spring Boot application. The `runApplication` function takes the main class and any command-line arguments as inputs.

3. **Writing a user data class `User`:** It is a simple data class that represents a user in a database.

   The following shows how it should look like:

   ```
   data class User(val id: Long, val name: String)
   ```

   It has two properties: an `id` of type `Long` and a `name` of type `String`.

4. **Writing a user repository class `UserRepository`:** This is a repository class that provides access to data storage. In the following example, it returns a list of users from a dummy database (`DATABASE`).

   In Spring Boot, a repository is a class that provides a way to access and manipulate data from a data source, such as a database, file, or Web service. It is typically responsible for performing **Create, Read, Update**, and **Delete** (**CRUD**) operations on data entities.

   Repositories are usually implemented as interfaces that extend Spring's `CrudRepository` or `JpaRepository` interfaces. These interfaces provide a set of methods that can be used to interact with the data source, such as `save`, `findById`, `findAll`, `deleteById`, and so on. By implementing these methods, a repository can abstract away the details of data storage and provide a clean and consistent API for accessing and manipulating data.

   The following shows how our `UserRepository` looks like:

   ```
   @Repository
   class UserRepository {
   ```

```kotlin
    private val DATABASE = mapOf(
        "users" to listOf(
            User(1, "Mounir BOUSSETTA"),
            User(2, "John Doe"),
            User(3, "Jane Smith")
        ),
        "profile" to listOf()
    )

    fun getUsers(): List<User>? = DATABASE["users"]

}
```

5. **Writing a user service class UserService:** This is a service class that provides business logic for the application. It has a dependency on the **UserRepository**, which it uses to retrieve the list of users. The **UserService** is responsible for manipulating the data returned by the **UserRepository**, if necessary, before returning it to the **UserController**.

   ```kotlin
   @Service
   class UserService(private val userRepository: UserRepository) {

       fun getUsers():List<User>? = userRepository.getUsers()
   }
   ```

   Generally, a service is a class that provides business logic and acts as an intermediary between the presentation layer (such as a Web controller) and the data access layer (such as a repository). A service is typically responsible for performing more complex operations on data than a repository, such as aggregating data from multiple sources or transforming data into different formats.

   Services are often used to implement use cases or business processes in an application. They encapsulate the logic of a particular use case and provide a clear and focused API for the rest of the application to interact with. They may also have dependencies on other services or repositories, which they use to perform their operations.

6. **Writing a user controller class UserController**: In a Spring Boot application, controllers are responsible for handling *HTTP requests* and returning *HTTP responses*. They act as the middleman between the client making the request and the application's business logic.

A controller in Spring Boot is a class annotated with **@RestController** or **@Controller**. The **@RestController** annotation indicates that the class will handle HTTP requests and return the response in the format of the request, typically JSON. The **@Controller** annotation is similar, but it returns a view (typically a Thymeleaf template or a JSP page) rather than JSON.

Thymeleaf and **JavaServer Pages** (**JSP**) are both server-side template engines that allow you to dynamically generate HTML pages in a Web application.

Thymeleaf is a modern XML/XHTML/HTML5 template engine that is designed to work with Spring Framework. It allows you to create dynamic Web pages by writing HTML templates that can be populated with dynamic data at runtime. Thymeleaf templates can be used to generate HTML, XML, or any other text-based format. Thymeleaf is popular among Spring Boot developers because of its tight integration with Spring and ease of use.

On the contrary, JSP is an older technology that has been around for a long time. It is a technology for creating dynamic Web pages using Java as the programming language. With JSP, you have to write HTML templates with embedded Java code, which is executed on the server side to generate dynamic content. JSP is still widely used, especially in legacy applications that were built before Spring Boot and other modern Web frameworks became popular.

Both Thymeleaf and JSP allow you to create dynamic Web pages that can be rendered on the server side and sent to the client's Web browser. They both support the use of variables, expressions, loops, and conditionals, which makes it easy to generate dynamic content based on data retrieved from a database or other data source.

This is just a brief introduction to controllers. Now, let us create a basic controller that returns a list of users as a response to an HTTP **GET** request from the user:

```
@RestController
class UserController(private val userService: UserService) {

    @GetMapping("/users")
    fun getUsers(): List<User>? = userService.getUsers()
}
```

In this example, we have created a controller named **UserController**. The **@GetMapping** annotation maps the HTTP **GET** request to the **/users** endpoint.

The **getUsers** method returns a list of users as a JSON response.

Controllers act as the middleman between the client and the application's business logic. By using controllers, we can separate the concerns of handling HTTP requests and processing data. This allows us to easily modify or extend the HTTP endpoints without affecting the application's core functionality.

In addition, by using Spring Boot's built-in annotations, such as **@GetMapping**, **@PostMapping**, **@PutMapping**, and **@DeleteMapping**, we can quickly and easily define HTTP endpoints without having to write boilerplate code for handling HTTP requests and responses.

Overall, controllers are an essential component of a Spring Boot application and play a crucial role in handling HTTP requests and responses.

7. **Running the application:** To run your Spring Boot application, you can use the Gradle wrapper included in the project. Open a terminal or command prompt, navigate to your project directory, and run the following command:

   `PS C:\Users\mouni\chapter_12\spring_demo> .\gradlew bootRun`

Your output should look like this:

```
PS C:\Users\mouni\chapter_12\spring_demo> .\gradlew bootRun
Starting a Gradle Daemon (subsequent builds will be faster)


> Task :app:bootRun


  .   ____          _            __ _ _
 /\\ / ___'_ __ _ _(_)_ __  __ _ \ \ \ \
( ( )\___ | '_ | '_| | '_ \/ _` | \ \ \ \
 \\/  ___)| |_)| | | | | || (_| |  ) ) ) )
  '  |____| .__|_| |_|_| |_\__, | / / / /
 =========|_|==============|___/=/_/_/_/
 :: Spring Boot ::                (v3.0.3)


2023-03-05T15:31:59.729+01:00  INFO    19176   ---   [main]   com.mb.SpringDemoApplicationKt    : Starting SpringDemoApplicationKt using Java 17.0.1 with PID 19176
2023-03-05T15:31:59.735+01:00  INFO    19176   ---   [main]   com.mb.SpringDemoApplicationKt    : No active profile set, falling back to 1 default profile: "default"
2023-03-05T15:32:00.807+01:00 INFO 19176 --- [main] o.s.b.w.embedded.tomcat.TomcatWebServer     : Tomcat initialized with port(s): 8080 (http)
```

```
2023-03-05T15:32:00.818+01:00 INFO 19176 --- [main] o.apache.catalina.
core.StandardService     : Starting service [Tomcat]
2023-03-05T15:32:00.818+01:00 INFO 19176 --- [main] o.apache.catalina.
core.StandardEngine      : Starting Servlet engine: [Apache Tomcat/10.1.5]
2023-03-05T15:32:00.931+01:00 INFO 19176 --- [main] o.a.c.c.C.[Tomcat].
[localhost].[/]          : Initializing Spring embedded WebApplicationContext
2023-03-05T15:32:00.932+01:00 INFO 19176 --- [main]
w.s.c.ServletWebServerApplicationContext : Root WebApplicationContext:
initialization completed in 1123 ms
2023-03-05T15:32:01.238+01:00 INFO 19176 --- [main] o.s.b.w.embedded.
tomcat.TomcatWebServer   : Tomcat started on port(s): 8080 (http) with
context path ''
2023-03-05T15:32:01.244+01:00    INFO    19176   ---   [main]    com.
mb.SpringDemoApplicationKt   : Started SpringDemoApplicationKt in 1.929
seconds (process running for 2.293)
<============--> 87% EXECUTING [49s]
> :app:bootRun
> IDLE
```

You will notice in the startup log that Spring uses the Tomcat Web server. Tomcat is a widely used Web server and servlet container in the Java ecosystem, and it is commonly used as the default Web server in Spring Boot applications.

In a Spring Boot application, Tomcat is used to host the application and serve incoming HTTP requests. When you start a Spring Boot application, it starts an embedded Tomcat server that listens for incoming requests on a specified port (**8080** by default in Spring Boot, which you can change in the **application.properties** by setting **server.port=YOUR_PORT**). The embedded server is included in the application's runtime dependencies and is started automatically when the application starts up.

Tomcat provides several benefits for Spring Boot applications, including the following:

- **Easy deployment:** Tomcat can be easily deployed to a variety of platforms and operating systems, making it a popular choice for Web applications.
- **Security:** Tomcat includes built-in security features, such as support for SSL encryption and HTTP request/response filtering.
- **Scalability:** Tomcat is designed to handle large numbers of concurrent requests, making it a good choice for applications that need to scale up quickly.
- **Stability:** Tomcat is a mature and stable Web server with a large community of developers contributing to its development and maintenance.

Overall, Tomcat is a reliable and robust choice for hosting Spring Boot applications, and it provides a solid foundation for building scalable and maintainable Web applications.

Now you will be able to make requests from your browser and get the users as a JSON response, as shown in *Figure 12.3*:

Figure 12.3: HTTP response from UserController

Now that we have covered the basics of creating a Spring Boot application let us dive into the next section into some more advanced features of Spring Reactive programming. In the context of Spring Boot, we can use the **Mono** and **Flux** classes to implement reactive programming and build applications that are both efficient and scalable. In the next section, we will explore how to use **Mono** and **Flux** in Spring Boot and see how they can help us to build reactive applications.

Flux and Mono

In the context of Spring Reactive programming, **Mono** and **Flux** are two classes that are used to implement reactive streams. Reactive streams are a way of processing and responding to asynchronous events in a non-blocking manner. **Mono** represents a stream of zero or one element, whereas **Flux** represents a stream of zero or more elements. These classes allow us to write code that can handle asynchronous events in a more efficient and scalable way.

To use **Mono** and **Flux** in a Spring Boot application, we first need to add the appropriate dependencies to our project. We can do this by adding the **spring-boot-starter-webflux** dependency to our Gradle build file like the following:

```
dependencies {
    implementation("org.springframework.boot:spring-boot-starter-webflux")
    implementation("com.fasterxml.jackson.module:jackson-module-kotlin")
    implementation("org.jetbrains.kotlin:kotlin-reflect")
    testImplementation("org.springframework.boot:spring-boot-starter-test")
}
```

Once we have added the necessary dependencies, we can start using **Mono** and **Flux** in our application. For example, let us update our **UserController** class, which is responsible for handling HTTP requests related to users. We can modify this class to use **Mono** and **Flux** as follows:

```
@RestController
class UserController(private val userService: UserService) {

    @GetMapping("/users/{id}")
    fun getUserById(@PathVariable id: Long): Mono<User> =
                                        userService.getUserById(id)

    @GetMapping("/users")
    fun getUsers(): Flux<User> = userService.getUsers()
}
```

We have added the **getUserById** method to return a **Mono<User>**. This allows us to handle asynchronous events in a non-blocking manner. Similarly, we have modified the **getUsers** method to return a **Flux<User>** instead of a list of **User** objects.

In the same way, we can modify the **UserService** and the **UserRepository** classes as follows:

```
@Service
class UserService(private val userRepository: UserRepository) {

    fun getUsers(): Flux<User> = userRepository.getUsers()
    fun getUserById(id: Long): Mono<User> = userRepository.findUserById(id)
}

@Repository
class UserRepository {

    private val DATABASE = mapOf(
        "users" to listOf(
            User(1, "Mounir BOUSSETTA"),
            User(2, "John Doe"),
```

```
            User(3, "Jane Smith")
        ),
        "profile" to listOf()
    )

    fun getUsers(): Flux<User> = Flux.fromIterable(DATABASE["users"]!!)
    fun findUserById(id: Long): Mono<User> {
        val user: User? = DATABASE["users"]?.find { it.id == id }
        return if (user != null) Mono.just(user) else Mono.empty()
    }

}
```

By using **Mono** and **Flux** in our Spring Boot application, we can build more efficient and scalable applications that can handle a large number of concurrent requests.

You can run the application the same way, using the same command in the previous section. You will notice one difference from the basic output in the previous section, which is the **Netty** server instead of **Tomcat**. Spring Reactive uses Netty as its default embedded Web server instead of Tomcat because Netty is a highly performant and scalable asynchronous event-driven network application framework that is specifically designed for high-performance and high-concurrency applications. Netty is built using a non-blocking I/O model and supports reactive programming out-of-the-box, making it an ideal choice for building reactive Spring applications.

In contrast, Tomcat is a traditional synchronous Web server that is not built to handle large numbers of concurrent requests in a non-blocking manner compared to Tomcat. Tomcat is optimized for traditional request-response-style Web applications that do not require the performance benefits of reactive programming.

Netty's non-blocking I/O model and support for reactive programming allow it to handle large numbers of concurrent requests efficiently and without blocking, making it a better choice for building reactive Spring applications. Therefore, Spring Reactive uses Netty as its default embedded Web server instead of Tomcat. However, Spring Reactive also provides the option to use other embedded Web servers, such as *Undertow* or *Jetty*, depending on the needs of the application.

Spring Data Reactive

Spring Data Reactive is an extension of the popular Spring Framework that offers reactive support for data access. Reactive programming emphasizes asynchronous and non-blocking data processing. This implies that instead of waiting for the data to arrive, reactive programs can continue to process other requests, which leads to better resource utilization and improved performance.

Spring Data Reactive offers a set of tools and APIs that allow developers to build reactive applications that can work with various types of data stores, including PostgreSQL, MongoDB, Cassandra, and Redis. In this chapter, we will focus on using Spring Data Reactive with MongoDB.

The requirement for the following example is to have MongoDB installed on your own machine or in the virtual machine. If you have Docker installed, you can run MongoDB in a container.

To use Spring Data Reactive with MongoDB, we need to add the following dependency to our project:

```
dependencies {
    implementation("org.springframework.boot:spring-boot-starter-webflux")
    implementation("com.fasterxml.jackson.module:jackson-module-kotlin")
    implementation("org.jetbrains.kotlin:kotlin-reflect")
    implementation("org.springframework.boot:spring-boot-starter-data-mongodb-reactive")
    testImplementation("org.springframework.boot:spring-boot-starter-test")
}
```

This will pull in all the necessary dependencies for using Spring Data Reactive with MongoDB.

Another additional thing is to create an **application.properties** file in the resources folder so that it will be accessed by spring boot, where we need to set the MongoDB connection information as follows:

```
spring.data.mongodb.uri=mongodb://localhost:27017/
spring.data.mongodb.database=users
```

Next, we need to update our simple model class **User** that represents our data as a document in MongoDB collection as follows:

```
@Document
data class User(@Id val uid: String?, val name: String)
```

The **@Document** annotation tells Spring Data that this class represents a MongoDB document, **uid**: an optional String that represents the unique identifier of the user. The **@Id** annotation indicates that this property is the ID field of the MongoDB document.

To interact with MongoDB using Spring Data Reactive, we need to update our repository **UserRepository** to be an interface instead of a class that extends the **ReactiveCrudRepository** interface:

```
interface UserRepository: ReactiveCrudRepository<User, String>
```

This repository interface extends the **ReactiveCrudRepository** interface and specifies that we want to work with the User class and use the String type for the document ID.

The last thing to modify in our project is the **UserService**, and we will use methods provided by the **ReactiveCrudRepository** like **findAll** and **findById** instead of **getUsers** and **getUserById**, respectively, without changing the return type. We need to change the **UserService** to the following:

```
@Service
class UserService(private val userRepository: UserRepository) {

    fun getUsers(): Flux<User> = userRepository.findAll()
    fun getUserById(id: String): Mono<User> = userRepository.findById(id)
}
```

So far, our basic Spring reactive application is working with the Spring data reactive using the MongoDB database without making a lot of changes. However, we did not see how to create a new User and how to update or delete one. Let us take a look to understand how we can implement these operations without effort.

In the following **UserService** code, we add the methods to perform the create, update, and delete operations:

```
@Service
class UserService(private val userRepository: UserRepository) {

    fun getUsers(): Flux<User> = userRepository.findAll()
    fun getUserById(id: String): Mono<User> = userRepository.findById(id)

    fun createUser(user: User): Mono<User> = userRepository.save(user)
    fun deleteUserById(id: String) = userRepository.deleteById(id)
```

```kotlin
    fun updateUser(user: User) = userRepository.save(user)
}
```

Then, in the **UserController** class, we will add the endpoints to handle the HTTP **POST** method for the creation of the user, the HTTP **PUT** method for the update, and the HTTP **DELETE** method for the deletion using the annotations **@PostMapping**, **@PutMapping**, and the **@DeleteMapping** respectively as follows:

```kotlin
@RestController
class UserController(private val userService: UserService) {

    @GetMapping("/users/{id}")
    fun getUserById(@PathVariable id: String): Mono<User> = userService.getUserById(id)

    @GetMapping("/users")
    fun getUsers(): Flux<User> = userService.getUsers()

    @PostMapping("/users/create")
    fun createUser(@RequestBody user: User): Mono<User> = userService.createUser(user)

    @DeleteMapping("/users/delete/{id}")
    fun deleteUser(@PathVariable id: String) = userService.deleteUserById(id)

    @PutMapping("/users/update")
    fun updateUser(@RequestBody user: User): Mono<User> = userService.updateUser(user)
}
```

In this code, we created three methods to handle the corresponding HTTP method:

- **createUser**: This method handles a **POST** request to the **/users/create** endpoint and creates a new user.

- **deleteUser**: This method handles a `DELETE` request to the **/users/delete/{id}** endpoint and deletes a user by their ID.
- **updateUser**: This method handles a `PUT` request to the **/users/update** endpoint and updates a user.

All of these methods return reactive types, specifically **Mono<User>** and **Flux<User>**, which allow for non-blocking, asynchronous handling of the request and response. The actual implementation of the functionality for each endpoint is delegated to the **UserService** instance that is injected into the controller by the spring framework.

To test these operations, you need a tool like *Postman* or a command lines tool such as *curl* or *http* to make all different kinds of HTTP requests with the data required.

The following are the outputs of the tests using an integrated HTTP client in IntelliJ IDEA:

- **Create a new user**

    POST Request:

    ```
    ###
    POST http://localhost:8080/users/create
    Content-Type: application/json

    {
      "name": "Demo Name"
    }
    ```

    Response:

    ```
    HTTP/1.1 200 OK
    Content-Type: application/json
    Content-Length: 52

    {
      "id": "64098f2d671dac2f4f939d46",
      "name": "Demo Name"
    }
    ```

- **Update a user**
  PUT Request:

  ```
  ###
  PUT http://localhost:8080/users/update
  Content-Type: application/json

  {
    "id": "64098f2d671dac2f4f939d46",
    "name": "Demo Name updated"
  }
  ```

  Response:

  ```
  HTTP/1.1 200 OK
  Content-Type: application/json
  Content-Length: 60

  {
    "id": "64098f2d671dac2f4f939d46",
    "name": "Demo Name updated"
  }
  ```

- **Get user by ID.**
  GET Request:

  ```
  ###
  GET http://localhost:8080/users/64098f2d671dac2f4f939d46
  ```

  Response:

  ```
  HTTP/1.1 200 OK
  Content-Type: application/json
  Content-Length: 60

  {
    "id": "64098f2d671dac2f4f939d46",
    "name": "Demo Name updated"
  }
  ```

- **Get all users**

    GET request:

    ```
    ###
    GET http://localhost:8080/users
    ```

    Response:

    ```
    HTTP/1.1 200 OK
    transfer-encoding: chunked
    Content-Type: application/json

    [
      {
        "id": "64098f2d671dac2f4f939d46",
        "name": "Demo Name updated"
      }
    ]
    ```

- **Delete a user by ID.**

    DELETE request:

    ```
    ###
    DELETE http://localhost:8080/users/delete/64098f2d671dac2f4f939d46
    ```

    Response:

    ```
    HTTP/1.1 200 OK
    content-length: 0

    <Response body is empty>
    ```

    The user has been deleted successfully. Now if you try to get the users, you will have the following response:

    ```
    HTTP/1.1 200 OK
    transfer-encoding: chunked
    Content-Type: application/json

    []
    ```

Conclusion

Spring Boot is a powerful and popular framework for developing Web applications. It offers a wide range of features and tools that help developers build robust, scalable, and efficient applications with ease. The use of Kotlin and Gradle makes development even more streamlined and efficient.

Controllers play a crucial role in defining the behavior of our Web application and serve as a bridge between the user interface and the business logic. Services and repositories are used to handle the application's business logic and data persistence, respectively.

With the introduction of reactive programming in Spring Boot, we can achieve higher performance and scalability by making our application non-blocking and asynchronous. **Mono** and **Flux** are the two main types of reactive streams that can be used in our application to handle data asynchronously.

Finally, Spring Data Reactive provides a set of powerful tools and APIs for working with databases in a reactive programming style, making it easier for developers to build reactive applications with Spring Boot.

Overall, Spring Boot is an excellent choice for building modern Web applications that require high performance, scalability, and flexibility. By using its various features and tools, developers can create efficient and reliable applications in a relatively short amount of time.

Points to remember

The following are some points to remember when working with Spring Boot:
- Spring Boot is a popular framework for building Web applications.
- Spring Boot makes it easy to set up a project with minimal configuration.
- Kotlin and Gradle can be used with Spring Boot to improve development efficiency.
- Controllers define the behavior of the Web application and are responsible for handling HTTP requests.
- Services and repositories handle the business logic and data persistence, respectively.
- Reactive programming with Mono and Flux can improve application performance and scalability.
- Spring Data Reactive provides powerful tools and APIs for working with databases in a reactive programming style.
- Tomcat is the default Web server used with Spring Boot, but Netty is used in reactive applications for better performance.
- Spring Boot offers many features and tools for building robust, scalable, and efficient applications.
- Spring Boot is an excellent choice for modern Web applications that require high performance, scalability, and flexibility.

CHAPTER 13
Asynchronous Programming and Coroutines

Introduction

In the previous chapter, we learned that asynchronous programming is a programming paradigm that allows multiple tasks to be executed simultaneously without blocking the main thread. In traditional programming, when a thread is blocked by a long-running task, it can cause the application to become unresponsive, leading to poor user experience. Asynchronous programming can help solve this problem by allowing multiple tasks to be executed in parallel, improving application performance and responsiveness. We also discussed how to perform asynchronous programming using schedulers. However, Kotlin also provides another powerful tool for asynchronous programming called coroutines. Coroutines are a way of writing asynchronous code more sequentially and naturally, making it easier to reason about and maintain.

Structure

In this chapter, we will cover the following topics:
- Why multithreading?
- Handling work completion using callbacks

- Understanding coroutines
- Jobs
- UI threads

Objectives

Upon completing this chapter, readers will have acquired several essential skills and insights. Firstly, they will have a solid understanding of the challenges inherent in concurrent programming and the advantages that both multithreading and coroutines bring to the table. Readers will also grasp the art of handling work completion through the effective utilization of callbacks—a powerful tool for signaling the conclusion of asynchronous tasks. The chapter will demystify the concept of coroutines, showcasing how they streamline the process of writing asynchronous code by abstracting away the intricacies of multithreading. Furthermore, readers will become proficient in employing jobs to efficiently manage the execution of multiple tasks. Lastly, they will gain a clear understanding of the pivotal role played by UI threads in graphical user interface (GUI) applications, appreciating how they facilitate seamless user interface updates and responsive interactions with user input.

Overview

This chapter will explore the concepts of multithreading, callbacks, coroutines, jobs, and UI threads. We will begin by discussing why multithreading is important in modern software development, including the benefits of improved performance, scalability, and responsiveness. We will then dive into the topic of handling work completion using callbacks, which are a powerful mechanism for signaling the completion of asynchronous tasks.

Next, we will explore the concept of coroutines, which are a higher-level abstraction for managing asynchronous programming. We will examine how coroutines can simplify writing asynchronous code by abstracting away the complexity of multithreading.

After that, we will discuss jobs, which are units of work that can be executed asynchronously. We will explore how jobs can be used to manage the execution of multiple tasks. Finally, we will discuss the topic of UI threads, which are dedicated threads used in **graphical user interface** (**GUI**) applications to update the user interface and respond to user input before seeing it in real-world examples in an upcoming chapter.

Why multithreading?

Multithreading is a technique in computer programming where multiple threads of execution are created within a single process. Each thread runs independently and can perform a separate task simultaneously, improving the application's overall performance and responsiveness. For example, a program that needs to download multiple files from the internet can use multithreading to download the files concurrently, significantly reducing the download time.

By using multithreading, a program can take advantage of the multiple cores available in modern CPUs and distribute tasks across multiple threads, which can improve the overall performance.

Reason behind multithreading use

The following are some of the reasons why we need multithreading:

- **Using multi-core processors**: Many modern CPUs have multiple cores, which means they can execute multiple threads simultaneously. By using multithreading, we can take advantage of these cores and distribute the workload across them to achieve faster performance.
- **Improving responsiveness**: Multithreading allows an application to remain responsive even while performing time-consuming tasks. By separating a long-running task into multiple threads, we can ensure that the user interface remains responsive to user input.
- **Better resource utilization**: By using multithreading, we can better use system resources such as memory and CPU time. For example, if we have multiple threads that need to access a shared resource, we can use synchronization techniques to ensure that they access the resource in a controlled and efficient manner.
- **Simplifying complex operations**: Some operations can be simplified by breaking them down into smaller, independent parts that can be executed concurrently. For example, image processing operations can be split into multiple threads, each processing a separate image section.

Overall, multithreading is a powerful technique that can improve applications' performance and responsiveness while efficiently using system resources.

However, multithreading can also introduce new challenges, such as synchronization and race conditions, which must be carefully managed to ensure that the program runs correctly.

Challenges

The following are some of the challenges of multithreading:

- **Concurrency issues**: When multiple threads access shared data concurrently, it can lead to concurrency issues such as race conditions, deadlocks, and livelocks. These issues can result in unpredictable behavior and can be difficult to diagnose and debug.

- **Synchronization overhead**: To prevent concurrency issues, we need to use synchronization techniques such as locks and semaphores, which can introduce overhead and reduce performance.
- **Increased complexity**: Multithreaded programs can be more complex than single-threaded programs, requiring careful design and implementation to ensure correct behavior and avoid concurrency issues.
- **Debugging difficulties**: Multithreaded programs can be difficult to debug, as concurrency issues can be intermittent and dependent on timing and scheduling.
- **Resource contention**: When multiple threads compete for the same resources, such as CPU time or memory, it can lead to resource contention and reduced performance.

Overall, multithreading requires careful consideration and design to ensure correct behavior and avoid the challenges that it presents.

Solutions

The following are some strategies that can help address these challenges.

Use thread-safe data structures and synchronization mechanisms

When multiple threads in a program access the same shared resource, such as a piece of memory or a file, it can create a situation where they compete and cause concurrency issues. Two common concurrency issues are race conditions and deadlocks.

A race condition is a situation where the behavior of the program depends on the timing or order in which the threads execute. For example, if two threads access the same variable and both try to modify it at the same time, the result may be unpredictable.

A deadlock is a situation where two or more threads are blocked and unable to proceed because they are waiting for each other to release a resource. This can happen when threads are not properly synchronized, leading to the program becoming unresponsive.

To avoid these issues, we need to use thread-safe data structures and synchronization mechanisms to control access to shared resources. A thread-safe data structure is a data structure that is designed to be accessed by multiple threads concurrently without causing issues. For example, a concurrent collection is a thread-safe collection that can be accessed by multiple threads without causing a race condition.

Synchronization mechanisms such as locks and semaphores can be used to control access to shared resources. A lock is a mechanism that allows only one thread to access a shared resource at a time, whereas a semaphore is a mechanism that allows a limited number of threads to access a shared resource at a time. By using locks and semaphores, we can ensure that threads access shared resources in a controlled and safe manner, which helps prevent race conditions and deadlocks.

In summary, using thread-safe data structures and synchronization mechanisms such as locks and semaphores is important to avoid concurrency issues such as race conditions and deadlocks when multiple threads in a program access a shared resource.

Use atomic operations

When multiple threads in a program try to access the same variable or resource, they can interfere with each other and cause issues, such as race conditions. A race condition is a situation where the behavior of the program depends on the timing or order in which the threads execute.

To avoid race conditions and ensure that a particular operation is performed as a single, indivisible unit, we can use atomic operations. An atomic operation is an operation that is guaranteed to be performed as a single, indivisible operation without any interference from other threads.

For example, let us say two threads in a program try to increment a counter variable simultaneously. Without any synchronization mechanism, they may interfere with each other and cause a race condition where the value of the counter is unpredictable. But if we use an atomic operation to increment the counter, it will ensure that the increment operation is performed as a single, indivisible operation without interference from other threads.

Using atomic operations can help avoid race conditions and improve performance because they eliminate the need for synchronization mechanisms like locks or semaphores, which can be expensive and cause contention. Atomic operations can be more efficient because they do not require locking or blocking other threads, so they can improve the performance of multithreaded applications.

In summary, atomic operations are operations that are guaranteed to be performed as a single, indivisible operation without interference from other threads. Using atomic operations can help avoid race conditions and improve the performance of multithreaded applications.

Use thread pools

Creating and destroying threads in a multithreaded program can be time-consuming and resource-intensive. Additionally, creating too many threads at once can lead to resource contention, where threads compete for resources such as CPU time, memory, or I/O bandwidth, which can reduce performance.

To address these issues, you can use a thread pool, which is a collection of threads that can be used to execute tasks concurrently. When a task needs to be executed, it is assigned to an available thread in the thread pool. Once the task is completed, the thread is returned to the pool and can be reused for another task.

Using a thread pool can avoid the overhead of creating and destroying threads for each task. This can lead to improved performance because you do not need to spend time and resources creating new threads each time a task needs to be executed. Additionally, because the number of threads in the pool is limited, you can avoid resource contention and ensure that the threads are used efficiently.

For example, let us say you have a program that needs to process a large number of requests. Without a thread pool, you may create a new thread for each request, which can be inefficient and lead to resource contention. But with a thread pool, you can limit the number of threads that are active at any given time and reuse threads that have completed previous tasks, which can improve performance.

To recapitulate, a thread pool is a collection of threads that can be used to execute tasks concurrently. By using a thread pool, you can avoid the overhead of creating and destroying threads for each task, and you can limit the number of threads that are active at any given time, which can help avoid resource contention and improve performance.

Use message passing

In a multithreaded program, threads often need to communicate with each other to coordinate their work or share data. One way to do this is by accessing shared data directly, but this can lead to concurrency issues like race conditions or deadlocks.

Another way to communicate between threads is by using message passing. Message passing is a communication method where threads communicate by exchanging messages rather than accessing shared data directly. When a thread wants to communicate with another thread, it sends a message containing the data or instructions it wants to share. The receiving thread then processes the message and sends a response if necessary.

Using message passing can help avoid concurrency issues because threads do not access shared data directly. Instead, they communicate by exchanging messages, which ensures that each thread has exclusive access to its own data. This can simplify program design because threads do not need to coordinate their access to shared data or worry about synchronization issues.

For example, let us say you have a program with two threads: one thread that generates data and another thread that processes the data. Without message passing, the processing thread may need to access the data directly, which can lead to concurrency issues. But with message passing, the generating thread can send the data to the processing thread as a message, which ensures that the data is only accessed by one thread at a time.

In summary, message passing is a communication method where threads communicate by exchanging messages rather than accessing shared data directly. This can help avoid concurrency issues and simplify program design.

Use profiling and debugging tools

When developing multithreaded applications, it can be difficult to identify and diagnose issues that arise from the interaction between threads. Performance issues, concurrency issues, and other problems can all impact the behavior of your application in complex ways.

Profiling and debugging tools can help you identify these issues and diagnose them more quickly and effectively. These tools allow you to monitor your application's behavior in real-time and identify performance bottlenecks, concurrency issues, and other problems that may be affecting your application's behavior.

For example, a profiling tool may allow you to see how much CPU time each thread in your application is using and which parts of your code are taking the most time to execute. This can help you identify performance bottlenecks and optimize your code for better performance.

Similarly, a debugging tool can help you identify concurrency issues like race conditions or deadlocks by allowing you to pause your program's execution and inspect the state of each thread and the shared data they are accessing.

By using these tools, you can save time and effort by identifying issues more quickly and effectively. This can help you optimize your code and avoid issues that could cause problems for your users.

Overall, by using these solutions, you can address the challenges of multithreading and build more reliable and efficient applications.

In conclusion, multithreading is a crucial technique that enables us to take advantage of the parallel processing capabilities of modern computing environments. By improving performance, responsiveness, resource utilization, simplifying code, and enabling scalability, multithreading provides a significant advantage to developers and end-users alike. As such, it is essential to understand and incorporate multithreading into our applications to achieve optimal performance and user experience.

Handling work completion using callbacks

In asynchronous programming, tasks are executed independently from the main thread, allowing the program to continue running while the task is being executed. However, this also creates a challenge—the program needs to know when the task is complete before moving on to the next task.

In a traditional programming model, the program would simply wait for the task to be completed before moving on to the next task. However, this is not feasible in an asynchronous programming model because the program needs to keep running while the task is being executed.

To solve this challenge, callbacks are used. A callback is a function that is passed as an argument to another function. The callback function is then called when the original function completes. In the case of asynchronous programming, the callback function is called when the task is complete.

For example, let us say you need to download an image from the internet in your program. Instead of waiting for the image to download, you can initiate the download and pass a callback function as an argument. When the download is complete, the callback function is called, allowing you to continue with the next task in your program.

Using callbacks in this way can be extremely useful in asynchronous programming, as it allows the program to continue running while tasks are being executed. However, it can also create some challenges of its own, such as managing callbacks for multiple tasks and the potential for callback hell—a situation where the code becomes difficult to read and maintain due to a large number of nested callbacks.

To address these challenges, newer programming paradigms such as Promises, async/await, and reactive programming have been developed, providing more sophisticated ways of managing asynchronous programming. However, callbacks remain an important part of the asynchronous programming toolbox, and understanding them is essential for any beginner programmer looking to work with asynchronous programming.

The following are some examples of how callbacks are used in Kotlin in real-world scenarios:

Asynchronous programming

In asynchronous programming, callbacks are commonly used for operations that take time to complete, such as network calls, file I/O, or database operations. Callbacks can be used to signal the completion of these operations so that the program can continue execution without blocking the main thread.

For example, consider the following code snippet that uses callbacks to handle reading files asynchronously:

```
import java.io.File
import java.lang.Thread.sleep
```

```kotlin
fun readFileAsync(file: File, callback: (String) -> Unit) {
    Thread {
        val content = file.readText()
        sleep(5000)
        callback(content)
    }.start()
}

fun main() {

    println("Start")

    val file = File("tasks.csv")
    readFileAsync(file) { content ->
        println("File content: $content")
    }

    println("End")
}
```

The following will be the output:

```
Start
End
File content: Go to the market,12:00,Completed
Do homeworks,15:30,""
Feed cats,16:30,Archived
```

The **readFileAsync** function takes a **File** object and a callback function as arguments. It reads the contents of the file in a separate thread using a **Thread** object, which allows the program to continue executing without blocking the main thread. The sleep method is called with a delay of 5,000 milliseconds (5 seconds) to simulate a long-running operation. Finally, the **callback** function is called with the content of the file as an argument.

When the program is run, **Start** is printed first, followed by **End**. The **readFileAsync** function is executed asynchronously, so the program does not wait for it to finish before printing **End**. After a delay of 5 seconds, the content of the file **tasks.csv** is printed to the console.

Asynchronous file I/O using CompletableFuture

When reading or writing files asynchronously, callbacks can be used to notify the calling code when the operation is complete. In Kotlin, you can use the **CompletableFuture** class to define a callback function and pass it as a parameter to an asynchronous function.

For example, consider the following code snippet that uses the **CompletableFuture** class to read a file asynchronously:

```kotlin
import java.io.File
import java.util.concurrent.CompletableFuture

fun readFileAsync(file: File): CompletableFuture<String> {
    return CompletableFuture.supplyAsync {
        val content = file.readText()
        Thread.sleep(5000)
        content
    }.exceptionally {
        println(it.message)
         null
    }
}

fun main() {
    println("Start")

    val file = File("tasks.csv")
    readFileAsync(file).thenAccept { content ->
        println("File content: $content")
    }

    println("End")
    Thread.sleep(6000) // Wait for the CompletableFuture to complete

    println("Done")
}
```

In this example, `CompletableFuture.supplyAsync` reads the file content asynchronously and returns a `Future`. The `thenAccept` method is used to define a callback function that is called when the future completes successfully. If the future fails, the exceptional method is used to handle the exception and return null.

Understanding coroutines

Coroutines are a way to write asynchronous, non-blocking code in a more readable and sequential manner. They are essentially lightweight threads that can be started and stopped quickly and easily, making them ideal for tasks that need to run concurrently.

In traditional programming, when a task is executed, the program waits for that task to finish before moving on to the next one. This can be time-consuming and inefficient, especially for tasks that involve I/O operations such as network requests or file operations. Coroutines allow you to start a task and then move on to the next task while the first one is still running in the background. When the first task finishes, it signals the program to continue where it left off, allowing you to write code that appears to be executed sequentially but is actually running concurrently.

Coroutines are designed to be easy to use and understand. They allow you to write asynchronous code in a more natural, sequential way without the complexity and overhead of traditional concurrency mechanisms such as threads and locks. In Kotlin, coroutines are built-in and can be used without any additional libraries or frameworks.

When programming with coroutines, you first define a scope in which the coroutine will run. Think of this scope as a container for the coroutine. Then, within that scope, you can start a coroutine, which is like a block of code that can run independently of the rest of the program. It is similar to starting a new thread, but with coroutines, you do not necessarily need to create a new thread for each coroutine.

Once a coroutine is started, it can run in the background while the rest of the program continues to execute. This is useful when you have tasks that take a long time to complete, but you do not want to block the main thread of the program. For example, you might use a coroutine to download an image from the internet while the user continues to interact with the app.

Example:

```kotlin
import kotlinx.coroutines.delay
import kotlinx.coroutines.launch
import kotlinx.coroutines.runBlocking

fun main() = runBlocking {
    println("Started")
```

```
    launch {
        delay(1000)
        println("Coroutine 1 finished")
    }

    launch {
        delay(2000)
        println("Coroutine 2 finished")
    }

    println("Finished")
}
```

The following will be the output:

Started

Finished

Coroutine 1 finished

Coroutine 2 finished

In this example, we create a coroutine scope using the **runBlocking** function. Within that scope, we launch two coroutines using the launch function. Each coroutine simply delays for a certain amount of time using the delay function to simulate intensive work and then prints a message to the console.

When we run this program, we first see the message **Started** printed on the console. Then, both coroutines are launched and run concurrently. However, because each coroutine is delayed for a different amount of time, they do not necessarily finish in the order they were launched. Finally, we see the message **Finished** printed to the console once all the coroutines have finished executing.

When the coroutine is finished, it can return a value or signal the program to continue where it left off. This can be done through a concept called **suspending**, which allows the coroutine to pause its execution until some condition is met, such as a network request completing; we will see that in the upcoming chapters. Once the condition is met, the coroutine can resume its execution, return the result, or continue executing the next set of instructions.

Coroutines offer a significant benefit in that they are highly effective and have minimal resource overhead. They can be started and stopped quickly and easily, and they use fewer system resources than traditional threads. This makes them ideal for tasks that need to be executed quickly and frequently, such as network requests or database queries.

In summary, coroutines are a powerful and efficient way to write asynchronous, non-blocking code in Kotlin. They allow you to write code that appears to be executed sequentially but is actually running concurrently in the background. They are lightweight, easy to use, and can be used for a wide range of tasks, making them an essential tool for modern application development.

Jobs

In the context of asynchronous programming, a **Job** is a unit of work that can be launched as a coroutine. You can think of a job as a task that you want to execute asynchronously without blocking the main thread. When you launch a job, it will be executed in the background, allowing your program to continue executing other tasks.

A job can have different states, such as *active*, *completed*, or *canceled*. When a job is active, it means that it is currently running. When a job is completed, it means that it has finished executing. When a job is canceled, it means that it has been stopped before completion.

One of the benefits of using jobs in coroutines is that you can easily cancel them if needed. For example, if a user decides to cancel a task, you can cancel the corresponding job, which will stop the task from continuing to run in the background. This can help improve the performance of your program by avoiding unnecessary work.

When a coroutine is started, it returns a job object that can be used to manage the coroutine. The job object can be used to check if the coroutine is still active or has been completed. If the coroutine has not been completed, the job can also be used to cancel the coroutine.

To create a job in Kotlin, you can use the launch function, which returns a job object; the code snippet is as follows:

```
val job: Job = launch {
    // Coroutine code goes here
}

if (job.isActive) {
    // coroutine is still running
} else {
    // coroutine not running
}
```

The `launch` function starts a new coroutine and returns a `job` object that can be used to manage the coroutine. You can use the `job` object to check the status of the coroutine, cancel the coroutine, or wait for the coroutine to complete.

For example, you can use the `isActive` property of the `job` object to check if the coroutine is still running.

You can also use the `cancel` method of the `job` object to cancel the coroutine:

```
job.cancel()
```

The `cancel` method cancels the coroutine, causing it to stop executing. You can also provide a reason for the cancellation by passing an exception to the `cancel` method.

Finally, you can use the `join` method of the `job` object to wait for the coroutine to complete:

```
job.join()
```

The `join` method blocks the current thread until the coroutine completes. Once the coroutine has been completed, the join method returns, allowing the program to continue.

UI threads

UI threads are responsible for rendering the user interface of an application. This includes everything from displaying buttons and text fields to processing user input and responding to events. Because the UI is such a crucial aspect of most applications, it is important that it remains responsive and does not freeze or become unresponsive during long-running tasks.

In an asynchronous application, it is common for tasks to run on separate threads to avoid blocking the UI thread. This can help ensure that the UI remains responsive while the application performs other tasks. However, it is important to remember that UI elements can only be accessed from the UI thread. This means that if you need to update the UI from a separate thread, you will need to use a mechanism to marshal the call back to the UI thread.

When an asynchronous task needs to update the UI, it cannot do so directly from the thread it is running on (usually a background thread). This is because UI elements can only be accessed from the UI thread. Therefore, in order to update the UI from an asynchronous task, the task needs to somehow communicate with the UI thread.

One common approach to achieving this communication is to use a message loop. A message loop is a mechanism that allows threads to communicate with each other by sending messages. In the context of user interfaces, the message loop is typically associated with the UI thread.

When an asynchronous task needs to update the UI, it can post a message to the message loop. The message contains information about the update that needs to be performed, such as the new value of a text field or the position of a graphical element. The message is then placed in a queue of messages that are waiting to be processed on the UI thread.

The UI thread continually monitors the message queue and processes each message in turn. When the UI thread encounters a message that contains an update to a UI element, it performs the update and redraws the display. Once all messages in the queue have been processed, the UI thread returns to its normal event loop, waiting for new user input or other events.

By using a message loop to marshal UI updates back to the UI thread, asynchronous tasks can update the UI without blocking the UI thread. This allows the UI to remain responsive and ensures the user experience is smooth and seamless.

Another important consideration when dealing with UI threads is thread synchronization. Because multiple threads may be accessing the UI thread simultaneously, it is important to ensure that access to UI elements is synchronized in order to avoid race conditions and other issues. This can be accomplished using locks or other synchronization mechanisms.

The following are some real-world examples when you can use UI threads:

- **Updating the user interface in response to user input**: When a user interacts with a GUI application, the application must respond quickly to provide feedback to the user. For example, when a user clicks a button or types text into a text box, the UI thread must quickly update the user interface to reflect the user's input.
- **Displaying animations or videos**: When displaying animations or videos in a GUI application, the UI thread must update the user interface quickly and frequently to provide a smooth, seamless experience. If the UI thread becomes blocked, the animation or video may stutter or pause, leading to poor user experience.
- **Loading data from a database or network**: When a GUI application needs to load data from a database or network, it can take some time to complete. If the UI thread is blocked during this time, the user interface can become unresponsive. By executing these tasks asynchronously on a separate thread, the UI thread can remain free to update the user interface and respond to user input.

Performing complex calculations or processing large amounts of data: When performing complex calculations or processing large amounts of data in a GUI application, the UI thread can become blocked, leading to poor user experience. By executing these tasks asynchronously on a separate thread, the UI thread can remain free to update the user interface and respond to user input.

In conclusion, UI threads are a critical aspect of many applications, and managing them in an asynchronous context can be challenging. However, with careful planning and attention to detail, it is possible to create responsive and efficient applications that take full advantage of the power of asynchronous programming. By understanding the principles of thread synchronization and message passing, developers can create robust applications that provide a great user experience.

Conclusion

In conclusion, this chapter has provided a comprehensive overview of the concepts of multithreading, callbacks, coroutines, jobs, and UI threads in modern software development. We have explored the benefits and potential drawbacks of each of these concepts, as well as practical examples of their application in real-world scenarios.

Through this chapter, we have learned that multithreading is an important tool for improving performance, scalability, and responsiveness in modern software applications. We have also explored the use of callbacks for handling work completion, coroutines as a higher-level abstraction for managing asynchronous programming, and jobs for managing the execution of multiple tasks.

Finally, we have discussed the role of UI threads in **graphical user interface** (**GUI**) applications and how they are used to update the user interface and respond to user input.

Points to remember

The following are some points to remember:

- Multithreading is an important tool for improving performance, scalability, and responsiveness in modern software applications.
- Callbacks are a powerful mechanism for signaling the completion of asynchronous tasks.
- Coroutines are a higher-level abstraction for managing asynchronous programming and can simplify the process of writing asynchronous code.
- Jobs are units of work that can be executed asynchronously and can be used to manage the execution of multiple tasks.
- UI threads are dedicated threads used in GUI applications to update the user interface and respond to user input.

Join our book's Discord space

Join the book's Discord Workspace for Latest updates, Offers, Tech happenings around the world, New Release and Sessions with the Authors:

https://discord.bpbonline.com

CHAPTER 14
Suspending Functions and Async/Await

Introduction

In the previous chapter, we learned about asynchronous programming and coroutines in Kotlin. We learned that coroutines are a way to write asynchronous code that is concise, readable, and efficient.

In this chapter, we will learn more about suspending functions and async/await. Suspending functions are a type of function that can be paused and resumed at a later time. Async/await are keywords that can be used to write asynchronous code in a more concise and readable way. By the end of this chapter, you will be able to write asynchronous code in Kotlin using suspending functions and async/await.

Structure

In this chapter, we will cover the following topics:
- Suspending versus non-suspending
- Creating suspendable API
- Async/await
- Deferred values
- Combination of deferred values

Objectives

This chapter is focused on providing a comprehensive understanding of Kotlin's suspending functions and their applications. It starts by introducing the concept of suspending functions and then delves into the creation of suspendable APIs. Readers will learn how to employ the "async" and "await" keywords to craft asynchronous code effectively. Additionally, the chapter covers the essential skill of using deferred values to manage and represent the results of asynchronous operations. Finally, it demonstrates the art of combining these deferred values to tackle more complex asynchronous tasks. By the end of this chapter, readers will be equipped with the expertise to confidently write asynchronous Kotlin code using suspending functions and async/await, efficiently handle deferred values to depict asynchronous outcomes, and successfully orchestrate intricate asynchronous operations.

Overview

In this chapter, we will learn about suspending functions and `async`/`await`. Suspending functions are a powerful tool that can be used to write asynchronous code in Kotlin. They allow you to write code that is more concise, readable, and efficient.

In the real world, suspending functions can be used to write code that performs network requests, database queries, and other asynchronous operations. For example, you could use suspending functions to write code that fetches data from a web service, updates a database, or plays a sound file.

Suspending functions can also be used to write code that is more responsive to user input. For example, you could use suspending functions to write code that displays a progress bar while an asynchronous operation is in progress.

Overall, suspending functions are a powerful tool that can be used to write asynchronous code in Kotlin.

The following are some examples of how *suspending* functions can be used in the real world:
- A Web application that fetches data from a Web service could use suspending functions to make the requests and display the results in a timely manner.
- A mobile application that updates a database could use suspending functions to ensure that the data is always up-to-date.
- A game that plays sound files could use suspending functions to ensure that the sound files are played smoothly.

Suspending functions can be used to write asynchronous code in any situation where you need to perform an operation that takes some time to complete. By using suspending functions, you can write code that is more concise, readable, efficient, and responsive to user input.

Suspending versus non-suspending

In programming, functions are an important building block for creating robust and efficient code. Two types of functions commonly used in programming are suspending and non-suspending functions. In this section, we will explore the differences between the two, along with real-world examples.

Non-suspending functions

A non-suspending function is a function that runs synchronously from start to finish without pausing or yielding control until it has completed its task. These functions are typically used for tasks that do not require any asynchronous operations, such as simple mathematical calculations or basic string manipulations.

The following is an example of a non-suspending function in Kotlin:

```kotlin
fun sumNumbers(numbers: List<Int>): Int {
    return numbers.sum()
}

fun main() {
    println(sumNumbers((1..10).toList()))
}
```

The function **sumNumbers** takes a list of integers as input, which is specified by the parameter numbers. The function then returns the sum of all the integers in the list using the **sum()** function, which is a built-in function in Kotlin for calculating the sum of all elements in a collection.

So, when **sumNumbers** is called with a list of integers, it simply adds up all the numbers in the list and returns the resulting sum as an integer.

Suspending functions

In contrast to non-suspending functions, suspending functions are used for tasks that require asynchronous operations, such as I/O or network calls. A suspending function can suspend its execution and yield control to another part of the program, allowing other tasks to continue running until the suspending function is ready to resume.

In Kotlin, suspending functions are defined with the **suspend** keyword. The following is an example of a suspending function in Kotlin:

```kotlin
suspend fun fetchData(): List<String> {
    // simulate network request execution time
    delay(2500)
    return listOf("data chunk 1", "data chunk 2", "data chunk 3")
}
```

This function simulates a network request by suspending its execution for 2.5 seconds using the **delay** function, which is a built-in suspending function in the Kotlin Coroutines library. Once the delay is completed, the function returns a list of strings (or chunked data).

Some real-world examples

Let us consider some real-world examples where suspending functions can be useful in mobile development using Kotlin multiplatform.

Example 1: Fetching data from an API

In mobile development, it is common to make network requests to fetch data from an API. As network requests can take some time to complete, suspending functions can be used to handle these operations asynchronously without blocking the main thread of the application. The following is an example of a suspending function that fetches data from an API:

```kotlin
suspend fun fetchDataFromAPI(): List<User> {
    val response = httpClient.get("https://example.com/users")
    return response.jsonArray.map { User.fromJson(it) }
}
```

In this example, the **httpClient.get** function sends a network request to the specified URL and suspends the execution of the **fetchDataFromAPI** function until the response is received. Once the response is received, the function maps the JSON data to a list of **User** objects and returns it.

Example 2: Saving data to a local database

In mobile development, it is also common to save data to a local database for offline access. Since database operations can also take some time to complete, suspending functions can be used to handle these operations asynchronously without blocking the application's main thread. The following is an example of a suspending function that saves data to a local database:

```kotlin
suspend fun saveDataToDatabase(data: List<User>) {
    withContext(Dispatchers.IO) {
        database.userDao().insertAll(data)
```

```
            }
    }
```

In this example, the **withContext** function is used to switch the context of the execution to the I/O dispatcher, which is optimized for I/O operations. The function then inserts the data into the local database using Kotlin multiplatform. The following is an example of how the same function can be used in both the Android and iOS platforms:

```
expect class UserDao {
    fun insertAll(data: List<User>)
}

suspend fun saveDataToDatabase(data: List<User>) {
    withContext(Dispatchers.IO) {
        UserDao().insertAll(data)
    }
}
```

In this example, we define an expected class, **UserDao**, which represents a **Data Access Object (DAO)** for accessing the local database. We then implement this class separately for each platform. The **saveDataToDatabase** function can then be called on both platforms using the same code because the **UserDao** implementation is platform-specific.

In conclusion, suspending and non-suspending functions are two types of functions commonly used in programming. Non-suspending functions are used for synchronous operations while suspending functions are used for asynchronous operations. In mobile development using Kotlin multiplatform, suspending functions are particularly useful for handling network requests and database operations asynchronously without blocking the main thread of the application. By using Kotlin multiplatform, we can write platform-specific implementations for platform-specific code while keeping the common codebase as uniform as possible.

Creating suspendable API

In modern programming, asynchronous operations are crucial for building responsive and efficient applications. Kotlin, with its powerful coroutine support, provides a convenient way to work with asynchronous code. One of the key features of Kotlin coroutines is the ability to create suspendable APIs. In this section, we will explore the concept of suspendable APIs and discuss how they can simplify and enhance asynchronous operations.

Understanding suspendable APIs

A suspendable API, often implemented as a suspending function, is an API that can be seamlessly integrated into Kotlin coroutines. It allows you to perform long-running operations, such as network requests or disk I/O, without blocking the main thread or requiring explicit callback mechanisms. Suspendable APIs can suspend their execution at certain points, allowing other coroutines to run in the meantime and resume when the required resources or conditions are met.

To define a suspendable API in Kotlin, you use the **suspend** modifier before the function declaration, as shown in the following example:

```
suspend fun fetchUserData(userId: String): User {
    // Perform network request or other asynchronous operation
    // ...
    return user
}
```

In this example, **fetchUserData** is a suspendable API that fetches user data based on the provided **userId**. It can be called from a coroutine and suspends its execution until the network request is completed. Once the data is fetched, the function returns the **User** object.

Advantages of suspendable APIs

Suspendable APIs offer several advantages over traditional asynchronous programming models, and these advantages are given as follows:

- **Simplicity and readability**: By using suspendable APIs, you can write asynchronous code in a more sequential and linear style, similar to synchronous code. This improves the readability and maintainability of your code, as you do not need to deal with complex callback chains or nested structures. Coroutines and suspending functions provide a natural and intuitive way to express asynchronous behavior.
- **Integration with coroutines**: Suspendable APIs, when used in conjunction with Kotlin coroutines, provide seamless integration that allows you to leverage the full range of features offered by coroutines. These features include structured concurrency, cancellation, and exception handling, which greatly enhance the development of robust and efficient asynchronous code. Let us dive into each of these features and explore them with examples.
- **Structured concurrency**: Structured concurrency is a pattern facilitated by coroutines that helps you manage concurrent tasks in a structured and controlled manner. With suspendable APIs, you can easily create structured concurrent code that ensures all

child coroutines are complete before the parent coroutine completes. This helps prevent resource leaks and ensures that all necessary cleanup operations are performed.

Example:

```
suspend fun main() {
    coroutineScope {
        launch {
            // Child coroutine 1
            delay(1000)
            println("Task 1 completed")
        }
        launch {
            // Child coroutine 2
            delay(2000)
            println("Task 2 completed")
        }
        println("Performing other operations...")
    }
    println("All tasks completed")
}
```

In this example, the **coroutineScope** creates a structured concurrency scope where two child coroutines are launched. These child coroutines perform their respective tasks and print their completion messages. The parent coroutine waits for all child coroutines to complete before printing the **All tasks completed** message. Structured concurrency ensures that child coroutines are properly managed and executed within the defined scope.

- **Cancellation**: Coroutines offers built-in support for cancellation, allowing you to gracefully cancel or stop the execution of suspendable APIs when they are no longer needed. Cancellation is a cooperative mechanism where coroutines check for cancellation requests and terminate their execution when requested. This helps prevent unnecessary work and frees up system resources.

Example:

```
suspend fun performTask() {
    try {
        repeat(1000) { index ->
```

```
                println("Task in progress: $index")
                delay(500)
            }
        } finally {
            println("Task cancelled or completed")
        }
    }

    suspend fun main() {
        val job = GlobalScope.launch {
            performTask()
        }
        delay(2500)
        job.cancel()
    }
```

In this example, the **performTask** function is a suspendable API that performs a time-consuming task. The main function launches the **performTask** in a coroutine and cancels it after a delay of 2.5 seconds. The **performTask** function checks for cancellation requests using **coroutineContext.isActive** and terminates its execution gracefully when canceled. This allows for efficient cancellation of long-running operations.

- **Exception handling**: Exception handling is crucial for building robust and fault-tolerant asynchronous code. Kotlin coroutines provide a convenient and structured way to handle exceptions within suspendable APIs. You can use **try-catch** blocks or handle exceptions using the **CoroutineExceptionHandler** to catch and handle exceptions occurring within suspendable APIs.

Example:
```
    val exceptionHandler = CoroutineExceptionHandler { _, exception ->
        println("Exception caught: $exception")
    }

    suspend fun performWork() {
        try {
            throw RuntimeException("Something went wrong")
        } catch (e: Exception) {
```

```kotlin
            println("Caught exception: $e")
        }
    }

    suspend fun main() {
        val job = GlobalScope.launch(exceptionHandler) {
            performWork()
        }
        job.join()
    }
```

In this example, the **performWork** function deliberately throws a **RuntimeException**. The main function launches the **performWork** in a coroutine and provides an exception handler using **CoroutineExceptionHandler**. The exception is caught within the **performWork** function's **try-catch** block. The caught exception is then printed within the **catch** block, allowing for proper handling and logging of the exception.

By leveraging the exception-handling mechanisms provided by Kotlin Coroutines, you can effectively handle and manage exceptions that occur within suspendable APIs, ensuring your code remains resilient and capable of recovering from errors.

Overall, suspendable APIs seamlessly integrate with Kotlin coroutines, enabling you to harness the full power of coroutines' features, such as structured concurrency, cancellation, and exception handling. With coroutines, you can write asynchronous code that is concise, readable, and efficient, leading to improved code quality and maintainability.

Whether you need to coordinate concurrent tasks, gracefully cancel operations, or handle exceptions, suspendable APIs combined with Kotlin coroutines provide a lightweight and efficient solution for building robust and efficient asynchronous code. Adopting these practices allows you to streamline your asynchronous programming workflow and create more reliable and responsive applications.

Thread safety

When working with suspendable APIs and Kotlin coroutines, you do not have to explicitly manage thread synchronization or be concerned about race conditions. This is because coroutines handle thread switching and execution context preservation automatically, simplifying concurrent programming and reducing the likelihood of threading issues.

To understand this in more detail, let us explore an example that demonstrates the automatic thread switching and context preservation within coroutines given as follows:

```
import kotlinx.coroutines.*

suspend fun printData() {
    println("Printing data from coroutine: ${Thread.currentThread().name}")
    delay(1000)
    println("Data printing complete")
}

fun main() {
    println("Main thread: ${Thread.currentThread().name}")
    runBlocking {
        launch {
            printData()
        }
    }
    println("Coroutine execution complete")
}
```

In this example, we have a suspendable function called **printData()** that prints some data and simulates a delay of one second. The **main()** function sets up a coroutine using **runBlocking** and launches the **printData()** function within the coroutine.

When we run this code, we will observe the following output:

Main thread: main

Printing data from coroutine: main

Data printing complete

Coroutine execution complete

What is happening is given in detail as follows:

1. The **main()** function is executed in the main thread. We print the name of the current thread, which will be the **main**.
2. Within the **runBlocking** block, we launch a coroutine using the launch builder. This creates a new coroutine within the context of the **runBlocking** coroutine scope.
3. Inside the coroutine, we call the **printData()** function. Within the **printData()** function, we print the name of the current thread, which will also be the **main** as it is executed within the coroutine.

4. The `delay(1000)` suspends the coroutine for one second, but during this time, the thread is not blocked. The coroutine is suspended, and the underlying thread is freed to perform other tasks.
5. After the delay, the coroutine resumes execution, and we print the `Data printing complete`. Again, this happens within the same thread.
6. Finally, outside the coroutine, we print the `Coroutine execution complete` in the main thread.

In this example, you can see that the coroutines automatically handle the switching between threads without the need for explicit thread management. The *launch* builder launches a new coroutine that is scheduled to run in a thread pool managed by Kotlin coroutines. The underlying thread is reused for other tasks while the coroutine is suspended, and it resumes execution when the suspension is over.

This automatic thread switching and context preservation simplify concurrent programming by abstracting away the complexities of thread management. Coroutines provide a higher-level abstraction that allows you to focus on writing sequential code while benefiting from concurrent execution.

Furthermore, the automatic handling of thread switching and context preservation helps eliminate common threading issues such as race conditions or thread synchronization problems. Coroutines ensure that the execution context, including local variables and state, is preserved when a coroutine is suspended and resumed, preventing data corruption or inconsistent states.

By leveraging suspendable APIs and coroutines, you can write concurrent code that is cleaner, more readable, and less error-prone, as the underlying coroutines framework takes care of thread management and synchronization concerns for you.

Testing and debugging

Suspendable APIs offer significant benefits when it comes to testing and debugging asynchronous code. They simplify the testing process by allowing suspending functions to be run synchronously, enabling comprehensive and deterministic test cases without the need for complex mocking or asynchronous testing frameworks. Additionally, suspending functions provide clear points of suspension, making it easier to debug and trace the flow of asynchronous code. Let us explore these advantages in more detail with the following examples:

- **Simplified testing**: Suspendable APIs simplify testing by allowing suspending functions to be run synchronously. This means that you can execute suspending functions as regular function calls in test scenarios, making the testing process more straightforward and deterministic.

Example:

```kotlin
suspend fun fetchDataFromAPI(url: String): String {
    // Perform network request or other asynchronous operation
    delay(1000)
    return "Response from API"
}

suspend fun processResponse(response: String): String {
    // Process the response asynchronously
    delay(500)
    return "Processed: $response"
}

// Test function
suspend fun testFunction() {
    val response = fetchDataFromAPI("https://example.com")
    val processedResponse = processResponse(response)
    // Assert the processed response
}
```

In this example, the **fetchDataFromAPI** and **processResponse** functions are suspending functions. During testing, you can invoke the **testFunction** synchronously, allowing you to write comprehensive tests without the need for complex mocking frameworks. This simplifies the testing process, making it easier to verify the behavior and outputs of the suspending functions.

- **Clear points of suspension**: Suspended functions have explicit points of suspension, making it easier to debug and trace the flow of asynchronous code. These suspension points represent the locations where the execution of the function can be paused and resumed later. This provides better visibility into the sequence of operations and allows for more precise debugging.

Example:

```kotlin
suspend fun performTaskA() {
    println("Task A started")
    delay(1000)
    println("Task A completed")
```

```
    }

    suspend fun performTaskB() {
        println("Task B started")
        delay(500)
        println("Task B completed")
    }

    // Main function
    suspend fun main() {
        println("Execution started")
        performTaskA()
        performTaskB()
        println("Execution completed")
    }
```

In this example, the **performTaskA** and **performTaskB** functions represent two independent suspending tasks. During debugging, you can observe the precise points where suspension occurs, allowing you to track the flow of execution and identify any issues or unexpected behavior more easily.

The output of the example would be as follows:

Execution started

Task A started

Task A completed

Task B started

Task B completed

Execution completed.

By providing clear points of suspension, suspending functions offer better visibility into the asynchronous code execution, facilitating debugging and reducing the time required to diagnose and fix issues.

Suspendable APIs greatly simplify the testing and debugging of asynchronous code. By allowing suspending functions to be run synchronously during testing, you can write comprehensive and deterministic test cases without the need for complex mocking or asynchronous testing frameworks. Additionally, suspending functions provide clear points of suspension, enabling better debugging and tracing of asynchronous code execution. These features enhance the overall development experience and help ensure the reliability and correctness of your asynchronous code.

Async/await

Kotlin, a versatile programming language, offers a powerful feature called *async/await* that simplifies and streamlines asynchronous programming. In this section, we will explore the *async/await* syntax in Kotlin, its benefits, and how it can enhance your asynchronous code.

Understanding Async/Await

The **async/await** syntax in Kotlin provides a structured and concise way to write asynchronous code that appears more sequential and intuitive. It is built on top of coroutines, which are lightweight threads that enable asynchronous programming.

With **async/await**, you can mark a block of code as asynchronous using the **async** keyword. The **async** block returns a **Deferred** object, which represents a future result. By using the **await** keyword on a **Deferred** object, you can suspend the coroutine until the result is available, allowing for sequential execution.

Syntax and usage:

The syntax for using **async/await** in Kotlin is as follows:

```
suspend fun performTask1(): Int {
    delay(1000)
    return 42
}


suspend fun performTask2(): String {
    delay(500)
    return "Hello, World!"
}

  fun main() {
      runBlocking {
```

```kotlin
        val deferredA: Deferred<Int> = async { performTask1() }
        val deferredB: Deferred<String> = async { performTask2() }

        val resultA: Int = deferredA.await()
         val resultB: String = deferredB.await()

        println("Result A: $resultA")
        println("Result B: $resultB")
    }
}
```

In this example, the **performTask1** and **performTask2** functions are suspendable and represent two independent asynchronous tasks. Inside the main function, we use the async block to execute these tasks concurrently, obtaining **Deferred** objects—described in the next section—that represent the future results. The await calls suspend the coroutine until the results are available, allowing sequential access to the results.

Benefits of async/await

The following are the benefits of async/await:

- **Simplified asynchronous code**: The **async/await** syntax provides a more sequential and structured way to write asynchronous code. It eliminates the need for callbacks or complex chaining of asynchronous operations, making the code more readable and easier to reason about. Structuring code in a sequential manner simplifies control flow and reduces the cognitive load associated with asynchronous programming.
- **Improved performance**: The **async/await** allows for concurrent execution of independent tasks. By executing tasks concurrently and waiting for their results asynchronously, you can significantly improve the overall performance and efficiency of your application. It enables better utilization of system resources and reduces the time required to complete multiple asynchronous operations.
- **Error handling**: The **async/await** syntax integrates seamlessly with exception handling in Kotlin. Exceptions thrown within **async** blocks can be caught and handled in a structured manner, making it easier to manage errors and maintain code robustness. Error handling becomes more natural and similar to handling synchronous code, enhancing code maintainability.

The **async/await** syntax in Kotlin is a powerful tool for simplifying and enhancing asynchronous programming. By providing a more sequential and intuitive way to write asynchronous code, it improves code readability, maintainability, and performance. With **async**/**await**, you can leverage the full potential of coroutines and build responsive and efficient applications.

Asynchronous programming is increasingly crucial in today's software landscape, and Kotlin's async/await feature empowers developers to write cleaner.

Deferred values

Deferred values in Kotlin, which you just encountered in the previous section, are representations of asynchronous computations. They are similar to Promises or Futures in other programming languages, offering a way to obtain the result of an asynchronous operation. Deferred values allow you to work with the result of an asynchronous computation before it becomes available, providing a seamless integration with coroutines.

Creating a Deferred value

To create a **Deferred** value, you typically use the async coroutine builder, which returns a **Deferred** object representing the result of the asynchronous computation. The computation can be performed using a suspending function like you have seen in the previous example or a lambda expression.

```
import kotlinx.coroutines.*

suspend fun performAsyncTask(): Int {
    delay(1000)
    return 42
}

suspend fun main() {
   val deferredValue: Deferred<Int> = GlobalScope.async { performAsyncTask() }
}

    // Perform other operations

    val result: Int = deferredValue.await()
    println("Result: $result")
}
```

The preceding code demonstrates the usage of **async** and **await** functions. In this example, the **performAsyncTask** function represents an asynchronous task that delays for 1 second and returns the value **42**. Within the main function, a **Deferred** object named **deferredValue** is created using async, which starts the execution of the **performAsyncTask** function asynchronously. While the asynchronous task is running, other operations can be performed. The **await** function is then used on the **Deferred** object to suspend the coroutine until the result is available. Finally, the result is retrieved and printed. This way, the **Deferred** value is obtained by launching the asynchronous task with async and awaiting its completion with await, allowing for concurrent execution and retrieval of the result when it becomes available.

Error handling with Deferred values

Deferred values seamlessly integrate with exception handling in Kotlin coroutines. You can use **try-catch** blocks to handle exceptions that may occur during the asynchronous computation.

```kotlin
    suspend fun performTaskX(): String {
        delay(1000)
        throw RuntimeException("Task failed")
    }


    fun main() {
        val deferredValue: Deferred<String> = GlobalScope.async { performTaskX() }
}

        runBlocking {
            try {
                val result: String = deferredValue.await()
                println("Result: $result")
            } catch (e: Exception) {
                println("Error occurred: ${e.message}")
            }
        }
    }
```

In the preceding example, the **performTaskX** function intentionally throws a **RuntimeException**. We **catch** the exception within a **try-catch** block and handle it accordingly.

Deferred values in Kotlin provide a powerful mechanism for working with the results of asynchronous computations. By leveraging **Deferred** values, you can seamlessly integrate asynchronous code within coroutines, enabling clean and readable code that is easy to reason about.

Combination of deferred values

Deferred values in Kotlin represent asynchronous computations that may produce results at a later time. Combining deferred values allows you to orchestrate multiple asynchronous tasks and merge their results into a single value or perform further computations based on the combined results. This capability is particularly useful when dealing with complex asynchronous workflows, such as parallel computations, dependent tasks, or data aggregation.

- **Combining deferred values using awaitAll**: Kotlin provides a convenient function called **awaitAll** that allows you to combine multiple **Deferred** values and await their completion. It takes a vararg of **Deferred** objects and suspends the coroutine until all the **Deferred** values have been completed.

```kotlin
suspend fun performTask_1(): Int {
    delay(1000)
    return 42
}

suspend fun performTask_2(): String {
    delay(500)
    return "Hello, World!"
}

fun main() {
    runBlocking {
      val deferredA: Deferred<Int> = async { performTask_1() }
      val deferredB: Deferred<String> = async { performTask_2() }

      val results: List<Any> = awaitAll(deferredA, deferredB)

      println("Result 1: ${results[0]}")
      println("Result 2: ${results[1]}")
    }
```

}

In the preceding example, we combine two **Deferred** values, **deferredA**, and **deferredB**, using the **awaitAll** function. The **awaitAll** function suspends the coroutine until both Deferred values are complete and returns a list of their results. We can then access the individual results using index-based retrieval.

- **Combining deferred values with transformations**: Besides awaiting the completion of multiple Deferred values, you can also apply transformations or computations on the combined results. Kotlin provides functions such as **map**, **flatMap**, and **zip** that enable you to transform, merge, or process the results of **Deferred** values.

```kotlin
suspend fun performTaskC(): Int {
    delay(1000)
    return 42
}

suspend fun performTaskD(): String {
    delay(500)
    return "Hello, World!"
}

fun main() {
    runBlocking {
        val deferredC: Deferred<Int> = async { performTaskC() }
        val deferredD: Deferred<String> = async { performTaskD() }

        val result: String = deferredC.await().let { a ->
            deferredD.await().let { b ->
                "Result: $a, $b"
            }
        }

        println(result)
    }
}
```

In this example, we use the let function to access the individual results of the Deferred values and perform computations on them. We combine the results of **deferredC** and **deferredD** to create a meaningful string result.

- **Error handling with combined deferred values**: When combining Deferred values, it is essential to consider error handling. If any of the Deferred values in the combination throws an exception, the combined result will be an exception as well. To handle errors, wrap the combined operation with a **try-catch** block:

```
suspend fun performTaskM(): Int {
    delay(1000)
    return 42
}

suspend fun performTaskN(): String {
    delay(500)
    throw RuntimeException("Task N failed")
}

fun main() {
    runBlocking {
        val deferredM: Deferred<Int> = async { performTaskM() }
        val deferredN: Deferred<String> = async { performTaskN() }
        try {
            val results: List<Any> = awaitAll(deferredM, deferredN)
            println("Result M: ${results[0]}")
            println("Result N: ${results[1]}")
        } catch (e: Exception) {
            println("Error occurred: ${e.message}")
        }
    }
}
```

In the preceding example, the **performTaskN** function intentionally throws a **RuntimeException** to simulate an error. We handle the exception by wrapping the **awaitAll** operation in a **try-catch** block. If any of the Deferred values within **awaitAll** throws an exception, the **catch** block will be executed, allowing us to handle the error gracefully.

In conclusion, the combination of Deferred values in Kotlin provides a powerful toolset for building complex asynchronous workflows. By leveraging functions like awaitAll and transformations, you can orchestrate multiple asynchronous tasks and merge their results into meaningful outcomes. The ability to handle errors during the combination process ensures robustness in your asynchronous code.

Conclusion

In this chapter, we have explored several key concepts related to asynchronous programming in Kotlin. We started by understanding the fundamentals of suspending functions, which allow us to write asynchronous code in a sequential and concise manner. Suspended functions can be used with Kotlin coroutines to leverage their features, such as structured concurrency, cancellation, and exception handling.

We touched upon the concept of async and await functions in Kotlin, which are essential building blocks for working with deferred values. These functions enable us to launch asynchronous tasks and await their completion, ensuring that our code flows smoothly and efficiently.

We then delved into the world of deferred values, which represent asynchronous computations that may produce results at a later time. Deferred values offer a convenient way to work with asynchronous code, allowing us to start asynchronous tasks, combine their results, and handle errors gracefully.

By combining deferred values, we can orchestrate multiple asynchronous tasks and merge their results in a meaningful way. We explored techniques such as using **awaitAll** to await the completion of multiple deferred values simultaneously, as well as performing transformations on the combined results.

Finally, we discussed how deferred values simplify testing and debugging of asynchronous code. As *suspending* functions can be run synchronously in tests, it becomes easier to write comprehensive and deterministic test cases without the need for complex mocking or asynchronous testing frameworks. Suspended functions also provide clear points of suspension, aiding in debugging and tracing the flow of asynchronous code.

Points to remember

The following are some key points to remember:
- *Suspending* functions allow for sequential and concise asynchronous code by allowing suspension and resumption of execution. They are an integral part of Kotlin coroutines and enable the use of powerful coroutine features.
- *Deferred values* represent asynchronous computations that may produce results at a later time. They are a way to work with asynchronous code and provide mechanisms to await the completion of asynchronous tasks and retrieve their results.

- *Combining deferred* values allows for the orchestration of multiple asynchronous tasks and the merging of their results. Functions like `awaitAll` and transformations provide ways to combine, transform, and process the results of deferred values effectively.

- *Suspending* functions and *deferred* values simplify testing and debugging of asynchronous code. Suspended functions can be run synchronously in tests, enabling comprehensive and deterministic test cases. Additionally, suspended functions provide clear points of suspension, aiding in debugging and tracing the flow of asynchronous code.

- *async* and *await* are essential functions in Kotlin for working with *Deferred* values. *async* starts an asynchronous task and returns a *Deferred* object, while *await* suspends the coroutine until the result of the *Deferred* value is available.

- Kotlin *coroutines* provide features such as *structured concurrency*, *cancellation*, and *exception handling*. They offer a lightweight and efficient way to manage and coordinate concurrent tasks, simplifying the development of robust and efficient asynchronous code.

Join our book's Discord space

Join the book's Discord Workspace for Latest updates, Offers, Tech happenings around the world, New Release and Sessions with the Authors:

https://discord.bpbonline.com

Chapter 15
Contexts and Dispatchers

Introduction

In the previous chapter, we have explored some fundamentals of asynchronous programming in Kotlin, focusing on suspending functions, deferred values, and their combination. We also discussed the benefits of Kotlin coroutines in simplifying concurrent and asynchronous code. Building upon that foundation, we will now delve into more advanced topics related to coroutine management and control flow. This chapter will cover task scheduling, dispatcher types, exception propagation, coroutine cancellation, and various techniques to effectively manage and handle cancellations.

Structure

In this chapter, we will cover the following topics:
- Task scheduling
- Dispatchers types
- Exception propagation and its handling
- Coroutine cancellation
- Manage cancellation

Objectives

In this chapter, readers will achieve several key objectives. They will gain a comprehensive understanding of Kotlin coroutines, including their fundamentals and usage in different contexts. Additionally, readers will learn how to effectively handle concurrency challenges and write asynchronous code using Kotlin coroutines. By the end of the chapter, they will have the knowledge and skills necessary to leverage coroutines for efficient and responsive concurrent programming in Kotlin, making their code more robust and maintainable.

By achieving these objectives, readers will have a solid understanding of how to manage and control the flow of Kotlin coroutines, enabling them to write robust and efficient asynchronous code. They will be equipped with the knowledge to handle exceptions, control task execution contexts using dispatchers, and effectively manage coroutine cancellations, ensuring their applications are responsive, maintainable, and error-resilient.

Overview

This chapter focuses on the management and control flow aspects of Kotlin coroutines. We will explore how coroutines are scheduled and executed, the different types of dispatchers available, and how exceptions propagate within coroutines. Additionally, we will delve into the critical topic of coroutine cancellation, understanding the mechanisms behind it and exploring techniques to effectively manage and handle cancellations.

Task scheduling

Asynchronous programming can be a challenging topic to grasp, but Kotlin's coroutines offer a streamlined approach that simplifies concurrent programming. One of the key aspects of coroutines is task scheduling, which determines how and when coroutines are executed. In this section, we will explore the basics of coroutine scheduling, including execution flow, coroutine contexts, and the impact of coroutine builders on scheduling.

Understanding coroutine scheduling and execution flow

Coroutines execute in a cooperative manner, which means that they rely on each other to yield control of the execution thread. This is in contrast to threads, which can run simultaneously and independently of one another. When a coroutine is suspended, it yields control of the execution thread to another coroutine that is ready to run. This is possible because coroutines are not tied to any specific thread and can run on any thread that is associated with a coroutine context.

In Kotlin coroutines, the parent–child relationship between coroutines determines their execution flow. This relationship is established when a coroutine is launched from another coroutine using a coroutine builder like **launch** or **async**.

When a coroutine is launched, it becomes a child of the coroutine that launched it. This means that the *parent* coroutine is responsible for managing the execution of its *child* coroutines, including suspending and resuming them as needed. If the parent coroutine is cancelled or encounters an unhandled exception, all of its child coroutines are also cancelled.

For example, consider the following code snippet:

```
import kotlinx.coroutines.*

fun main() = runBlocking {
    launch {
        delay(1000)
        println("Child coroutine completed")
    }
    println("Parent coroutine completed")
}
```

In this example, a parent coroutine is launched using **runBlocking**. Inside this coroutine, a child coroutine is launched using **launch**. The child coroutine simply waits for one second and then prints a message to the console.

When the program is run, the output will be the following:

```
Parent coroutine completed
Child coroutine completed
```

Here, we can see that the parent coroutine completes before the child coroutine because it is not waiting for the child coroutine to complete before exiting. The parent–child relationship between coroutines also affects error handling. If a child coroutine encounters an unhandled exception, it will cancel its parent coroutine and all of its sibling coroutines. This can be seen in the following modified example:

```
import kotlinx.coroutines.*

fun main() = runBlocking {
    launch {
        delay(1000)
```

```
            throw RuntimeException("Child coroutine failed")
        }
        println("Parent coroutine completed")
    }
```

In this example, the child coroutine throws an exception instead of printing a message. When the program is run, the output will be the following:

```
Parent coroutine completed


Exception in thread "main" java.lang.RuntimeException: Child coroutine failed
at chapter_15.Execution_flow_exceptionKt$main$1$1.invokeSuspend(execution_flow_exception.kt:8)
at                           kotlin.coroutines.jvm.internal.BaseContinuationImpl.resumeWith(ContinuationImpl.kt:33)
at kotlinx.coroutines.DispatchedTaskKt.resume(DispatchedTask.kt:234)
at kotlinx.coroutines.DispatchedTaskKt.dispatch(DispatchedTask.kt:166)
at kotlinx.coroutines.CancellableContinuationImpl.dispatchResume(CancellableContinuationImpl.kt:397)
at kotlinx.coroutines.CancellableContinuationImpl.resumeImpl(CancellableContinuationImpl.kt:431)
at kotlinx.coroutines.CancellableContinuationImpl.resumeImpl$default(CancellableContinuationImpl.kt:420)
at kotlinx.coroutines.CancellableContinuationImpl.resumeUndispatched(CancellableContinuationImpl.kt:518)
    at kotlinx.coroutines.EventLoopImplBase$DelayedResumeTask.run(EventLoop.common.kt:500)
    at kotlinx.coroutines.EventLoopImplBase.processNextEvent(EventLoop.common.kt:284)
    at kotlinx.coroutines.BlockingCoroutine.joinBlocking(Builders.kt:85)
    at kotlinx.coroutines.BuildersKt__BuildersKt.runBlocking(Builders.kt:59)
    at kotlinx.coroutines.BuildersKt.runBlocking(Unknown Source)
    at   kotlinx.coroutines.BuildersKt__BuildersKt.runBlocking$default(Builders.kt:38)
```

```
    at kotlinx.coroutines.BuildersKt.runBlocking$default(Unknown Source)
    at chapter_15.Execution_flow_exceptionKt.main(execution_flow_exception.kt:5)
    at chapter_15.Execution_flow_exceptionKt.main(execution_flow_exception.kt)
```

Here, we can see that the child coroutine encountered an unhandled exception and caused the parent coroutine to be cancelled, resulting in an exception being thrown.

Overall, understanding the parent–child relationship between coroutines is important for managing their execution flow and error handling. By properly managing parent–child relationships, we can ensure that our coroutines execute correctly and avoid issues such as unhandled exceptions and cancellations.

Coroutine contexts and their role in determining the execution context

Coroutine contexts provide a way to define the execution context of a coroutine, which includes the thread that the coroutine runs on, as well as other configuration options. A coroutine context is essentially a set of rules that govern how a coroutine behaves. By default, coroutines inherit their parent's context, but it is also possible to create a new context for a coroutine.

A coroutine context is a set of key-value pairs that provide additional information about how the coroutine should be executed, such as which thread pool to use, which dispatcher to use, and so on. By default, coroutines run on a shared pool of threads, but using different dispatchers can allow coroutines to run on different threads and thread pools.

The **Dispatcher** objects in Kotlin provide several built-in coroutine contexts, including **Dispatchers.Default**, **Dispatchers.IO**, and **Dispatchers.Main**. The default dispatcher is used for CPU-bound tasks, such as sorting, filtering, or parsing data. The IO dispatcher is used for IO-bound tasks, such as reading from or writing to a file or making network requests. Finally, the main dispatcher is used for tasks that interact with the UI, such as updating views or listening to user input.

The following is an example of using the **Dispatchers.Default** dispatcher to perform a CPU-bound task of calculating the sum of a large list of numbers:

```
import kotlinx.coroutines.*

suspend fun calculateSum(numbers: List<Int>): Int
    = withContext(Dispatchers.Default) {
    numbers.sum()
}
```

```kotlin
suspend fun main() {
    val numbers = (1..100000).toList()
    val sum = calculateSum(numbers)
    println("The sum is: $sum")
}
```

The following will be the output:

The sum is: 705082704

In this example, we use the **withContext** function to switch to the **Dispatchers.Default** dispatcher and then call the **numbers.sum()** function to calculate the sum of the list. By using the appropriate dispatcher, we ensure that the CPU-bound task runs efficiently and does not block other coroutines.

It is important to choose the appropriate dispatcher for your task to ensure that it runs efficiently and does not block other coroutines. Choosing the wrong dispatcher can lead to poor performance, deadlocks, or even crashes. Therefore, it is important to understand the characteristics of each dispatcher and choose the one that best fits your use case.

Coroutine builders and their impact on scheduling

Coroutine builders are functions that are used to launch a new coroutine. They include **launch**, **async**, and **runBlocking**, among others. Each builder has its own impact on scheduling, which determines how the coroutine will be executed.

The launch builder is used to start a new coroutine that does not return a value. It runs the coroutine on the current thread or a thread from the default dispatcher and returns a Job object that can be used to manage the lifecycle of the coroutine.

The async builder is used to start a new coroutine that returns a Deferred value. It runs the coroutine on the current thread or a thread from the default dispatcher and returns a Deferred object that can be used to retrieve the value once the coroutine completes.

The **runBlocking** builder is used to start a new coroutine that blocks the current thread until it completes. It is primarily used for testing and for wrapping synchronous code in a coroutine context.

In conclusion, understanding coroutine scheduling is essential for writing efficient and responsive asynchronous code. By understanding how coroutines execute, how coroutine contexts determine the execution context and the impact of coroutine builders on scheduling, you can write robust and efficient concurrent programs that take full advantage of Kotlin's coroutine library.

Dispatcher's types

Kotlin coroutines provide a variety of dispatchers to handle different types of tasks. A dispatcher determines which thread or threads will execute a coroutine and manages its execution context. Understanding the characteristics and use cases of each dispatcher type is essential for efficient and effective coroutine programming.

Kotlin Coroutines provide several built-in dispatchers that are optimized for different types of tasks. Some of the most commonly used dispatchers are as follows:

Dispatchers.Default

This is the default dispatcher for CPU-bound tasks, as we saw in the previous section, that does not involve any IO operations. It is backed by a shared pool of threads and is suitable for computationally intensive tasks such as sorting, searching, or data processing. It is the default dispatcher used by all coroutine builders unless you specify a different dispatcher explicitly.

The following is an example of using the **Default** dispatcher:

```
fun performCPUIntensiveTask() = withContext(Dispatchers.Default) {
    // Perform CPU-bound task
}
```

Dispatchers.IO

This dispatcher is optimized for IO-bound tasks such as reading or writing to files, network operations, or database queries. It is backed by a pool of threads that grows on demand and automatically shrinks when idle. It is so important to limit the number of tasks running concurrently to avoid overloading the system.

The following is an example of using the IO dispatcher:

```
fun performIOBoundTask() = withContext(Dispatchers.IO) {
    // Perform IO-bound task
}
```

Dispatchers.Main

This dispatcher is used for tasks that interact with the UI, such as updating the user interface, processing touch events, or handling animations. It is always available and optimized for low-latency and responsive user interactions, and it is backed by the UI thread on Android and the event loop on other platforms.

The following is an example of using the **main** dispatcher:

```
fun updateUI() = withContext(Dispatchers.Main) {
    // Update UI
}
```

Dispatchers.Unconfined

In Kotlin coroutines, the **Dispatchers.Default** dispatcher is used for CPU-bound tasks, and **Dispatchers.IO** is used for blocking IO tasks, but there are times when you may need to switch the thread a coroutine is running on. That is where the **Dispatchers.Unconfined** dispatcher comes in handy.

This dispatcher is not tied to any specific thread or thread pool and allows the coroutine to start on one thread and resume on another. It is useful for cases where you want a coroutine to inherit the context of its parent coroutine but not necessarily the thread pool.

The following is an example:

```
import kotlinx.coroutines.*

fun main() = runBlocking<Unit> {
    launch(Dispatchers.Unconfined) {
        // This coroutine will run on the main thread,
        // but may switch to another thread later
        println("Started on thread ${Thread.currentThread().name}")
        delay(500)
        println("Resumed on thread ${Thread.currentThread().name}")
    }
    println("Hello,")
    delay(1000)
    println("world!")
}
```

In this example, we launch a coroutine on the **Dispatchers.Unconfined** dispatcher. The coroutine starts on the main thread and prints its name but may switch to another thread later. We delay the coroutine for half a second and then print the name of the thread it is resumed on. In the meantime, we print **Hello** and delay for one second before printing "world!."

The output of the program may look something like the following:

```
Started on thread main
Hello,
Resumed on thread kotlinx.coroutines.DefaultExecutor
world!
```

You will notice that the coroutine was resumed on a different thread than it started on, which is why the thread name is different in the second print statement.

Exception propagation and its handling

Kotlin coroutines provide a convenient way to handle exceptions that occur during asynchronous operations. Exceptions that occur within a coroutine are propagated up the call stack until they are caught and handled. In this section, we will explore how exceptions propagate within coroutines and the various ways to handle them.

- **How exceptions propagate within coroutines**: When an exception occurs within a coroutine, it propagates up the call stack until it is caught and handled by an enclosing **try-catch** block. If the exception is not caught, it will be propagated to the coroutine's parent, and so on, until it reaches the top-level coroutine. If an exception is not caught at the top level, it will result in an unhandled exception and may cause the application to crash.

    The following is an example that demonstrates how exceptions propagate within coroutines:

    ```
    import kotlinx.coroutines.*

    fun doSomething() {
        throw IllegalStateException("Something went wrong")
    }

    suspend fun main() {
        GlobalScope.launch {
            doSomething()
        }.join()
    }
    ```

    In this example, the **doSomething()** function throws an **IllegalStateException**. As there is no **try-catch** block to handle the exception, it is propagated up the call stack to the top-level coroutine. The result is an unhandled exception that will cause the program to crash.

- **Handling exceptions within coroutines using try-catch blocks**: To handle exceptions within a coroutine, you can use a **try-catch** block. The **try** block contains the code that may throw an exception, and the **catch** block handles the exception if it occurs. The following is an example:

    ```
    import kotlinx.coroutines.*

    fun doSomethingElse() {
        throw IllegalStateException("Something went wrong")
    }

    suspend fun main() {
        GlobalScope.launch {
            try {
                doSomethingElse()
            } catch (e: Exception) {
                println("Exception caught: ${e.message}")
            }
        }.join()
    }
    ```

    The following will be the output:

    ```
    Exception caught: Something went wrong
    ```

    In this example, the **doSomethingElse()** function throws an **IllegalStateException**. However, the exception is caught and handled by the **catch** block, which prints a message to the console.

- **Propagating exceptions across coroutine hierarchies**: When a coroutine launches another coroutine, the launched coroutine becomes a child of the parent coroutine. If an exception occurs within a child coroutine, it will propagate up the coroutine hierarchy until it is caught and handled by an enclosing try-catch block. If the exception is not caught, it will be propagated to the parent coroutine, and so on, until it reaches the top-level coroutine.

    The following is an example that demonstrates how exceptions propagate across coroutine hierarchies:

```
import kotlinx.coroutines.*

suspend fun doAnotherWork() {
    throw IllegalStateException("Something went wrong")
}

suspend fun doSomeWork() {
    doAnotherWork()
}

suspend fun main() {
    GlobalScope.launch {
        try {
            doSomeWork()
        } catch (e: Exception) {
            println("Exception caught: ${e.message}")
        }
    }.join()
}
```

In this example, the **doAnotherWork()** function throws an **IllegalStateException**. However, the exception is caught and handled by the catch block in the **main()** coroutine, which prints a message to the console.

Understanding how exceptions propagate within coroutines and how to handle them is crucial for writing robust and reliable asynchronous code. With the **try-catch** block and coroutine hierarchies, Kotlin coroutines provide a powerful mechanism for handling exceptions during asynchronous operations.

Coroutine cancellation

Coroutines are a powerful way to write asynchronous and concurrent code in Kotlin. They allow us to write code that looks like sequential and synchronous code but can run on multiple threads and suspend and resume without blocking.

However, sometimes we need to cancel a coroutine when it is no longer needed or when it takes too long to complete. For example, if a user closes the app or navigates away from a screen, we might want to stop any network requests or background tasks that were started by a coroutine.

In this section, we will learn how to cancel coroutines in Kotlin and what are the best practices for doing so.

Coroutine cancellation is cooperative

The first thing to understand about coroutine cancellation is that it is cooperative. This means that a coroutine has to cooperate to be cancellable. It has to check for cancellation and stop its execution when it is cancelled.

Kotlin provides the following two ways for a coroutine to check for cancellation:

- Calling a suspending function that is cancellable: All the suspending functions in **kotlinx.coroutines** are cancellable. They check for cancellation of the coroutine and throw a **CancellationException** when cancelled. For example, **delay()**, **yield()**, **withTimeout()**, **await()**, and so on are all cancellable suspending functions.

- Calling the **isActive** property of the coroutine's **CoroutineScope** or **CoroutineContext**. This property returns true if the coroutine is still active, has not been cancelled, and false otherwise. A coroutine can use this property to check its own cancellation status and exit gracefully if it is cancelled.

If a coroutine does not call any suspending function or check the **isActive** property, it cannot be cancelled. It will keep running until it finishes its work or until the whole application is terminated.

Let us see an example of a *non-cancellable* coroutine:

```
import kotlinx.coroutines.*

suspend fun main() {
    val job = GlobalScope.launch {
        // This loop is not cancellable
        while (true) {
            println("I'm working hard")
        }
    }
```

```
        delay(1000)
        println("I'm tired of waiting")
        job.cancel() // This will not cancel the job
        job.join()
        println("Now I can quit")
    }
```

The preceding code will print **I'm working hard** indefinitely, even after we call **job.cancel()**. This is because the loop does not check for cancellation or call any suspending function. The only way to stop this coroutine is to kill the whole application.

Now, let us see an example of a cancellable coroutine:

```
import kotlinx.coroutines.*

suspend fun main() {
    val job = GlobalScope.launch {
        // This loop is cancellable
        while (isActive) {
            println("I'm working hard")
            delay(100) // This suspending function checks for cancellation
        }
    }

    delay(1000)
    println("I'm tired of waiting")
    job.cancel() // This will cancel the job
    job.join()
    println("Now I can quit")

}
```

The preceding code will print **I'm working hard** for about 10 times, then stop after we call **job.cancel()**. This is because the loop checks the **isActive** property and exits when it becomes false. The **delay()** function also checks for cancellation and throws a **CancellationException** when cancelled.

How to cancel a coroutine?

There are following two ways to cancel a coroutine:

- Calling the **cancel()** method on the **Job** object that represents the coroutine. This method cancels the job and all its children recursively. It also cancels the parent's job if all its children are cancelled.

- Using a cancellation scope such as **coroutineScope**, **supervisorScope**, or **withContext**. These functions create a new scope for the coroutines that are launched inside them and cancel them automatically when they complete normally or exceptionally.

Let us see some examples of using these methods to cancel coroutines.

- **Cancelling a job**: When we launch a coroutine using one of the coroutine builders, such as **launch**, **async**, or **runBlocking**, we get a **Job** object that represents the coroutine. We can use this object to cancel the coroutine by calling its **cancel()** method.

    For example:

    ```
    import kotlinx.coroutines.*

    suspend fun main() {
        val job = GlobalScope.launch {
            repeat(10) { i ->
                println("I'm sleeping $i ...")
                delay(500)
            }
        }

        delay(1300)
        job.cancel()
        println("Job cancelled")
    }
    ```

    After calling **cancel()** on the **Job** object, the coroutine will be cancelled and will stop executing. In this example, the coroutine will only print **I'm sleeping 0 ...**, **I'm sleeping 1 ...**, and **I'm sleeping 2 ...** before being cancelled. The **println("Job cancelled")** statement will be executed after the coroutine has been cancelled.

- **Cancelling a scope**: Another way to cancel coroutines is to use a cancellation scope such as **coroutineScope**, **supervisorScope**, or **withContext**. These functions create a new scope for the coroutines that are launched inside them and cancel them automatically when they complete normally or exceptionally.

For example:

```
import kotlinx.coroutines.*

suspend fun main() {

    runBlocking {
        // This is a cancellation scope
        coroutineScope {
            launch {
                repeat(10) { i ->
                    println("I'm sleeping $i ...")
                    delay(500)
                }
            }
            launch {
                delay(1300)
                println("I'm tired of waiting")
                // This cancels all the coroutines in this scope
                cancel()
            }
        }
        println("Now I can quit")
    }

}
```

This code will print **I'm sleeping** ... for about three times, then stop after the second coroutine calls **cancel()**. This is because **coroutineScope** cancels all the coroutines in its scope when one of them fails or cancels.

The following are some differences between the different cancellation scopes:

- **coroutineScope** is a regular scope that propagates cancellation to its parent and children. It also waits for all its children to complete before returning.

- **supervisorScope** is a scope that does not propagate cancellation to its parent but still cancels its children. It also waits for all its children to complete before returning.
- **withContext** is a scope that changes the context of the coroutines in its block. It also propagates cancellation to its parent and children but does not wait for them to complete before returning.

Manage cancellation

When a coroutine is cancelled, it throws a **CancellationException**. This exception is a subclass of **RuntimeException**, so it does not need to be declared or caught explicitly. However, sometimes we might want to handle this exception or perform some cleanup actions before the coroutine terminates.

The following are two ways to handle cancellation exceptions:

- Using a **try-catch** block to catch the exception and handle it. This is useful when we want to perform some specific actions based on the exception or its cause.
- Using a **finally** block to execute some code regardless of the exception. This is useful when we want to perform some general cleanup actions, such as closing resources or cancelling other jobs.

Let us see some examples of using these blocks to handle cancellation exceptions.

Using a try-catch block

We can use a **try-catch** block to catch the **CancellationException** and handle it. For example:

```
import kotlinx.coroutines.*

suspend fun main() {
    val job = GlobalScope.launch {
        try {
            repeat(10) { i ->
                println("I'm sleeping $i ...")
                delay(500)
            }
        } catch (e: CancellationException) {
            println("I was cancelled")
            // We can access the cause of the cancellation
```

```
            println("The cause was: ${e.localizedMessage}")
        }
    }
    delay(1300)
    println("I'm tired of waiting")
    // We can pass an optional cause for the cancellation
    job.cancel(CancellationException("Timeout"))
    job.join()
    println("Now I can quit")
}
```

The following will be the output:

```
I'm sleeping 0 ...
I'm sleeping 1 ...
I'm sleeping 2 ...
I'm tired of waiting
I was cancelled
The cause was: Timeout
Now I can quit
```

This code will print "I'm sleeping…" for about three times, then print "I was cancelled" and "The cause was: Timeout" after we call job.cancel(). This is because we catch the CancellationException and handle it in the catch block.

Note that catching a CancellationException does not resume the coroutine. It still terminates after the catch block.

Using a finally block

We can use a **finally** block to execute some code regardless of the cancellation exception. For example:

```
import kotlinx.coroutines.*

suspend fun main() {
    val job = GlobalScope.launch {
        try {
```

```
                repeat(10) { i ->
                    println("I'm sleeping $i ...")
                    delay(500)
                }
            } finally {
                println("I'm running finally")
            }
        }
        delay(1300)
        println("I'm tired of waiting")
        job.cancel()
        job.join()
        println("Now I can quit")
    }
```

This code will print **I'm sleeping** for about three times, then print **I'm running finally** after we call **job.cancel()**. This is because we execute some code in the final block regardless of the cancellation exception.

Note that if we want to call a suspending function in the **finally** block, we need to wrap it with **withContext(NonCancellable)** or check the **isActive** property. Otherwise, it will throw another **CancellationException** and skip the rest of the code. For example:

```
import kotlinx.coroutines.*

suspend fun main() {
    val job = GlobalScope.launch {
        try {
            repeat(10) { i ->
                println("I'm sleeping $i ...")
                delay(500)
            }
        } finally {
            // This will throw a CancellationException and skip the println
            // delay(1000)
                // This will run the suspending function without throwing an exception
```

```kotlin
            withContext(NonCancellable) {
                delay(1000)
                println("I'm running finally")
            }
            // This will check the cancellation status before running the
            suspending function
            if (isActive) {
                delay(1000)
                println("I'm still active")
            }
        }
    }

    delay(1300)
    println("I'm tired of waiting")
    job.cancel()
    job.join()
    println("Now I can quit")
}
```

This code will print **I'm sleeping** for about three times, then print **I'm running finally** after a delay of 1 second. This is because we use **withContext(NonCancellable)** to run the suspending function in the final block without throwing an exception. The code after the if (**isActive**) block will not run because the coroutine is already cancelled.

Conclusion

In this chapter, we explored the fundamentals of task scheduling in Kotlin coroutines, including coroutine task scheduling and execution flow, coroutine contexts, and coroutine builders. We also looked at different dispatchers available in Kotlin coroutines and their use cases, including the default dispatcher, IO dispatcher, and main dispatcher. Furthermore, we discussed the importance of handling exceptions within coroutines using try-catch and, finally, blocks and propagating exceptions across coroutine hierarchies.

By mastering these concepts, developers can write efficient and error-free asynchronous code using Kotlin coroutines.

Points to remember

The following are some points to remember:
- Coroutines are launched within a parent–child relationship, with the parent responsible for managing the execution of their child's coroutines.
- The appropriate coroutine context and dispatcher should be chosen based on the type of task to ensure efficiency and avoid blocking other coroutines.
- Different dispatchers are available for different scenarios, with each dispatcher type having its own characteristics and use cases.
- The `Dispatchers.Default` dispatcher is used for CPU-bound tasks, `Dispatchers.IO` is used for blocking IO tasks, and `Dispatchers.Main` is used for tasks that interact with the UI.
- Exceptions can be propagated within coroutines and across coroutine hierarchies, with *try-catch* blocks used for handling exceptions within coroutines.
- Unhandled exceptions can cause the cancellation of a coroutine and its child coroutines.
- Coroutines can be cancelled using either cooperative cancellation or forceful cancellation.
- Cancellation is important for preventing resource leaks and ensuring efficient use of system resources.
- The *withContext* and *coroutineScope* functions can be used to manage coroutine cancellation.

By understanding these concepts and their applications, developers can leverage Kotlin coroutines to write efficient and responsive asynchronous code.

Join our book's Discord space

Join the book's Discord Workspace for Latest updates, Offers, Tech happenings around the world, New Release and Sessions with the Authors:

https://discord.bpbonline.com

CHAPTER 16
Coroutines Channels

Introduction

In the previous chapters, we have learned about some basic concepts of Kotlin coroutines, including their creation, scheduling, and cancellation. We have also explored how to handle exceptions and manage coroutine contexts.

In this chapter, we will delve into another powerful feature of coroutines: channels. Channels provide a way for coroutines to communicate with each other in a safe and efficient manner. We will explore how to create, send, and receive data through channels, as well as their different types and use cases. By the end of this chapter, you will have a solid understanding of how to leverage channels to build concurrent and responsive applications.

Structure

In this chapter, we will cover the following topics:
- Generators and sequences
- Pipelines
- Send and offer
- Receive and poll

- Channels versus Java queues
- Broadcast channels
- Producers and actors

Objectives

By the end of this chapter, readers will grasp the essence of channels in Kotlin coroutines. They'll become proficient in employing channels for various communication patterns like generators and pipelines. The distinction between sending and receiving operations in channels will be clear, along with insights into broadcast channels' unique characteristics. Readers will also gain an understanding of producers and actors and their roles in managing data flow within channels.

Overview

The concept of channels is an important part of Kotlin coroutines. Channels can be used to implement communication patterns between coroutines, allowing data to be passed between them in a safe and efficient way. In this chapter, we will explore the various features of channels, including generators, pipelines, and broadcast channels. We will also discuss the different types of operations that can be performed on channels, such as send and receive and learn about producers and actors, which can be used to control the flow of data in channels. By the end of this chapter, you will have a strong understanding of how channels work and how they can be used in your Kotlin coroutine applications.

Generators and sequences

A generator is a function that can produce a sequence of values without storing them all in memory. A generator can be implemented using the **yield** keyword, which suspends the execution of the function and returns the next value to the caller.

For example, the following function generates the **fibonacci** sequence:

```kotlin
fun fibonacci(): Sequence<Int> = sequence {
    var a = 0
    var b = 1
    while (true) {
        yield(a)
        val tmp = a + b
        a = b
```

```
            b = tmp
        }
    }
```

A *sequence* is an interface that represents a lazily evaluated collection of elements. A sequence can be created from a generator function using the sequence builder or from an existing collection using the **asSequence** extension function. A sequence can be iterated overusing a **for** loop or transformed using functional operators such as **map**, **filter**, **take**, and so on.

For example, the following code prints the first 10 even **fibonacci** numbers:

```
fun main() {
    val evenSequence = fibonacci().filter { it % 2 == 0 }.take(10)
    evenSequence.forEach { println(it)}
}
```

Sequences in Kotlin are a way of representing a potentially infinite collection of data in a memory-efficient manner. Sequences are evaluated lazily, meaning that they only compute the next element when it is requested. This allows for better performance and memory efficiency, as only the necessary elements are computed at a time. Sequences are particularly useful when dealing with large collections of data that do not fit in memory or that are expensive to compute.

For example, consider a sequence of prime numbers. It is possible to represent an infinite sequence of prime numbers in a memory-efficient way by only computing the next prime number when it is requested. A sequence can be created using the **generateSequence** function, which takes a lambda function that computes the next element in the sequence.

```
fun generatePrimes(): Sequence<Int> = generateSequence(2) { current ->
    generateSequence(current + 1) { it + 1 }.first { next ->
        (2 until next).none { next % it == 0 }
    }
}

fun main() {
    val primes = generatePrimes().take(10).toList()
    println(primes) // Output: [2, 3, 5, 7, 11, 13, 17, 19, 23, 29]
}
```

In the preceding code, **generateSequence** is used to create a sequence of prime numbers starting from 2. The lambda function passed to **generateSequence** takes the current prime number and computes the next prime number by finding the first number greater than the current number, which is also a prime number.

While sequences are useful for lazy evaluation of potentially infinite collections, they are not suitable for concurrent programming. This is because sequences are not thread-safe and do not support cancellation. If a sequence is being evaluated on multiple threads concurrently, it may result in unexpected behavior and data corruption. In addition, sequences do not support cancellation, meaning that once a sequence has started evaluation, it cannot be canceled or stopped until all elements have been computed.

Overall, sequences are a powerful tool in Kotlin for representing and computing potentially infinite collections of data in a memory-efficient and performant manner. However, they should be used with caution in concurrent programming scenarios, where other data structures, such as channels, may be more appropriate.

Pipelines

A pipeline is a pattern of concurrent programming that involves splitting a task into multiple stages that run in parallel and communicate through channels. A channel is a data structure that allows coroutines to send and receive values asynchronously. A channel can be created using the Channel constructor, which takes an optional capacity argument that specifies how many values can be buffered in the channel before it suspends the sender.

A coroutine can send a value to a channel using the send method, which suspends until there is space in the buffer or the channel is closed. A coroutine can receive a value from a channel using the receive method, which suspends until there is a value available or the channel is closed. A channel can be closed using the close method, which indicates that no more values will be sent.

One important aspect of working with channels is being able to check whether a channel is closed or not. A channel can be closed explicitly by calling the **close()** function on it or implicitly when a producer or consumer coroutine is canceled. When a channel is closed, it can no longer accept any more data, and any attempts to send or receive data will result in an exception.

To check whether a channel is closed for sending data, you can use the **isClosedForSend** property. This property returns true if the channel has been closed for sending and false otherwise. The following is an example:

```
val channel = Channel<Int>()
channel.close()
println(channel.isClosedForSend) // Output: true
```

In this example, we create a new channel of type **Int** and immediately close it using the **close()** function. We then check whether the channel is closed for sending data using the **isClosedForSend** property, which returns true since we just closed the channel.

Similarly, to check whether a channel is closed for receiving data, you can use the **isClosedForReceive** property. This property returns true if the channel has been closed for receiving and false otherwise. The following is an example:

```
val channel = Channel<Int>()
channel.cancel()
println(channel.isClosedForReceive) // Output: true
```

The following code creates a pipeline that generates prime numbers using an unbound channel:

```
import kotlinx.coroutines.*
import kotlinx.coroutines.channels.Channel

fun main() = runBlocking {
    // Create an unbounded channel for numbers
    val numbers = Channel<Int>()

    // Launch a coroutine that sends numbers from 2 to 1000 to the channel
    launch {
        for (x in 2..1000) {
            if (!numbers.isClosedForSend) {
                numbers.send(x)
            }
        }
        numbers.close() // Close the channel when done
    }

    // Launch another coroutine that receives numbers from the channel and
    filters out multiples of 2
    val multiplesOfTwo = Channel<Int>()
    launch {
        for (x in numbers) { // Receive values until the channel is closed
            if (x % 2 != 0) {
```

```kotlin
                if (!multiplesOfTwo.isClosedForSend) {
                    multiplesOfTwo.send(x) // Send values to another channel
                }
            }
        }
        multiplesOfTwo.close() // Close the channel when done
    }

    // Launch another coroutine that receives numbers from the channel and
    filters out multiples of 3
    val multiplesOfThree = Channel<Int>()
    launch {
        for (x in multiplesOfTwo) {
            if (x % 3 != 0) {
                if (!multiplesOfThree.isClosedForSend) {
                    multiplesOfThree.send(x)
                }
            }
        }
        multiplesOfThree.close()
    }

    // Print the remaining numbers from the channel, which are prime
    for (x in multiplesOfThree) {
        println(x)
    }
}
```

The following example shows how to use **isClosedForReceive** to check if the channel is closed for receiving data and the **receive()** method to get the data sent on the channel.

```kotlin
fun main(): Unit = runBlocking {
    val channel = Channel<Int>()
```

```kotlin
    // Launch a coroutine to send data to the channel
    launch {
        for (i in 1..5) {
            println("Sending $i")
            channel.send(i)
        }
        channel.close()
    }

    // Launch a coroutine to receive data from the channel
    launch {
        while (!channel.isClosedForReceive) {
            val data = channel.receive()
            println("Received $data")
        }
    }
}
```

Pipelines are useful when dealing with streams of data that need to be processed in parallel by different stages.

Send and offer (trySend)

The **send** method is a suspending function that sends an element to the channel, blocking the calling coroutine if the channel is full. The **trySend** method (replacing the **offer** method, which was deprecated starting from Kotlin version 1.6), on the other hand, is a non-suspending function that tries to send an element to the channel, returning true if the element was successfully sent and false if the channel is full and the element could not be sent.

The send method is useful when the caller can afford to be blocked until the channel is ready to accept the element, whereas **trySend** is useful when the caller wants to avoid blocking and handle the case when the channel is full separately.

The following is an example of using **send** and **trySend**:

```kotlin
fun main() = runBlocking {
    val channel = Channel<Int>(capacity = 3) // Create a channel with a
    capacity of 3
```

```
launch {
    channel.send(1) // This will succeed immediately
    channel.send(2) // This will succeed immediately
    channel.send(3) // This will succeed immediately
    channel.send(4) // This will block until another coroutine
    receives an element from the channel
    channel.close()
}

for (i in 1..4) {
    val result = channel.trySend(i)
    if (result.isSuccess) {
        println("Successfully sent $i")
    } else {
        println("Failed to send $i: channel is full")
    }
}

for (element in channel) {
    println("Received: $element")
}
}
```

In this example, we create a channel with a capacity of 3 and launch a coroutine that sends four elements to the channel. Since the channel has a capacity of 3, the fourth send call will block until another coroutine receives an element from the channel.

We then loop through the numbers 1 to 4 and use the **trySend** method to send each number to the channel. The first three numbers are successfully sent, while the fourth number fails because the channel is full.

Finally, we loop through the channel and print each element as it is received. The output of the program will be the following:

```
Successfully sent 1
Successfully sent 2
```

```
Successfully sent 3
Failed to send 4: channel is full
Received: 1
Received: 2
Received: 3
Received: 1
Received: 2
Received: 3
Received: 4
```

Receive and poll (tryReceive)

The receive method is a suspending function that waits until there is a value available in the channel or the channel is closed. Sometimes, it may be desirable to receive a value without suspending, for example, when the receiver has a timeout or a cancellation mechanism. In that case, the poll method can be used instead, which returns a nullable value indicating whether there was a value available or not.

But the poll method in Kotlin channels is deprecated in favor of the **tryReceive** method, which returns a **ChannelResult** object that contains either the received value or null. The **tryReceive** method is used to receive a value without suspending, which is useful when the receiver has a timeout or cancellation mechanism or when the receiver does not want to block on an empty channel.

For example, consider the following code that creates a pipeline that receives numbers from a channel with a capacity of 10 and stops after 1 second. The sender coroutine sends numbers from 1 to 1,000 to the channel, whereas the receiver coroutine uses the **tryReceive** method to receive values without suspending and printing them. After 1 second, the receiver coroutine is canceled, and the sender coroutine is joined.

```
import kotlinx.coroutines.channels.Channel
import kotlinx.coroutines.*

fun main() = runBlocking {
    // Create a channel with a capacity of 10
    val channel = Channel<Int>(10)
```

```kotlin
        // Launch a coroutine that sends numbers from 1 to 1000 to the channel
        val sender = launch {
            for (x in 1..1000) {
                channel.send(x) // Suspend until there is space in the buffer
                println("Sent $x")
            }
            channel.close() // Close the channel when done
        }

        // Launch another coroutine that receives numbers from the channel and prints them
        val receiver = launch {
            while (isActive) {
                val result = channel.tryReceive() // Try to receive without suspending
                if (result.isSuccess) {
                    val x = result.getOrNull()
                    println("Received $x")
                } else {
                    println("Channel is empty")
                }
                delay(100) // Wait for 100 ms
            }
        }

        // Wait for 1 second and cancel the receiver
        delay(1000)
        receiver.cancel()
        println("Receiver cancelled")

        // Wait for the sender to finish sending all the values to the channel
        sender.join()
        println("Sender done")
    }
```

In this example, the **tryReceive** method is used to receive values from the channel without suspending, which allows the receiver to periodically check for new values while waiting for a timeout or cancellation. The **isActive** property is used to check if the coroutine is still active, which is necessary for the cancellation mechanism to work.

The **tryReceive** method is useful when the receiver does not want to block on an empty channel but rather returns **ChannelResult**, which holds the sent value or null.

Channels versus Java queues

Channels are used for communication and data transfer between coroutines, just like queues in other concurrency models. However, channels are more expressive and flexible than queues because they provide several different features that make them more versatile.

One important feature of channels is that they support different kinds of buffers. A buffer is a storage area that temporarily holds data while it is being transferred from one coroutine to another. Channels can be unbounded, meaning they can hold an unlimited number of items, or they can be bounded, meaning they have a fixed size limit. Additionally, channels can be rendezvous or conflated. Rendezvous channels do not have any buffer at all and require both the sender and the receiver to be ready at the same time to communicate, whereas conflated channels keep only the latest value sent to them and discard previous values.

Another important feature of channels is that they support different kinds of operations. In addition to the standard send and receive operations, channels also support **trySend** and **tryReceive** operations. The offer operation tries to send an item to the channel without blocking, whereas the **tryReceive** operation tries to receive an item from the channel without blocking. Channels also support the close operation to signal that no more items will be sent to the channel, which is useful for termination or cleanup.

Channels also support different kinds of semantics, such as fan-out, fan-in, and broadcast. Fan-out channels allow multiple coroutines to receive the same value from a single channel, whereas fan-in channels allow multiple coroutines to send values to a single channel. Broadcast channels allow a single value to be sent to multiple coroutines simultaneously.

Let us consider an example of using channels to implement a fan-out operation. Suppose we have a single producer coroutine that generates a sequence of numbers, and we want to distribute those numbers to multiple consumer coroutines. We can use a fan-out channel to accomplish this:

```
import kotlinx.coroutines.*
import kotlinx.coroutines.channels.*

fun main() = runBlocking {
```

```kotlin
        val numbers = produceNumbers() // Create a producer coroutine
        val squares = List(5) { // Create 5 consumer coroutines
            launch { consumeNumbers(numbers) }
        }
        squares.forEach { it.join() } // Wait for all the consumers to finish
    }

    fun CoroutineScope.produceNumbers() = produce<Int> {
        for (x in 1..10) {
            send(x) // Send the numbers to the channel
        }
    }

    suspend fun consumeNumbers(numbers: ReceiveChannel<Int>) {
        for (x in numbers) { // Receive the numbers from the channel
            println("Square of $x is ${x * x}")
        }
    }
```

In this example, we define a producer coroutine **produceNumbers()** that generates a sequence of numbers and sends them to a channel using the send operation. We then create five consumer coroutines that receive numbers from the same channel using the **for**-loop syntax, which implicitly calls the receive operation. Each consumer coroutine squares the received number and prints the result.

By using a fan-out channel, we can distribute the numbers generated by the producer coroutine to multiple consumer coroutines. This makes our code more expressive and flexible than a simple queue.

Channels are a powerful abstraction that can simplify concurrent programming in Kotlin. They can be used to implement various patterns and algorithms that involve data flow and communication between coroutines.

Broadcast channels

A broadcast channel is a special kind of channel that allows multiple receivers to subscribe to the same values sent by a single sender. A broadcast channel can be created using the

BroadcastChannel constructor, which takes a capacity argument that specifies how many values can be buffered in the channel before it suspends the sender.

A coroutine can send a value to a broadcast channel using the **send** method, which suspends until there is space in the buffer or the channel is closed. A coroutine can subscribe to a broadcast channel using the **openSubscription** method, which returns a regular channel that receives the values from the broadcast channel. A coroutine can receive a value from a subscription channel using the receive method, which suspends until there is a value available or the channel is closed. A broadcast channel can be closed using the **close** method, which indicates that no more values will be sent. A broadcast channel can be checked for closure using the **isClosedForSend** property. For example, the following code creates a broadcast channel that sends random numbers to multiple subscribers:

```
import kotlinx.coroutines.channels.BroadcastChannel
import kotlinx.coroutines.*
import java.util.*

fun main() = runBlocking {
    // Create a broadcast channel with a capacity of 10
    val channel = BroadcastChannel<Int>(10)

    // Launch a coroutine that sends random numbers to the channel
    val sender = launch {
        val random = Random()
        repeat(20) {
            val x = random.nextInt(100)
            channel.send(x) // Suspend until there is space in the buffer
            println("Sent $x")
        }
        channel.close() // Close the channel when done
    }

    // Launch another coroutine that subscribes to the channel and prints
    the values
    val subscriber1 = launch {
```

```
            val subscription = channel.openSubscription() // Subscribe to the channel
        for (x in subscription) { // Receive values until the channel is closed
            println("Subscriber 1 received $x")
        }
    }

    // Launch another coroutine that subscribes to the channel and prints
    the values
    val subscriber2 = launch {
            val subscription = channel.openSubscription() // Subscribe to the channel
        for (x in subscription) { // Receive values until the channel is closed
            println("Subscriber 2 received $x")
        }
    }

    // Wait for all coroutines to finish
    sender.join()
    subscriber1.join()
    subscriber2.join()
}
```

Broadcast channels are useful when dealing with streams of data that need to be consumed by multiple receivers in parallel.

Producers and actors

A producer is a coroutine that produces a stream of values and sends them to a channel. A producer can be created using the produce builder, which takes a scope and a capacity argument and returns a channel that can be used to receive the values from the producer. For example, the following code creates a producer that generates the **Fibonacci** sequence:

```
import kotlinx.coroutines.CoroutineScope
import kotlinx.coroutines.channels.*
```

```kotlin
fun CoroutineScope.fibonacci(): ReceiveChannel<Int> = produce {
    var a = 0
    var b = 1
    while (true) {
        send(a) // Suspend until there is space in the buffer or the
        channel is closed
        val tmp = a + b
        a = b
        b = tmp
    }
}
```

An actor is a coroutine that receives a stream of messages and performs some action on them. An actor can be created using the **actor** builder, which takes a scope, a capacity, and a **block** argument and returns a channel that can be used to send messages to the actor. The **block** argument defines how the actor handles each message. For example, the following code creates an actor that prints the messages it receives:

```kotlin
fun CoroutineScope.printer(): SendChannel<String> = actor {
    for (msg in channel) { // Receive messages until the channel is closed
        println(msg)
    }
}
```

Producers and actors are useful abstractions that can simplify concurrent programming in Kotlin. They can be used to implement various patterns and algorithms that involve data flow and communication between coroutines.

Conclusion

In this chapter, we learned how to use generators and sequences to create lazy and asynchronous streams of data in Kotlin. We also learned how to use pipelines to process data in parallel and how to use channels to communicate between coroutines. Finally, we saw how to use broadcast channels, producers, and actors to implement common patterns of concurrent programming.

Points to remember

The following are some key takeaways from this chapter:

- *Generators* and *sequences* are a way to generate a potentially infinite sequence of values on demand, allowing for efficient handling of large or infinite data sets.
- *Pipelines* are a way to process data in a sequence of stages, where each stage performs some transformation on the input data and passes it on to the next stage.
- `Send` and `trySend` are methods for adding values to a channel, with send being a suspending function that blocks until there is space in the channel buffer and `trySend` being a non-suspending function that returns a `Result` indicating whether the value was added to the channel.
- `Receive` and `tryReceive` are methods for retrieving values from a channel, with receive being a suspending function that blocks until a value is available in the channel and `tryReceive` being a non-suspending function that returns a `ChannelResult` that holds a value indicating whether there was a value available in the channel.
- *Channels* in Kotlin are more expressive and flexible than Java queues, as they support different kinds of buffers, operations, and semantics, allowing for more efficient and expressive concurrent programming.
- *Broadcast channels* are a type of channel that allows multiple receivers to receive the same value, enabling fan-out semantics in channel communication.
- *Producers* are a way to encapsulate the logic of generating data for a channel, allowing for more modular and reusable code.
- *Actors* are a way to encapsulate state and behavior into a single entity, enabling more robust and fault-tolerant concurrent programming.

By understanding these concepts and how they relate to each other, developers can create efficient and flexible concurrent programs using Kotlin.

Join our book's Discord space

Join the book's Discord Workspace for Latest updates, Offers, Tech happenings around the world, New Release and Sessions with the Authors:

https://discord.bpbonline.com

CHAPTER 17
Coroutine Flows

Introduction

So far, we explored the powerful features of Kotlin coroutines and how they revolutionize asynchronous programming. We learned about task scheduling, different dispatchers, exception propagation, coroutine cancellation, and the features of coroutine channels. These concepts laid a solid foundation for writing efficient and concurrent code.

In this chapter, we will delve into a new dimension of Kotlin coroutines known as Coroutine Flows. While coroutines provide a powerful mechanism for managing concurrency and asynchrony, Coroutine Flows takes it a step further by providing a seamless way to handle data streams.

Coroutine Flows enables us to work with data streams in a more elegant and efficient manner, allowing us to control the flow of data, handle backpressure, and process streams asynchronously. They provide a declarative and sequential approach to working with data, making it easier to write expressive and maintainable code.

In the following pages, we will explore the concept of Coroutine Flows in depth. We will discuss their advantages over traditional approaches, understand their limitations, and learn how to apply flow constraints effectively. We will also explore various operators and techniques for manipulating and transforming data streams using Coroutine Flows.

By the end of this chapter, you will have a solid understanding of Coroutine Flows and how to leverage their power to handle complex data streams in your Kotlin applications. So, let us dive into the world of Coroutine Flows and unlock the full potential of asynchronous data processing.

Structure

In this chapter, we will cover the following topics:
- Data streams
- Streams limitations
- Flow constraints

Objectives

In this chapter, you will be introduced to Coroutine Flows in Kotlin, a powerful tool for handling data streams efficiently. The chapter's objectives include explaining the significance of data streams in asynchronous programming, highlighting the limitations of traditional approaches, and showcasing how Coroutine Flows overcome these limitations. It will provide an overview of Coroutine Flows' key features, such as flow constraints, operators, and backpressure handling, and demonstrate their practical use through examples and hands-on exercises. Advanced topics like flow composition, error handling, and integration with other concurrency mechanisms will also be discussed. Additionally, you'll receive guidance on best practices and design patterns for effective use of Coroutine Flows in Kotlin applications, including an exploration of flow constraints to maximize their potential.

Throughout this chapter, we will explore these objectives in a beginner-friendly manner, providing detailed explanations, practical examples, and hands-on exercises to reinforce your understanding of Coroutine Flows. So, let us embark on this exciting journey and unlock the power of Coroutine Flows in your Kotlin applications.

Overview

In this chapter, we will delve into the powerful concept of Coroutine Flows in Kotlin. Asynchronous programming often involves handling data streams that require efficient processing and management. Traditional approaches to stream processing may have limitations when it comes to handling backpressure, composing operators, and maintaining concurrency. Coroutine Flows offers a comprehensive solution to these challenges by providing a declarative and efficient way to work with data streams.

This chapter will also discuss the limitations of traditional data streams and the need for a more efficient approach. It will highlight the challenges of handling backpressure and cancellation effectively in traditional data streams and explain how Coroutine Flows provide built-in support for these features.

The chapter also explores the concept of flow constraints, which allow developers to fine-tune the behavior of data streams according to specific requirements. It provides examples of how to use flow constraints such as buffer size and concurrency to optimize resource utilization and control the flow of data.

It will provide a comprehensive overview of how Coroutine Flows can be used to handle data streams efficiently. By leveraging the power of coroutines and reactive programming, developers can overcome the limitations of traditional data streams and achieve better control, efficiency, and scalability when working with data streams.

Data streams

In the world of software development, data streams play a crucial role in handling continuous and potentially infinite streams of data. Whether it is processing sensor readings, handling user events, or consuming data from external sources, efficiently managing data streams is essential for building responsive and scalable applications.

In the context of Kotlin coroutines, data streams are elegantly handled using *Coroutine Flows*. Coroutine Flows provide a seamless way to represent and process asynchronous sequences of values. Unlike traditional approaches that involve callbacks or blocking operations, Coroutine Flows offers a more concise and structured way to work with data streams.

A Coroutine Flow can be thought of as a stream of values emitted over time. It starts emitting values when it is collected by a coroutine, and it can emit values one by one or in batches. With Coroutine Flows, you can represent both finite and infinite streams of data, making them highly flexible and suitable for a wide range of scenarios.

Let us consider a simple example to illustrate the concept of data streams using Coroutine Flows. Suppose we have a data source that emits a stream of integers asynchronously. We can create a Coroutine Flow to handle this stream as follows:

```kotlin
import kotlinx.coroutines.*
import kotlinx.coroutines.flow.Flow
import kotlinx.coroutines.flow.flow

fun streamOfIntegers(): Flow<Int> = flow {
    for (i in 1..10) {
        delay(100) // Simulate asynchronous delay
        emit(i) // Emit the next integer
```

      }
    }

In the preceding code, the **streamOfIntegers()** function returns a **Flow<Int>** representing a stream of integers from 1 to 10. Each value is emitted with a delay of 100 milliseconds to simulate an asynchronous source.

To consume the values emitted by the flow, we can use the collect operator within a coroutine scope as follows:

```
fun main() = runBlocking {
    streamOfIntegers().collect { value ->
        println(value) // Print each value
    }
}
```

In the **main()** function, we use the collect operator to consume the values emitted by the flow. The lambda function inside collect is invoked for each emitted value, allowing us to process the values as they arrive. In this example, we simply print each value to the console.

Let us consider a real-world example to demonstrate the usage of Coroutine Flows in handling data streams.

Imagine you are building a weather application that fetches weather data from an API and displays it to the user. The weather data updates periodically, and you want to continuously fetch the latest weather information and update the user interface accordingly.

To achieve this, you can use Coroutine Flows to represent the stream of weather updates. The following is an example implementation:

```
import kotlinx.coroutines.delay
import kotlinx.coroutines.flow.Flow
import kotlinx.coroutines.flow.flow
import kotlinx.coroutines.runBlocking

data class Weather(val temperature: Double, val description: String)

fun fetchWeatherUpdates(): Flow<Weather> = flow {
    while (true) {
        delay(5000) // Fetch weather every 5 seconds
```

```
        // Simulate API call to fetch weather data
        val temperature = getRandomTemperature()
        val description = getRandomWeatherDescription()

        // Emit the latest weather information
        emit(Weather(temperature, description))
    }
}

fun main() = runBlocking {
    // Collect weather updates from the flow
    fetchWeatherUpdates().collect { weather ->
        // Update UI with the latest weather information
        displayWeather(weather)
    }
}

fun displayWeather(weather: Weather) {
    // Code to update UI with the weather information
    println("Temperature: ${weather.temperature}°C, Description: ${weather.
    description}")
}

// Helper functions to generate random weather data for demonstration purposes
fun getRandomTemperature(): Double = (Math.random() * 30 + (-10)).toDouble()

fun getRandomWeatherDescription(): String = listOf("Sunny", "Cloudy",
"Rainy", "Snowy").random()
```

In this example, the **fetchWeatherUpdates()** function returns a Coroutine Flow of Weather objects. It uses a loop to continuously fetch weather data from the API every 5 seconds. The fetched data is then emitted through the flow using the **emit()** function.

In the `main()` function, we collect the weather updates from the flow using the collect operator. For each emitted Weather object, we call the `displayWeather()` function to update the UI with the latest weather information.

The `displayWeather()` function is a placeholder for the actual code to update the UI. In a real application, you would use appropriate UI frameworks or libraries to update the UI elements with the weather information.

By using Coroutine Flows, you can handle the continuous stream of weather updates efficiently. The flow is executed in a non-blocking manner, allowing your application to remain responsive while fetching and processing the updates. This example demonstrates how Coroutine Flows simplifies the management of data streams in real-world scenarios. With Coroutine Flows, you can easily handle periodic updates, respond to changes in external data sources, and keep your application up-to-date with the latest information.

By understanding and leveraging the power of Coroutine Flows, you can build robust and responsive applications that efficiently handle data streams with ease.

Streams limitations

It is crucial to understand the limitations of traditional data streams and recognize the need for a more efficient and flexible approach. In this section, we will explore the limitations of traditional data streams and discuss the importance of overcoming these challenges. In this section, you will have understood why Coroutine Flows in Kotlin offers a superior solution for handling data streams effectively.

Handling backpressure and cancellation

Traditional data streams often struggle to handle backpressure and cancellation effectively, which can lead to various issues. Let us dive deeper into these concepts and understand their significance.

Backpressure

Backpressure is a challenge that arises when the producer generates data at a higher rate than the consumer can handle. Imagine a scenario where a slow consumer is receiving data from a fast producer. If there is no mechanism to regulate the flow, the consumer can become overwhelmed, leading to memory overflow or resource exhaustion.

Let us delve deeper into addressing backpressure in Coroutine Flows and explore the various operators available for controlling the flow of data.

Coroutine Flows provides developers with built-in support for backpressure management, ensuring that data flow remains balanced between producers and consumers. This prevents overload situations and resource-related issues. The following are some operators commonly used to handle backpressure in Coroutine Flows:

- **Buffer**: The **buffer** operator allows the consumer to specify a buffer size, which acts as a temporary storage space for emitted values. It enables the producer to continue producing data even if the consumer is slower in processing it. By setting an appropriate buffer size, developers can achieve a balance between the producer's speed and the consumer's capacity, preventing overwhelming the consumer.

```kotlin
import kotlinx.coroutines.delay
import kotlinx.coroutines.flow.buffer
import kotlinx.coroutines.flow.flowOf

suspend fun main() {
    val flow = flowOf(1, 2, 3, 4, 5)
        .buffer(2) // Set buffer size to 2

    flow.collect { value ->
        println("Received: $value")
        delay(1000) // Simulate slow processing
    }
}
```

The following will be the output:

```
Received: 1
Received: 2
Received: 3
Received: 4
Received: 5
```

In the preceding example, the buffer operator sets a buffer size of 2. Even though the consumer processes the values with a delay, the producer continues emitting all the values. The buffer holds the extra values until the consumer is ready to process them, maintaining a balanced data flow.

- **Conflate**: The **conflate** operator allows the flow to skip intermediate values when the consumer is slower than the producer. It only emits the latest value, discarding any unprocessed intermediate values.

```
fun main() = runBlocking {
    val flow = flowOf(1, 2, 3, 4, 5)
        .conflate()

    flow.collect { value ->
        delay(1000) // Simulate slow processing
        println("Received: $value")
    }
}
```

The following will be the output:

```
Received: 1
Received: 5
```

In the preceding example, the **conflate** operator ensures that only the latest value (`` `1` `` and `` `5` ``) is emitted, whereas intermediate values (`` `2` `` to `` `4` ``) are skipped. This allows the consumer to keep up with the producer by processing only the most recent data.

- **CollectLatest**: The `collectLatest` operator is similar to conflate, but it cancels the processing of the previous value as soon as a new value arrives. It ensures that the consumer is always processing the latest value.

```
fun main() = runBlocking {
    val flow = flowOf(1, 2, 3, 4, 5)

    flow.collectLatest { value ->
        println("Received: $value")
        delay(1000) // Simulate slow processing
    }
}
```

The following will be the output:

Received: 1

Received: 2

Received: 3

Received: 4

Received: 5

In the preceding example, the **collectLatest** operator processes the values one by one. When a new value arrives, it cancels the processing of the previous value and immediately starts processing the latest value. This ensures that the consumer always works with the most up-to-date data.

By using these operators, developers can control the flow of data in Coroutine Flows effectively. The choice of which operator to use depends on the specific requirements and characteristics of the data stream. Whether it is buffering values, conflating intermediate values, or collecting only the latest values, these operators provide flexibility and control over backpressure management, enabling a more efficient and balanced data flow.

Cancellation

Cancellation is an essential feature when working with data streams. There are situations where a consumer needs to stop processing the stream either because it is no longer needed or an error has occurred. Without proper cancellation mechanisms, the stream may keep producing data, wasting system resources and causing memory leaks.

Coroutine Flows seamlessly integrates with the structured concurrency model provided by Kotlin coroutines, enabling graceful cancellation. When a flow is canceled, all the upstream operations are also canceled, ensuring proper cleanup. For example, by using the **cancellable** operator within a flow, you can handle cancellation signals and perform necessary cleanup tasks before the flow terminates:

```
fun main() = runBlocking {

    val flow = flow {
        repeat(1000) {
            emit(it)
            delay(100)
        }
    }

    val job = flow
        .onEach { println("Received: $it") }
        .onCompletion { println("Flow completed") }
        .cancellable()
        .launchIn(this)
```

```
        // Simulate cancellation after 500 ms
        delay(500)
        job.cancel()
    }
```

The following will be the output:

```
Received: 0
Received: 1
Received: 2
Received: 3
Received: 4
Flow completed
```

In the preceding example, the `cancellable` operator is used to handle cancellation. When the job is canceled, the flow stops emitting new values, and the `onCompletion` block is executed. This ensures that resources are properly released, avoiding potential leaks.

By incorporating backpressure handling and cancellation support into Coroutine Flows, developers can create more robust and resource-efficient stream processing pipelines. It allows for better control over data flow and ensures that streams are gracefully handled, preventing overload and resource-related issues.

Inefficient resource utilization

Traditional data streams often rely on blocking I/O operations, which can lead to inefficient resource utilization. Let us explore this limitation in more detail.

When a thread is blocked, it means that it is waiting for an I/O operation, such as reading data from a file or making a network request, to complete. During this waiting period, the thread is unable to perform any other tasks. In a traditional stream-based approach, if multiple threads are used to handle concurrent data streams, each thread may end up being blocked at different times, waiting for I/O operations to complete. As a result, the overall system resource utilization becomes suboptimal because threads are not actively processing tasks.

Consider an example where an application needs to download multiple files concurrently. Using traditional stream-based approaches, each download operation may block the thread until the file is fully downloaded. As a result, if there are multiple downloads happening simultaneously, each download operation may cause a thread to be blocked, leading to underutilization of system resources.

Coroutine Flows provides a solution to this limitation by leveraging non-blocking I/O operations and suspending functions. When using coroutines, instead of blocking a thread, a suspended coroutine can free up the underlying thread to perform other tasks while waiting for I/O operations to complete. This enables more efficient utilization of system resources, as multiple coroutines can be executed concurrently on a smaller number of threads.

Let us take a look at an example that demonstrates the efficient resource utilization of coroutine flows:

```
import kotlinx.coroutines.Dispatchers
import kotlinx.coroutines.delay
import kotlinx.coroutines.flow.flow
import kotlinx.coroutines.runBlocking
import kotlinx.coroutines.withContext

fun main() = runBlocking {
    val files = listOf("file1.txt", "file2.txt", "file3.txt")

    withContext(Dispatchers.IO) {
        files.forEach { file ->
            // Use coroutine flow to download files concurrently
            flow {
                // Simulate downloading the file
                val content = downloadFile(file)
                emit(content)
            }.collect { content ->
                // Process the downloaded content
                processContent(content)
            }
        }
    }
}

suspend fun downloadFile(file: String): String {
    // Simulate downloading file asynchronously
    delay(1000)
```

```
        return "Content of $file"
}

fun processContent(content: String) {
    println("Processing: $content")
}
```

The following will be the output:

```
Processing: Content of file1.txt
Processing: Content of file2.txt
Processing: Content of file3.txt
```

In this example, the **files** list represents multiple files to be downloaded concurrently. By using a coroutine flow, each file download operation is executed asynchronously, allowing other coroutines to continue their execution while waiting for the I/O operation to complete. As a result, the system resources are used more efficiently, as coroutines are not blocking threads but rather suspending and allowing other tasks to be executed.

By leveraging coroutine flows and non-blocking I/O operations, developers can overcome the limitations of traditional data streams and achieve more efficient resource utilization, especially when dealing with concurrent data streams in large-scale applications.

The need for a coroutine flows approach

Given the limitations of traditional data streams, there is a clear need for a more efficient and flexible approach. Coroutine Flows in Kotlin provides a powerful solution by combining the benefits of coroutines and reactive programming. Coroutine Flows offers built-in support for backpressure and cancellation, enabling more controlled and efficient handling of data streams.

They also leverage non-blocking I/O operations, ensuring optimal resource utilization and scalability.

By recognizing the inefficiency in handling backpressure, cancellation, and resource utilization, we can appreciate the need for a more efficient approach. With Coroutine Flows, we can achieve better control, efficiency, and scalability when working with data streams.

Flows constraints

Let us dive into the concept of flow constraints and their importance in managing data streams.

Flow constraints refer to the properties and behaviors that can be applied to Coroutine Flows to control and manage the flow of data. These constraints allow developers to fine-tune the behavior of data streams according to specific requirements. By understanding and applying flow constraints, developers can optimize resource utilization, control buffer sizes, manage concurrency, and ensure efficient processing of data streams.

As you already saw in a previous example, one important flow constraint is the *buffer size*. The buffer represents a temporary storage space for emitted elements in a flow. By specifying a buffer size, developers can control how many elements can be buffered before the downstream operations consume them. This helps manage backpressure situations where the producer is faster than the consumer.

For example, consider a scenario where a producer emits elements at a high rate, but the consumer is slower in processing them. By using a buffer with an appropriate size, the producer can continue emitting elements even if the consumer is not ready to receive them immediately. This prevents overwhelming the consumer and provides a balanced flow of data.

The following is an example that demonstrates the use of buffer constraint in a Coroutine Flow:

```
import kotlinx.coroutines.delay
import kotlinx.coroutines.flow.asFlow
import kotlinx.coroutines.flow.buffer
import kotlinx.coroutines.runBlocking

fun main() = runBlocking {
    val numbers = (1..10).asFlow()

    numbers.buffer(3) // Specify a buffer size of 3

    numbers.collect { value ->
        delay(1000) // Simulate slow processing
        println("Received: $value")
    }
}
```

In this example, we have a Coroutine Flow called numbers that emits numbers from 1 to 10. By applying the **buffer(3)** constraint to the flow, we set the buffer size to 3. This means that the producer can emit up to 3 elements without waiting for the consumer to process them. The consumer then collects the elements and simulates slow processing using **delay(1000)**.

The **buffer** constraint ensures that the producer can continue emitting elements even if the consumer is slow. In this case, the output will show that the first three elements are received without any delay, whereas subsequent elements are delayed by 1 second each.

Another important flow constraint is concurrency, which controls how many coroutines can concurrently process the emitted elements. By limiting the concurrency level, developers can regulate the degree of parallelism in processing data streams.

Consider a scenario where you have a flow that performs CPU-intensive computations on the emitted elements. If the flow is allowed to execute all computations concurrently, it might overload the system and degrade performance. By limiting the concurrency level, you can control the number of coroutines executing concurrently, ensuring optimal resource utilization.

The following is an example that illustrates the use of concurrency constraints in a Coroutine Flow:

```
import kotlinx.coroutines.delay
import kotlinx.coroutines.flow.asFlow
import kotlinx.coroutines.flow.flatMapMerge
import kotlinx.coroutines.flow.flow
import kotlinx.coroutines.runBlocking

fun main() = runBlocking {
    val numbers = (1..10).asFlow()

    numbers.flatMapMerge(concurrency = 2) { value ->
        flow {
            delay(1000) // Simulate computation time
            emit(value * 2)
        }
    }.collect { value ->
        println("Processed: $value")
    }
}
```

In this example, we have a Coroutine Flow called numbers that emits numbers from 1 to 10. We use the **flatMapMerge** operator to perform a computation on each emitted element. By specifying a concurrency level of 2, we limit the maximum number of concurrent computations to 2.

This ensures that, at most 2, coroutines are executing the computations in parallel, preventing overload and excessive resource usage. The output will show that the elements are processed in a concurrent manner, with a maximum of 2 computations happening simultaneously.

By applying flow constraints like buffer size and concurrency, developers can fine-tune the behavior of Coroutine Flows to suit specific requirements. These constraints allow for efficient management of data streams, better resource utilization, and controlled processing of elements.

Conclusion

In conclusion, this chapter provided a detailed overview of how Coroutine Flows in Kotlin can be used to handle data streams efficiently. It discussed the limitations of traditional data streams and highlighted the need for a more efficient approach. By leveraging the power of coroutines and reactive programming, developers can overcome those limitations and achieve better control, efficiency, and scalability when working with data streams.

This chapter provided examples of how to use Coroutine Flows to represent and handle data streams in real-world scenarios. It demonstrated, as an example, how to fetch data periodically and update the user interface with the latest information using Coroutine Flows. The example illustrated the ease and efficiency with which data streams can be managed using Coroutine Flows.

The chapter also explored the concept of flow constraints, which allow developers to fine-tune the behavior of data streams according to specific requirements. It provided examples of how to use flow constraints such as buffer size and concurrency to optimize resource utilization and control the flow of data.

Furthermore, the chapter discussed the challenges of handling backpressure and cancellation effectively in traditional data streams. It explained how Coroutine Flows provides built-in support for these features, enabling more controlled and efficient handling of data streams.

Overall, this chapter provided a comprehensive understanding of how Coroutine Flows can simplify the management of data streams in real-world scenarios. By understanding and leveraging the power of Coroutine Flows, developers can build robust and responsive applications that efficiently handle data streams with ease.

Points to remember

The following are some points to remember:
- Coroutine Flows in Kotlin can be used to handle data streams efficiently.
- Traditional data streams have limitations in handling backpressure and cancellation effectively.
- Coroutine Flows provides built-in support for backpressure and cancellation.
- Flow constraints such as buffer size and concurrency can be used to fine-tune the behavior of data streams according to specific requirements.
- By leveraging the power of coroutines and reactive programming, developers can overcome the limitations of traditional data streams and achieve better control, efficiency, and scalability when working with data streams.

Join our book's Discord space

Join the book's Discord Workspace for Latest updates, Offers, Tech happenings around the world, New Release and Sessions with the Authors:

https://discord.bpbonline.com

CHAPTER 18
Multiplatform and Kotlin

Introduction

Throughout this book, we have explored various aspects of Kotlin development, from the basics of the language to advanced concepts such as coroutines and flows. We delved into important topics such as data streams, channels, and coroutine-based concurrency. We discussed how these concepts address the limitations of traditional approaches and enable efficient handling of data in asynchronous and concurrent scenarios. We have built a strong foundation of knowledge and practical skills in Kotlin programming.

Now, as we enter the final chapter of this book, we embark on a new journey exploring the world of multiplatform development with Kotlin. Multiplatform development has gained significant traction in recent years as a powerful approach to building cross-platform applications. With Kotlin's multiplatform capabilities, we can create applications that run on multiple platforms, such as Android, iOS, Web, and desktop, while sharing code and resources between them.

In this chapter, we will dive into the exciting realm of multiplatform development and explore the process of setting up Android Studio for multiplatform projects. We will learn how to harness the power of Kotlin's multiplatform features to write shared code that can be used across different platforms, saving time and effort in development. In addition, we will walk through a real-world application example: building a *Todo app* using *Compose multiplatform*, which showcases the practical implementation of multiplatform development in action. So, let us embark on this final chapter and unlock the potential of Kotlin's multiplatform capabilities.

Structure

In this chapter, we will cover the following topics:
- Setting up Android Studio
- Todo app in compose multiplatform (Android and desktop)

Objectives

In this chapter, the main focus is on understanding the principles and benefits of multiplatform development with Kotlin. We will delve into the concepts that make multiplatform development a powerful approach for building applications that can run on different platforms.

Our journey begins with configuring a Kotlin Compose multiplatform application for both Android and Desktop. We will explore the step-by-step process of setting up Android Studio specifically for multiplatform projects, ensuring a smooth development experience.

One of the key aspects we will cover is the idea of shared code and resources in multiplatform development. We will dive into how we can leverage common code across platforms to maximize code reuse and streamline development efforts.

A highlight of this chapter is the development of a real-world application, a Todo app, using Compose Multiplatform. This will allow us to witness the power and versatility of multiplatform development with Kotlin in action.

Furthermore, we will showcase the advantages offered by multiplatform development, such as increased code reuse, improved efficiency, and broader platform coverage. By understanding these benefits, developers will be equipped to make informed decisions about adopting multiplatform development for their projects.

To ensure a comprehensive learning experience, we will provide insights into best practices and considerations for multiplatform development with Kotlin. This will enable developers to write high-quality, maintainable code that adheres to industry standards and maximizes the potential of multiplatform development.

Ultimately, our aim is to initiate developers with the skills and knowledge needed to embrace multiplatform development and create versatile applications that cater to a wider range of platforms. By the end of this chapter, you will be well-prepared to embark on your multiplatform development journey and unlock the full potential of Kotlin's multiplatform capabilities.

Overview

In this final chapter of the book, we delve into the realm of multiplatform development with Kotlin. Multiplatform development has emerged as a powerful approach to building applications that can run on multiple platforms, enabling code sharing and reducing development effort. In this chapter, we explore the principles and benefits of multiplatform development and guide you through the process of setting up Android Studio for multiplatform projects.

We delve into the concepts of shared code and resources, which lie at the core of multiplatform development, and provide practical examples to illustrate their usage. A highlight of this chapter is the development of a real-world application: the *Todo* app. Using *Compose Multiplatform*, we demonstrate the process of building a cross-platform application that runs on both Android and desktop, leveraging the code-sharing capabilities of Kotlin.

Throughout the chapter, we emphasize the advantages of multiplatform development, such as increased code reuse, improved efficiency, and wider platform coverage. We also provide insights into best practices and considerations for successful multiplatform development with Kotlin. By the end of this chapter, you will have a solid understanding of multiplatform development principles and be equipped with the skills to embark on your own multiplatform projects. So, let us dive into the exciting world of multiplatform development with Kotlin and unleash the full potential of cross-platform application development.

Setting up the development environment

To build our cross-platform using Compose Multiplatform, we will need to use Android Studio and Gradle. These tools will facilitate the creation, design, and deployment of your application across both Android and Desktop platforms.

Android Studio is an **integrated development environment** (**IDE**) for Android app development, whereas Gradle is a build automation tool. Both are open-source and free to use. Android Studio provides a number of features that make it easier to develop Android apps, such as a code editor, graphical layout editor, debugger, testing framework, build system, and emulator. Gradle is especially popular for building Java, Kotlin, and Android applications, but it can be used for various other programming languages and project types as well. It provides a flexible and powerful build system that allows developers to define and manage their project's build process as code.

In this section, we are going to create a simple Android application with Jetpack Compose and migrate to Compose multiplatform without relying on any third-party plugins.

Creating a simple Android application with Jetpack Compose

To create a new project in Android Studio, go to **File** | **New** | **New project**. The following window will appears:

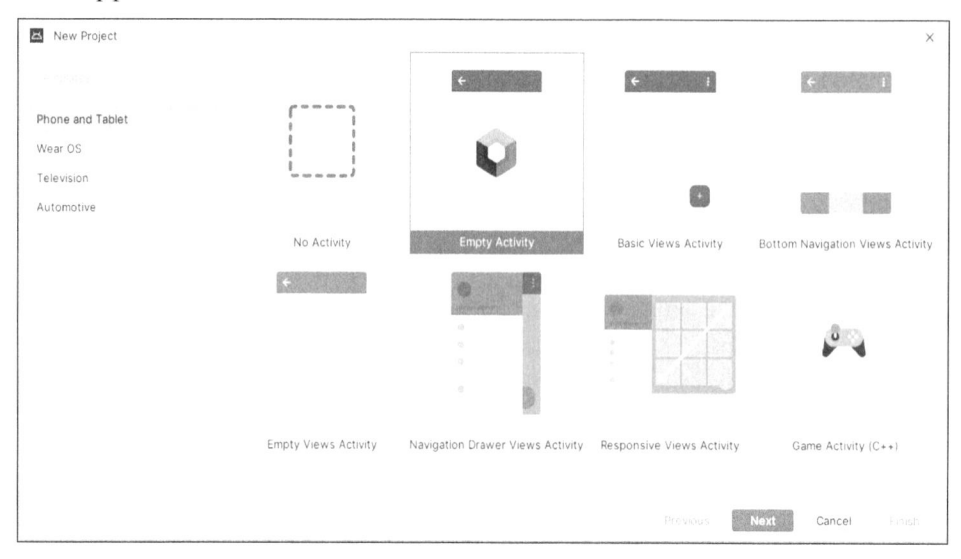

Figure 18.1: Android Studio new project dialog

In this step, you need to choose the **Empty Activity template**, then fill the form with the needed information as follows:

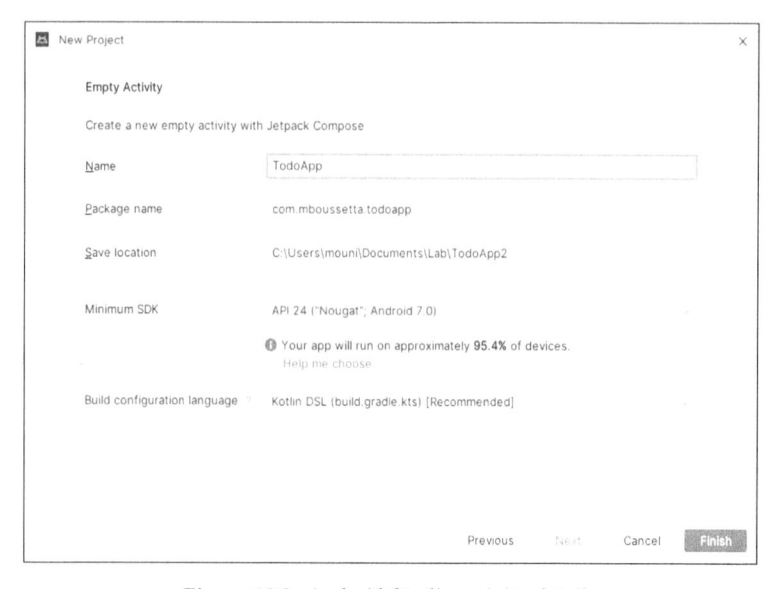

Figure 18.2: Android Studio activity details

Next, you click on **Finish** and wait until all the project dependencies are downloaded. The following is the Android project-generated structure:

Figure 18.3: Generated simple Android structure

And at the end of this step, we will rename the **app** module to **android** because it contains the Android platform-specific code.

Setting up the Compose multiplatform project structure

Within a Compose multiplatform project, we will typically have a shared module for common code that can be used on all platforms (Android and Desktop in our case). This module will contain our business logic, data models, and any utility functions. This allows us to share code between platforms, which can save time and effort. It also makes it easier to maintain the code, as changes made to the shared module will be reflected on both platforms.

The following are some of the benefits of using a shared module in a Compose multiplatform project:

- It saves time and effort by allowing you to share code between the two platforms.
- It makes it easier to maintain the code, as changes made to the **shared** module will be reflected on all platforms.
- It can improve the performance of our app, as the shared code can be compiled for each platform.
- It can make our app more portable, as it can be easily ported to other platforms.

The Kotlin Multiplatform plugin is a Gradle plugin that will help us migrate our Android application with Jetpack Compose to a Compose Multiplatform application. It does this by providing a number of tasks that can be used to generate the necessary code and resources for our multiplatform application.

In the top-level build file **build.gradle.kts**, we add the compose Gradle plugin to enable Jetpack compose development as follow:

```
// Top-level build file where you can add configuration options common to all sub- projects/modules.
plugins {
    id("com.android.application") version "8.2.0-beta04" apply false
    id("org.jetbrains.kotlin.android") version "1.9.0" apply false
    id("org.jetbrains.compose") version "1.5.0" apply false // jetpack compose plugin
}
```

Next, we should create a shared module for the common code of all platforms and also the **desktop** module. In the same hierarchy level as the **android** module, we create the modules **common** and **desktop**. Each module will have a **build.gradle.kts** Gradle build file.

The project structure should look like the following:

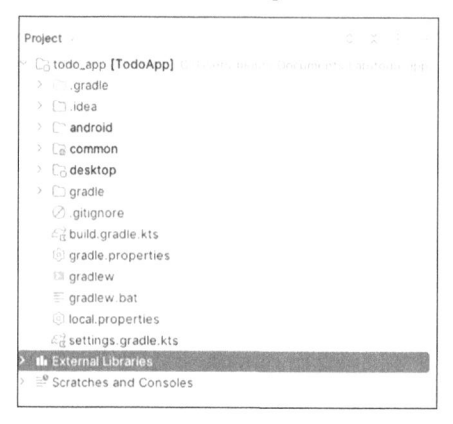

Figure 18.4: Compose multiplatform project structure

Now, let us see how to set up each module.

Setting up the common module

Within the common module, we need to create a directory named **src**, in which we should create three directories for source sets: **commonMain**, **desktopMain**, and **androidMain**. In a Compose multiplatform application, **commonMain**, **desktopMain**, and **androidMain** are source sets that contain code that is specific to each platform.

- **commonMain** contains code that is shared by all platforms. This can include business logic, data models, and common UI components.
- **desktopMain** contains code that is specific to desktop platforms. This can include code for interacting with the desktop windowing system, handling keyboard and mouse input, and displaying desktop-specific UI elements.
- **androidMain** contains code that is specific to Android platforms. This can include code for interacting with Android APIs, handling touch input, and displaying Android-specific UI elements.

In each source set, we need to have a **kotlin** directory in which we are going to create a package—for example: **com.mboussetta.todoapp**. Next, we should add the Kotlin multiplatform plugin to the **common** module build file. The following is how the **build.gradle.kts** of the common module will look like:

```
plugins {
    kotlin("multiplatform")
    id("com.android.library")
    id("org.jetbrains.compose")
}

kotlin {
    androidTarget {
        compilations.all {
            kotlinOptions {
                jvmTarget = "1.8"
            }
        }
    }
    jvm("desktop") {
        jvmToolchain(17)
```

```
        }



        sourceSets {
            val commonMain by getting {
                dependencies {
                    implementation(compose.foundation)
                     implementation(compose.runtime)
                    implementation(compose.material3)
                     implementation(compose.materialIconsExtended)
                }
             }


            val androidMain by getting {
                dependencies {
                    api(libs.appcompat)
                     api(libs.core.ktx)
                }
            }


            val desktopMain by getting {
                dependencies {
                    implementation(libs.sqldelight.native.driver)
                }
            }
        }
    }


    android {
```

```
    namespace = "com.mboussetta.todoapp"
    compileSdk = 34
    defaultConfig {
        minSdk = 24
    }


    compileOptions {
        sourceCompatibility = JavaVersion.VERSION_1_8
        targetCompatibility = JavaVersion.VERSION_1_8
    }
}
```

The following plugins were used in this project:

- **Kotlin multiplatform plugin `kotlin("multiplatform")`**: This plugin enables Kotlin multiplatform development.
- **Android library plugin `id("com.android.library")`**: This plugin enables Android library development.
- **Jetpack Compose plugin `id("org.jetbrains.compose")`**: This plugin enables Jetpack Compose development.

The Kotlin multiplatform project is defined in the Kotlin block. The Android target is configured in the **androidTarget** block. The desktop target is configured in the **jvm("desktop")** block.

The **sourceSets** block defines the source sets for the project. The **commonMain** source set contains code that is shared by both the Android and desktop targets. The **androidMain** source set contains code that is specific to the Android target. The **desktopMain** source set contains code that is specific to the desktop target.

The Android project is configured in the Android block. The namespace is set to **com.mboussetta.todoapp**, the compile SDK is set to 34, and the minimum SDK is set to 24. The source compatibility and target compatibility are also set to Java 8.

We should also make some changes to the **settings.gradle.kts** to include the maven repository from where all the compose libraries will be downloaded:

```
pluginManagement {
    repositories {
        google()
```

```
            mavenCentral()
            gradlePluginPortal()
            maven("https://maven.pkg.jetbrains.space/public/p/compose/dev")
        }
    }
    dependencyResolutionManagement {
        repositories {
            google()
            mavenCentral()
            maven("https://maven.pkg.jetbrains.space/public/p/compose/dev")
        }
    }
```

maven("https://maven.pkg.jetbrains.space/public/p/compose/dev") this line adds a Maven repository for compose libraries.

These repository declarations allow your Gradle build to fetch dependencies and plugins from multiple sources. Depending on our project's requirements.

Setting up the Android module

The early generated Gradle build script will be modified to the following:

```
    plugins {
        id("com.android.application")
        kotlin("android")
        id("org.jetbrains.compose")
    }

    android {
        namespace = "com.mboussetta.todoapp"
        compileSdk = 34

        defaultConfig {
            applicationId = "com.mboussetta.todoapp"
            minSdk = 24
```

```
        targetSdk = 34
        versionCode = 1
        versionName = "1.0"

        vectorDrawables {
            useSupportLibrary = true
        }
    }

    buildTypes {
        release {
            isMinifyEnabled = false
             proguardFiles(
                getDefaultProguardFile("proguard-android-optimize.txt"),
               "proguard-rules.pro"
            )
        }
    }
    compileOptions {
        sourceCompatibility = JavaVersion.VERSION_1_8
         targetCompatibility = JavaVersion.VERSION_1_8
    }
    kotlinOptions {
       jvmTarget = "1.8"
    }


    composeOptions {
       kotlinCompilerExtensionVersion = "1.5.1"
    }
    packaging {
        resources {
```

```
            excludes += "/META-INF/{AL2.0,LGPL2.1}"
        }
    }
}

dependencies {
    implementation(project(":common"))
     implementation("androidx.activity:activity-compose:1.7.2")
}
```

We just updated the dependencies block so that the Android module would add the **common** module as a dependency which should be compiled and packaged into our application's APK file for the Android platform.

Setting up the desktop module

Now, we have to create a Gradle build script for the desktop module. It will be configured as follows:

```
import org.jetbrains.compose.desktop.application.dsl.TargetFormat

plugins {
    kotlin("multiplatform")
    id("org.jetbrains.compose")
}

kotlin {
    jvm {
        jvmToolchain(17)
         withJava()
    }
    
    sourceSets {
        val jvmMain by getting {
            dependencies {
```

```
                implementation(project(":common"))

                    implementation(compose.desktop.common)
                    implementation(compose.desktop.currentOs)
                }
            }
        }
    }


    compose.desktop {
        application {
            mainClass = "mainKt"
             nativeDistributions {
                targetFormats(TargetFormat.Dmg, TargetFormat.Msi, TargetFormat.Deb)
                    packageName = "TodoApp"
            }
        }
    }
```

This Gradle build script configures the project to build a desktop application using Compose. The **jvmMain** source set contains the code that will be compiled and run on the JVM. The **jvmMain** source set depends on the **common** module and the Compose desktop libraries. This means that the code in the **jvmMain** source set can use the code in the common module and the Compose desktop libraries. To add code to the **jvmMain** source set, we create the main Kotlin file (**main.kt**) in the **src/jvmMain/kotlin** directory.

The **compose.desktop** block configures the project to build desktop applications using Compose. It specifies the main class for the application and the target formats for the native distributions. The target formats are the formats that will be used to create the native distributions of the application. The target formats can be as follows:

- **Dmg**: A macOS native distribution.
- **Msi**: A Windows native distribution.
- **Deb**: A Linux native distribution.

The **packageName** is the name that will be used for the application in the native distributions. Now, the final structure should look like the following:

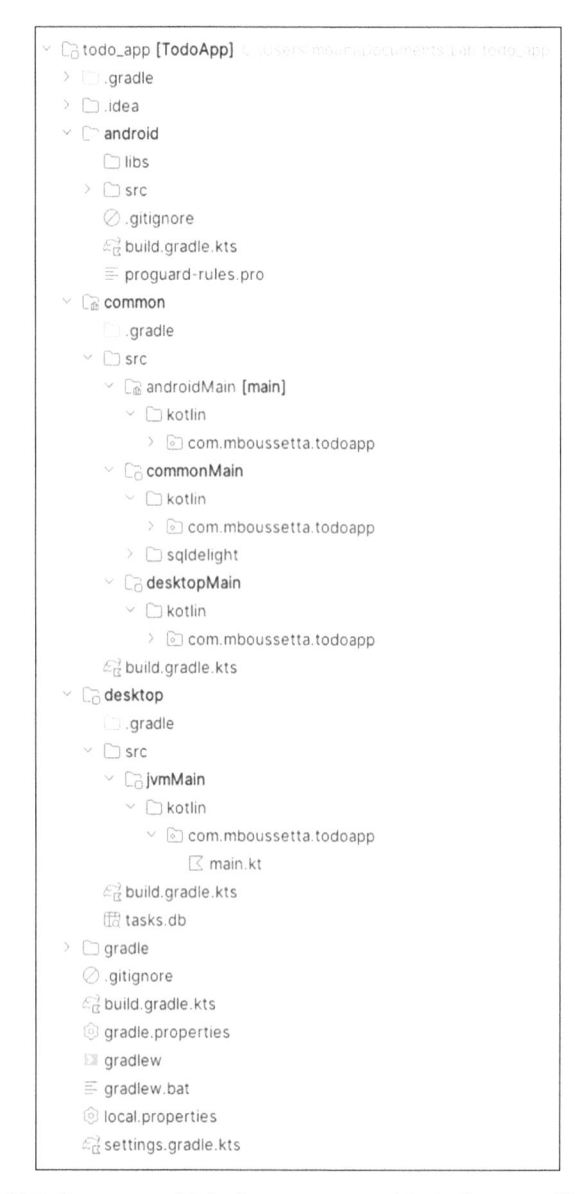

```
v 🗁 todo_app [TodoApp]
  > 🗀 .gradle
  > 🗀 .idea
  v 🗀 android
      🗀 libs
    > 🗀 src
      ⊘ .gitignore
      🗲 build.gradle.kts
      ≡ proguard-rules.pro
  v 🗁 common
      🗀 .gradle
    v 🗀 src
      v 🗁 androidMain [main]
        v 🗀 kotlin
          > 🗀 com.mboussetta.todoapp
      v 🗁 commonMain
        v 🗀 kotlin
          > 🗀 com.mboussetta.todoapp
        > 🗀 sqldelight
      v 🗁 desktopMain
        v 🗀 kotlin
          > 🗀 com.mboussetta.todoapp
      🗲 build.gradle.kts
  v 🗁 desktop
      🗀 .gradle
    v 🗀 src
      v 🗁 jvmMain
        v 🗀 kotlin
          v 🗀 com.mboussetta.todoapp
              🖾 main.kt
      🗲 build.gradle.kts
      🗎 tasks.db
  > 🗀 gradle
    ⊘ .gitignore
    🗲 build.gradle.kts
    ⓘ gradle.properties
    ⛶ gradlew
    ≡ gradlew.bat
    ⓘ local.properties
    🗲 settings.gradle.kts
```

Figure 18.5: *Compose multiplatform structure with platform-specific modules*

Todo app in Compose Multiplatform

Compose Multiplatform is a framework that allows building native applications for multiple platforms using a single codebase. It is based on Kotlin and uses the Kotlin Multiplatform plugin. The following are some of the benefits of using Compose Multiplatform:

- Building native applications for multiple platforms using a single codebase.
- Using Kotlin, which is a modern and expressive programming language.
- Using Kotlin Multiplatform Mobile libraries, which provide a lot of functionality for building native applications.
- Using Jetpack Compose UI toolkits.

Jetpack Compose is a modern toolkit for building native UI in Android. It is a declarative framework, which means that we describe what we want our UI to look like and Compose takes care of rendering it.

One of the benefits of using Jetpack Compose is that it is much simpler than using the traditional Android UI framework. With Compose, we can create complex UIs with just a few lines of code. Another benefit of using Jetpack Compose is that it is very performant. Compose uses a number of optimizations to render your UI as quickly as possible.

To create a Compose UI, you need to create a composable function. A composable function is a function that describes a UI element. For example, the following code defines a composable function for a text widget:

```
@Composable
fun TextWidget(text: String) {
    Text(text)
}
```

To render a composable function, you need to call it from another composable function. For example, the following code renders the **TextWidget** composable function:

```
@Composable
fun MyComposableFunction() {
    TextWidget("Hello, world!")
}
```

Overall, Jetpack Compose is a powerful tool for building native UIs in Android. It is a declarative framework that is simple, performant, and flexible.

To start creating our application, we are going to follow the following steps:

1. **Define the application UI theme**

    We created a new file, **Color.kt**, in the **common/src/commonMain/kotlin/com/mboussetta/todoapp/ui.theme/** directory. It will contain the colors of our theme with all the roles defined for both light and dark theme colors.

```kotlin
// Color.kt
import androidx.compose.ui.graphics.Color

val todo_light_primary = Color(0xFF006496)
val todo_light_onPrimary = Color(0xFFFFFFFF)
val todo_light_primaryContainer = Color(0xFFCCE5FF)
val todo_light_onPrimaryContainer = Color(0xFF001E31)
val todo_light_secondary = Color(0xFF50606F)
val todo_light_onSecondary = Color(0xFFFFFFFF)
val todo_light_secondaryContainer = Color(0xFFD4E4F6)
val todo_light_onSecondaryContainer = Color(0xFF0D1D2A)
val todo_light_tertiary = Color(0xFF66587B)
val todo_light_onTertiary = Color(0xFFFFFFFF)
val todo_light_tertiaryContainer = Color(0xFFECDCFF)
val todo_light_onTertiaryContainer = Color(0xFF211534)
val todo_light_error = Color(0xFFBA1A1A)
val todo_light_errorContainer = Color(0xFFFFDAD6)
val todo_light_onError = Color(0xFFFFFFFF)
val todo_light_onErrorContainer = Color(0xFF410002)
val todo_light_background = Color(0xFFFCFCFF)
val todo_light_onBackground = Color(0xFF1A1C1E)
val todo_light_surface = Color(0xFFFCFCFF)
val todo_light_onSurface = Color(0xFF1A1C1E)
val todo_light_surfaceVariant = Color(0xFFDEE3EB)
val todo_light_onSurfaceVariant = Color(0xFF42474E)
val todo_light_outline = Color(0xFF72787E)
val todo_light_inverseOnSurface = Color(0xFFF0F0F4)
val todo_light_inverseSurface = Color(0xFF2F3133)
val todo_light_inversePrimary = Color(0xFF91CDFF)
val todo_light_surfaceTint = Color(0xFF006496)
val todo_light_outlineVariant = Color(0xFFC2C7CE)
val todo_light_scrim = Color(0xFF000000)
```

```
val todo_dark_primary = Color(0xFF91CDFF)
val todo_dark_onPrimary = Color(0xFF003350)
val todo_dark_primaryContainer = Color(0xFF004B72)
val todo_dark_onPrimaryContainer = Color(0xFFCCE5FF)
val todo_dark_secondary = Color(0xFFB8C8D9)
val todo_dark_onSecondary = Color(0xFF22323F)
val todo_dark_secondaryContainer = Color(0xFF394856)
val todo_dark_onSecondaryContainer = Color(0xFFD4E4F6)
val todo_dark_tertiary = Color(0xFFD1BFE7)
val todo_dark_onTertiary = Color(0xFF372A4A)
val todo_dark_tertiaryContainer = Color(0xFF4E4162)
val todo_dark_onTertiaryContainer = Color(0xFFECDCFF)
val todo_dark_error = Color(0xFFFFB4AB)
val todo_dark_errorContainer = Color(0xFF93000A)
val todo_dark_onError = Color(0xFF690005)
val todo_dark_onErrorContainer = Color(0xFFFFDAD6)
val todo_dark_background = Color(0xFF1A1C1E)
val todo_dark_onBackground = Color(0xFFE2E2E5)
val todo_dark_surface = Color(0xFF1A1C1E)
val todo_dark_onSurface = Color(0xFFE2E2E5)
val todo_dark_surfaceVariant = Color(0xFF42474E)
val todo_dark_onSurfaceVariant = Color(0xFFC2C7CE)
val todo_dark_outline = Color(0xFF8C9198)
val todo_dark_inverseOnSurface = Color(0xFF1A1C1E)
val todo_dark_inverseSurface = Color(0xFFE2E2E5)
val todo_dark_inversePrimary = Color(0xFF006496)
val todo_dark_surfaceTint = Color(0xFF91CDFF)
val todo_dark_outlineVariant = Color(0xFF42474E)
val todo_dark_scrim = Color('0xFF000000)
```

To define a new theme, we are going to create a **nex** file in the same directory with the name **Theme.kt**; the following code is how it should look like:

```kotlin
private val LightColors = lightColorScheme(
    primary = todo_light_primary,
    onPrimary = todo_light_onPrimary,
    primaryContainer = todo_light_primaryContainer,
    onPrimaryContainer = todo_light_onPrimaryContainer,
    secondary = todo_light_secondary,
    onSecondary = todo_light_onSecondary,
    secondaryContainer = todo_light_secondaryContainer,
    onSecondaryContainer = todo_light_onSecondaryContainer,
    tertiary = todo_light_tertiary,
    onTertiary = todo_light_onTertiary,
    tertiaryContainer = todo_light_tertiaryContainer,
    onTertiaryContainer = todo_light_onTertiaryContainer,
    error = todo_light_error,
    errorContainer = todo_light_errorContainer,
    onError = todo_light_onError,
    onErrorContainer = todo_light_onErrorContainer,
    background = todo_light_background,
    onBackground = todo_light_onBackground,
    surface = todo_light_surface,
    onSurface = todo_light_onSurface,
    surfaceVariant = todo_light_surfaceVariant,
    onSurfaceVariant = todo_light_onSurfaceVariant,
    outline = todo_light_outline,
    inverseOnSurface = todo_light_inverseOnSurface,
    inverseSurface = todo_light_inverseSurface,
    inversePrimary = todo_light_inversePrimary,
    surfaceTint = todo_light_surfaceTint,
    outlineVariant = todo_light_outlineVariant,
    scrim = todo_light_scrim,
)
```

```kotlin
    private val DarkColors = darkColorScheme(
        primary = todo_dark_primary,
        onPrimary = todo_dark_onPrimary,
        primaryContainer = todo_dark_primaryContainer,
        onPrimaryContainer = todo_dark_onPrimaryContainer,
        secondary = todo_dark_secondary,
        onSecondary = todo_dark_onSecondary,
        secondaryContainer = todo_dark_secondaryContainer,
        onSecondaryContainer = todo_dark_onSecondaryContainer,
        tertiary = todo_dark_tertiary,
        onTertiary = todo_dark_onTertiary,
        tertiaryContainer = todo_dark_tertiaryContainer,
        onTertiaryContainer = todo_dark_onTertiaryContainer,
        error = todo_dark_error,
        errorContainer = todo_dark_errorContainer,
        onError = todo_dark_onError,
        onErrorContainer = todo_dark_onErrorContainer,
        background = todo_dark_background,
        onBackground = todo_dark_onBackground,
        surface = todo_dark_surface,
        onSurface = todo_dark_onSurface,
        surfaceVariant = todo_dark_surfaceVariant,
        onSurfaceVariant = todo_dark_onSurfaceVariant,
        outline = todo_dark_outline,
        inverseOnSurface = todo_dark_inverseOnSurface,
        inverseSurface = todo_dark_inverseSurface,
        inversePrimary = todo_dark_inversePrimary,
        surfaceTint = todo_dark_surfaceTint,
        outlineVariant = todo_dark_outlineVariant,
        scrim = todo_dark_scrim,
    )
```

```kotlin
@Composable
fun TaskAppTheme(
    darkTheme: Boolean = isSystemInDarkTheme(),
    content: @Composable () -> Unit
) {
    MaterialTheme(
        colorScheme = if (darkTheme) DarkColors else LightColors,
        content = content
    )
}
```

The **TaskAppTheme** function is a wrapper around the **MaterialTheme** composable that allows us to customize the look and feel of your app. It takes the following two parameters:

- **useDarkTheme**: This parameter controls whether the app should use a light or dark theme. It is tied to the function **isSystemInDarkTheme()** by default, so that the app will automatically switch to the dark theme if the system dark mode is enabled. However, you can also pass a Boolean value to this parameter to manually set the theme.

- **content**: This is the composable content to which the theme will be applied.

The **TaskAppTheme** function is a flexible way to theme our Jetpack Compose app. We can use it to theme the entire app or just specific parts of the app. We can also use it to switch between light and dark themes dynamically.

2. **Define the data model**

The first step in our journey is to define the data model for our application; we need to create a data class for our tasks in the **common/src/commonMain/kotlin/com/mboussetta/todoapp/domain/** directory:

```kotlin
data class Task(
    val id: Long?,
    val title: String,
    var complete: Boolean,
)
```

The data class **Task** has an **id**, a **title** for the task name and a **complete** field for the status of the task if it's done or not.

3. **Setting up database**

   In this section, we will explore how to set up a database for our Todo app using SQLDelight in a Compose Multiplatform application. SQLDelight is a powerful database library that allows to define a database schema in a type-safe manner, making it an excellent choice for modern multiplatform app development.

   Before we dive into setting up SQLDelight, we should add the **sqldelight** plugin to our project by including it in the project-level build script **build.grdale.kts**:

   ```
   plugins {
       // other plugins
       id("com.squareup.sqldelight") apply false
   }


   buildscript {
       dependencies {
           classpath("com.squareup.sqldelight:gradle-plugin:1.5.5")
       }
   }
   ```

   And add the SQLDelight and SQLDelight drivers in the common module Gradle build script:

   ```
   sourceSets {
       val commonMain by getting {
           dependencies {

               // Other dependencies ....

               // SqlDelight
               implementation("com.squareup.sqldelight:runtime:1.5.5")
               implementation("com.squareup.sqldelight:android-driver:1.5.5")
               implementation("com.squareup.sqldelight:sqlite-driver:1.5.5")
           }
       }

       val androidMain by getting {
   ```

```
            dependencies {
                // Other dependencies ...
                implementation("com.squareup.sqldelight:android-driver:1.5.5")
            }
        }

        val desktopMain by getting {
            dependencies {
                implementation("com.squareup.sqldelight:sqlite-driver:1.5.5")
            }
        }
    }
}
```

Next, we should prepare the database schema for our application, and we are going to create a file **tasks.sql** in the **common/src/commonMain/sqldelight/database/** directory:

```
CREATE TABLE IF NOT EXISTS taskEntity (
    id INTEGER NOT NULL PRIMARY KEY AUTOINCREMENT,
    title TEXT NOT NULL,
    complete INTEGER NOT NULL DEFAULT 0
);

getAllTasks:
SELECT *
FROM taskEntity;

insertTask:
INSERT OR REPLACE
INTO taskEntity (id, title)
VALUES (?,?);

deleteTask:
DELETE FROM taskEntity
WHERE id = ?;
```

```
completeTask:
UPDATE taskEntity
SET complete = 1
WHERE id = ?;
```

Now, we create a SQLDelight Gradle configuration by adding the following block to our **common** module's **build.gradle.kts**:

```
sqldelight {
    database("TaskDatabase") {
        packageName = "com.mboussetta.todoapp.database"
        sourceFolders = listOf("sqldelight")
    }
}
```

Android Studio will then automatically rebuild the Gradle project and generate the database for us. If it is not the case, we can generate the database manually by running the following Gradle task:

```
./gradlew :common:generateSqlDelightInterface
```

Next, we need to create a **DatabaseDriverFactory** class to set up the connection with the database. While we have a platform-specific implementation for the database driver, we are going to use "expect" and "actual" Kotlin features. Expect and actual are used to define and provide platform-specific implementations for certain code elements, allowing to write shared code in the **common** module while providing platform-specific implementations in platform-specific modules.

In the **commonMain/kotlin/com/mbousssetta/totoapp/data** directory, we create the following class:

```
import com.squareup.sqldelight.db.SqlDriver


expect class DatabaseDriverFactory {
    fun create(): SqlDriver
}
```

Then, we should provide the implementation of this class in the different platforms using the **actual** keyword. In the **desktopMain/kotlin/com/mboussetta/totoapp/data** directory:

```
import com.mboussetta.todoapp.database.TaskDatabase
import com.squareup.sqldelight.db.SqlDriver
import com.squareup.sqldelight.sqlite.driver.JdbcSqliteDriver

actual class DatabaseDriverFactory {
    actual fun create(): SqlDriver {
        val driver: SqlDriver = JdbcSqliteDriver("jdbc:sqlite:tasks.db")
        TaskDatabase.Schema.create(driver)
        return driver
    }
}
```

And in **androidMain/kotlin/com/mbousssetta/totoapp/data** directory:

```
import android.content.Context
import com.mboussetta.todoapp.database.TaskDatabase
import com.squareup.sqldelight.android.AndroidSqliteDriver
import com.squareup.sqldelight.db.SqlDriver

actual class DatabaseDriverFactory(private val context: Context) {
    actual fun create(): SqlDriver {
        return AndroidSqliteDriver(TaskDatabase.Schema, context, "tasks.db")
    }
}
```

These are the platform-specific implementations of the **DatabaseDriverFactory**.

4. **Configuring a DataSource**

   As a best practice, we are going to create a **TaskDataSource** Kotlin interface which will have the methods we are going to need to interact with the database. We use this interface so that it can be implemented by classes for different databases dialects.

   We create a new Kotlin interface with name **TaskDataSource** in the **commonMain/kotlin/com/mboussetta/todoapp/domain** directory:

```
interface TaskDataSource {
    fun deleteTask(id: Long)
    fun completeTask(id: Long)
    fun insertTask(task: Task)
    fun getAllTasks(): List<Task>
}
```

Now, let us create the **SqlDelightDataSource** class, which implements the **TaskDataSource** interface. In the **commonMain/kotlin/com/mboussetta/todoapp/data** directory, we create this class as follows:

```
import com.mboussetta.todoapp.database.TaskDatabase
import com.mboussetta.todoapp.domain.Task
import com.mboussetta.todoapp.domain.TaskDataSource

class SqlDelightTaskDataSource(db: TaskDatabase) : TaskDataSource {
    private val queries = db.tasksQueries

    override fun deleteTask(id: Long) {
        queries.deleteTask(id)
    }

    override fun getAllTasks(): List<Task> {
        return queries.getAllTasks().executeAsList().map {
            it.toTask()
        }
    }

    override fun completeTask(id: Long) {
        queries.completeTask(id)
    }

    override fun insertTask(task: Task) {
        queries.insertTask(
```

```
                id = task.id,
                title = task.title,
            )
        }
    }
```

The **SqlDelightTaskDataSource** class serves as an implementation of the **TaskDataSource** interface, providing a concrete way to interact with the database using SQLDelight. It encapsulates the details of how tasks are manipulated in the database, making it easier to work with tasks in the application's business logic without directly dealing with SQL queries.

In this implementation, the tasks list retrieved from the database using the method **queries.getAllTasks().executeAsList()** is of type **TaskEntity**, which is generated by the SQLDelight Gradle plugin.

```
override fun getAllTasks(): List<Task> {
    return queries.getAllTasks().executeAsList().map {
        it.toTask()
    }
}
```

To convert this to type **Task** we create a **TaskMapper.kt** file with an extension implementation of the **TaskEntity**:

```
import com.mboussetta.todoapp.domain.Task
import database.TaskEntity

fun TaskEntity.toTask(): Task {
    return Task(
        id,
        title,
        complete == 1L
    )
}
```

Next, we are going to create a **TaskViewModel**. Before going any further, let us get to know some design pattern development concepts: MVVM architecture.

5. **Configuring ViewModel**

   Model-View-ViewModel (**MVVM**) is a software design pattern that separates the user interface (View), the business logic (Model), and the state management (ViewModel). This makes the code more modular, reusable, and testable.

   In Jetpack Compose, the ViewModel can be used to hold the state of the UI and to provide methods for updating the state. The View can then observe the state of the ViewModel and update itself accordingly.

   To be able to use a ViewModel in our multiplatform application, we need a ViewModel implementation library that works in a compose multiplatform application. For this purpose, we are going to use the Moko MVVM library. Moko MVVM is a library that provides tools and architectural guidance for implementing the MVVM architectural pattern in Kotlin multiplatform projects.

   In the **common** module Gradle build script, we should add the Moko MVVM library dependencies as follows:

   ```
   dependencies {
       implementation("androidx.core:core-ktx:1.12.0")
       commonMainApi("dev.icerock.moko:mvvm-core:0.16.1")
       commonMainApi("dev.icerock.moko:mvvm-compose:0.16.1")
       commonMainApi("dev.icerock.moko:mvvm-flow:0.16.1")
       commonMainApi("dev.icerock.moko:mvvm-flow-compose:0.16.1")
   }
   ```

   Our application **TaskListViewModel** will be like the following:

   ```
   class TaskListViewModel(private val taskDataSource: TaskDataSource) : ViewModel() {

       var uiState by mutableStateOf(TaskListState())

       init {
           loadAllTasks()
       }

       private fun loadAllTasks() {
           uiState = uiState.copy(tasks = taskDataSource.getAllTasks())
   ```

```
        }

        fun changeTaskChecked(item: Task, checked: Boolean) =
            taskDataSource.completeTask(item.id!!)

        fun deleteTask(id: Long?) {
            taskDataSource.deleteTask(id!!).also { loadAllTasks() }
        }

        fun insertTask(task: Task) {
            taskDataSource.insertTask(task).also { loadAllTasks() }
        }

    }
```

Where **TaskListState** is a class to hold the state of the application, it is defined as follows:

```
data class TaskListState(
    var tasks: List<Task> = listOf(),
)
```

The **TaskListViewModel** uses Moko MVVM to manage the task list screen's state and interactions with the data source. It ensures that the UI state is updated appropriately when tasks are inserted, deleted, or when their completion status changes. Moko MVVM simplifies the process of handling UI-related logic in a Compose Multiplatform project by providing a consistent MVVM architecture across platforms.

6. **Creating the TaskListItem composable**

   We will write the code for a Composable function **TaskListItem**, used to render individual tasks in a task list. This Composable is typically used within a list component to display tasks along with options for marking them as completed or deleting them.

   In the **common** module, create a file **TaskListItem.kt** in the **commonMain/kotlin/com/mboussetta/todoapp/presentation/components** directory:

```
    @Composable
    fun TaskListItem(task: Task, onCheckedChange: (Boolean) -> Unit,
onDelete: () -> Unit) {
```

```
    Row(
        modifier = Modifier.padding(horizontal = 12.dp),
        verticalAlignment = Alignment.CenterVertically,
        horizontalArrangement = Arrangement.spacedBy(4.dp),
    ) {
        Checkbox(
            onCheckedChange = onCheckedChange,
            checked = task.complete,
        )
        Text(
            task.title,
            style = MaterialTheme.typography.bodyLarge,
            fontStyle = if (task.complete) FontStyle.Italic else
            FontStyle.Normal,
            textDecoration = if (task.complete) TextDecoration.
            LineThrough else TextDecoration.None,
            modifier = Modifier.weight(1f)
        )
        IconButton(onClick = onDelete) {
            Icon(
                Icons.Filled.Delete,
                contentDescription = "Delete",
                tint = MaterialTheme.colorScheme.error
            )
        }
    }

    Divider(
        thickness = 0.5.dp,
        color = MaterialTheme.colorScheme.surfaceVariant,
        modifier = Modifier.fillMaxWidth().padding(horizontal = 12.dp)
    )
}
```

The **TaskListItem** Composable function is designed to render a single task item. It takes the following three parameters:

- **task**: A **task** object representing the task to be displayed.
- **onCheckedChange**: A lambda function that takes a Boolean parameter to handle changes in the task's completion status (for example, when the user checks or unchecks the checkbox).
- **onDelete**: A lambda function to handle task deletion.

This code defines a Row Composable, which is a layout element for arranging child composable horizontally.

- **Modifier.padding(horizontal = 12.dp)** adds horizontal padding to the row to provide spacing between the task list item and the screen edges.
- **verticalAlignment = Alignment.CenterVertically** aligns the child composables vertically in the center.
- **horizontalArrangement = Arrangement.spacedBy(4.dp)** arranges the child composables horizontally with a spacing of 4.dp between them.

7. **Creating the TaskList composable**

To display the list of tasks, we will create a composable function to display items vertically using a **LazyColumn** composable function. It is a powerful tool for building scrollable lists in Jetpack Compose that can efficiently handle a wide range of use cases, from simple static lists to complex, dynamic, and large datasets.

In the same directory as **TaskListItem**, create a file **TasksList.kt** as follows:

```
@Composable
fun TasksList(
    modifier: Modifier = Modifier,
    tasks: List<Task>,
    onCheckedTask: (Task, Boolean) -> Unit,
    onCloseTask: (Task) -> Unit,
) {
    LazyColumn(
        modifier = modifier
    ) {
        item {
            Spacer(modifier = Modifier.height(24.dp))
```

```
            Text(
                text = "My Tasks (${tasks.size})",
              modifier = Modifier.fillMaxWidth().padding(horizontal = 16.dp),
                fontWeight = FontWeight.Normal,
            )
        }

        items(
            items = tasks,
            key = { task -> task.id!! }
        ) { task ->
            TaskListItem(task = task,
              onCheckedChange = { checked -> onCheckedTask(task, checked)
},
                onDelete = { onCloseTask(task) }
            )
        }
    }
}
```

The **TasksList** is a Composable function that displays a list of tasks. It takes the following parameters:

- **modifier**: A modifier for styling the **TasksList**.
- **tasks**: A list of tasks to display.
- **onCheckedTask**: A lambda function that is called when a task's completion status is changed (for example, when a checkbox is toggled). It takes a **Task** object and a Boolean indicating whether the task is checked.
- **onCloseTask**: A lambda function called when a task is closed or deleted. It takes a **Task** object.

Now, to let the user insert new tasks, we are going to need an input form for that.

8. **Create the InputTaskForm Composable**

    In the same directory as preceding, create a new file **InputTaskForm.kt** as follows:

```kotlin
@Composable
fun InputTaskForm(modifier: Modifier = Modifier, onSubmit: (Task) -> Unit) {
    Row(
        modifier = modifier,
        horizontalArrangement = Arrangement.spacedBy(8.dp),
        verticalAlignment = Alignment.CenterVertically
    ) {
        var taskValue by remember { mutableStateOf("") }
        OutlinedTextField(
            value = taskValue,
            singleLine = true,
            onValueChange = {
                taskValue = it
            },
            shape = RoundedCornerShape(12.dp),
            placeholder = { Text("Type here...") },
            modifier = Modifier.weight(1f),
            trailingIcon = {
                IconButton(
                    enabled = taskValue.isNotEmpty(),
                    onClick = {
                        onSubmit(Task(null, taskValue, false))
                        taskValue = ""
                    }) {
                    Icon(Icons.Filled.Send, contentDescription = "Clear search")
                }
            },
            leadingIcon = {
                Icon(
                    Icons.Filled.AddTask,
                    contentDescription = "Add Task",
```

```
                    modifier = Modifier.padding(start = 4.dp)
                )
            }
        )
    }

}
```

The **InputTaskForm** Composable is used to create an input form for adding new tasks in a Jetpack Compose UI. It consists of various Compose components and allows users to input task descriptions and submit them. It takes the following two parameters:

- **modifier**: A modifier for styling the form.
- **onSubmit**: A lambda function that takes a **Task** object and is called when the user submits a task.

9. **Create the TaskListScreen Composable**

    The **TaskListScreen** Composable represents a screen in a Compose multiplatform application for managing tasks. It integrates various Composable components to create a complete task list UI. It will be responsible for rendering the main task list screen.

    In the **commonMain/kotlin/com/mboussetta/todoapp/presentation** directory, create a new file **TaskListScreen.kt** as follows:

```
@Composable
fun TaskListScreen(taskListViewModel: TaskListViewModel) {
    Scaffold(
        topBar = {
            Row(
                modifier = Modifier
                    .height(56.dp)
                    .fillMaxWidth()
                    .background(
                        MaterialTheme.colorScheme.onPrimaryContainer
                    ),
                verticalAlignment = Alignment.CenterVertically,
                horizontalArrangement = Arrangement.Start
            ) {
```

```kotlin
                    Spacer(Modifier.width(24.dp))
                    Text(
                        "My Tasks",
                        textAlign = TextAlign.Center,
                        fontWeight = FontWeight.Bold,
                        color = Color.White,
                    )
                }
            }
        ) {
            Column(
                verticalArrangement = Arrangement.Top,
                modifier = Modifier.padding(bottom = 12.dp)
            ) {
                TasksList(
                    modifier = Modifier.weight(1f),
                    tasks = taskListViewModel.uiState.tasks,
                    onCheckedTask = { task, checked ->
                        taskListViewModel.changeTaskChecked(task, checked)
                    },
                    onCloseTask = { task -> taskListViewModel.
                    deleteTask(task.id) }
                )
                InputTaskForm(
                    modifier = Modifier.padding(horizontal = 16.dp),
                    onSubmit = {
                        taskListViewModel.insertTask(it)
                    }
                )
            }
        }
    }
```

It takes a **taskListViewModel** parameter of type **TaskListViewModel**. This ViewModel likely holds the business logic and state for the task list screen.

The **TaskListScreen** Composable creates a complete task list screen, including a custom app bar, a list of tasks, and an input form for adding new tasks. It integrates various Composable components and connects them to the **TaskListViewModel** to manage the tasks and user interactions efficiently.

10. **Creating the main App Composable**

    The **App** Composable will be the entry point for our compose multiplatform application. It uses several Composables to create the main user interface, applies the **TaskAppTheme**, and displays the **TaskListScreen**. And It will be instantiated by all different platforms.

    While the **TaskListScreen** needs a **TaskListViewModel** as a parameter, we are going to need a platform-specific class that has its own **TaskListViewModel** implementation and that can be passed as a parameter to the **App** composable.

    In the **commonMain/kotlin/com/mboussetta/todoapp** directory, create a new file **AppModule.kt** with the following content:

    ```
    expect class AppModule {
        val taskListViewModel: TaskListViewModel
    }
    ```

    Here, we use "expect" to tell that this class should be implemented by each platform. Now, let us create the actual implementation of this class on the desktop and the Android platform.

    In the **androidMain/kotlin/com/mboussetta/todoapp** directory, create a class with the **actual** keyword as follows:

    ```
    actual class AppModule(private val context: Context) {
        actual val taskListViewModel: TaskListViewModel by lazy {
            TaskListViewModel(SqlDelightTaskDataSource(
                db = TaskDatabase(driver = DatabaseDriverFactory(context).create())
            ))
        }
    }
    ```

    In the **desktopMain/kotlin/com/mboussetta/todoapp** directory, create a class with the **actual** keyword as follows:

```kotlin
actual class AppModule {
    actual val taskListViewModel: TaskListViewModel by lazy {
        TaskListViewModel(
            SqlDelightTaskDataSource(
                db = TaskDatabase(driver = DatabaseDriverFactory().create())
            )
        )
    }
}
```

Finally, in the **commonMain/kotlin/com/mboussetta/todoapp** we create the **App** composable as follows:

```kotlin
@Composable
fun App(appModule: AppModule) {
    TaskAppTheme {
        Surface(modifier = Modifier.background(MaterialTheme.colorScheme.surface)) {
            TaskListScreen(appModule.taskListViewModel)
        }
    }
}
```

In summary, the **App** Composable sets up the app's UI structure by applying a theme, creating a background **Surface**, and displaying the main content via the **TaskListScreen**. It passes the **taskListViewModel** from the **appModule** to the screen, indicating that the task list functionality is managed and displayed by the **TaskListScreen**.

11. **Setting up the platform-specific entry points**

    At this stage, we only need to update the entry point on the Android platform and create the one for desktop application platform.

    - **Update the MainActivity of the Android platform**

        To use the common code from our compose multiplatform application in the main entry point of the Android platform, we are going to need to update the **MainActifity.kt** to the following:

        ```kotlin
        class MainActivity : ComponentActivity() {
          override fun onCreate(savedInstanceState: Bundle?) {
              super.onCreate(savedInstanceState)
        ```

```
        setContent {
            App(AppModule(LocalContext.current.applicationContext))
        }
    }
}
```

- **Create the main entry point for the desktop application**

    For the desktop platform, we are going to create the main entry point that can use our **App** composable for a desktop application. To do so, we create a new file **main.kt** in the **desktop/src/jvmMain/kotlin/com/mboussetta/todoapp** directory as follows:

    ```
    fun main() = application {
        Window(onCloseRequest = ::exitApplication, title = "Todo App") {
            App(AppModule())
        }
    }
    ```

12. **Testing the final multiplatform application**

    To run the application for the desktop environment, we should execute the following Gradle task:

    ```
    .\gradlew jvmRun -DmainClass=MainKt --quiet
    ```

    The application should run as shown in the following screenshot:

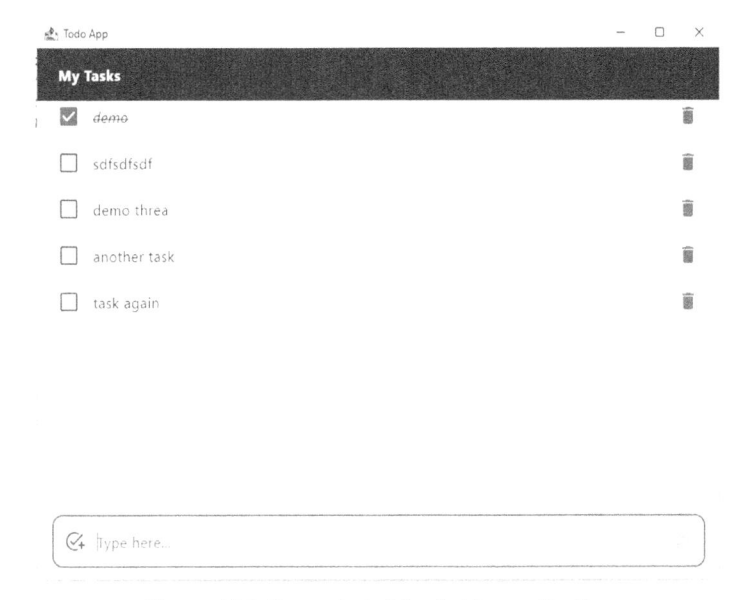

Figure 18.6: Screenshot of the desktop application

To run the application for the Android platform, we need to create an emulator in the Android Studio IDE, then click the button in the top right, shown as follows:

Figure 18.7: Android Studio launch button for Android emulator

Figure 18.8: Screenshot of the Android application

Conclusion

In conclusion, multiplatform development with Kotlin is a powerful approach to building cross-platform applications. It allows us to share code and resources between different platforms, saving time and effort in development. Additionally, it offers a number of advantages, such as increased code reuse, improved efficiency, and broader platform coverage.

We have explored the basics of multiplatform development with Kotlin in this chapter. We have learned how to set up Android Studio for multiplatform projects and how to write shared code that can be used across different platforms. We have also built a real-world application example: a Todo app using Compose Multiplatform.

Points to remember

The following are some points to remember:

- Multiplatform development with Kotlin is a powerful approach to building cross-platform applications.
- It allows us to share code and resources between different platforms, saving time and effort in development.
- Additionally, it offers a number of advantages, such as increased code reuse, improved efficiency, and broader platform coverage.
- To set up Android Studio for multiplatform projects, we must install the Kotlin Multiplatform plugin and enable the multiplatform support in the project settings.
- To write shared code that can be used across different platforms, we can use the Kotlin Multiplatform Shared Module.

Index

A

abstract class 59, 60
actor 303
Android application
  creating, with Jetpack
      Compose 324, 325
Android module
  setting up, in Compose
      multiplatform project 330-332
Android Studio 323
annotations 90
  annotation constructor 93, 94
  custom annotation, defining 91
  instantiation 94
  meta-annotations 92
  usage 90, 91
  use-site target 95
arrays 27
  primitive type arrays 27
assertComplete method 199

assertNoErrors method 199
assertValueAt method 200
assertValueCount method 200
assertValues method 199
async/await 260, 261
  benefits 261, 262
asynchronous file I/O
  CompletableFuture, using 240
asynchronous programming 231, 238, 239
  work completion, handing with callbacks
      237, 238
atomic operations
  using 235
average operator 162

B

backpressure 140-144
BehaviorProcessor 164, 165
BehaviorSubject 131-133
Boolean 26
break expression 38

broadcast channel 300-302
buffer operator 311

C

callable references 97
  Kotlin constructor references 98
  Kotlin function references 97
  Kotlin property references 98
cancellable operator 314
channels 299
  using 299, 300
  versus, Java queues 299
characters 22
classes 67
  data class 68
  inner class 69
  nested class 68, 69
  open class 67
  sealed class 70
  simple class 67
collectLatest operator 312
common module
  setting up, in Compose multiplatform project 327-330
@ComponentScan annotation 215
@Configuration annotation 215
Compare-and-Swap (CAS) 176
composable function 335
Compose Multiplatform 323, 334
  benefits 334, 335
  Todo app, creating 335-358
Compose Multiplatform project structure
  Android module, setting up 330-332
  common module, setting up 327-330
  desktop module, setting up 332, 333
  setting up 325, 326
concurrency 173, 174
  advantage 174
  best practices 176, 177

  challenges 175
  pitfalls 176
conditions 32
conflate operator 311
continue construct 39
coroutine builders 274
coroutine cancellation 279-281
  managing 284
  performing 282-284
coroutine cancellation exceptions
  handling 284
  handling, with finally block 285-287
  handling, with try-catch block 284, 285
coroutine context 273
Coroutine Flows 305, 306
coroutine flows approach
  need for 316
coroutines 231, 241
  example 241-243
coroutines channels 289
count operator 161, 162
CRUD operations 216
custom annotation
  defining 91

D

data class 68
data streams 307
  example 307-310
  limitations 310
data types 20
  arrays 27
  Boolean 26
  characters 22
  floating-point types 21
  integer types 20, 21
  string 23, 24
deadlock 175

debounce operator 158, 159
debugging tool
    using 237
declaration-site variance 82
    in keyword 82, 83
    out keyword 82
    use-site variance 83
Deferred values 262
    combining, with awaitAll 264
    combining, with transformations 265
    creating 262, 263
    error handling with 263
    error handling, with combined
        deferred values 266, 267
delegation pattern 71
deserialization 103
desktop module
    setting up, in Compose
        multiplatform project 332, 333
dispatchers 275
    default dispatcher 275
    Dispatchers.Unconfined dispatcher 276
    IO dispatcher 275
    main dispatcher 275, 276
displayWeather() function 310
distinct operator 155, 156
distinctUntilChanged operator 156
do…while loop 36

E

elementAt operator 156
Elvis operator (?:) 29
@EnableAutoConfiguration
    annotation 215
error handling 119-123, 168
error-handling operators
    onErrorResumeNext operator 169, 170
    onErrorReturn operator 169
exception handling 43
exception propagation 277
    handling 277-279

extensions
    extension functions 40, 41
    extension properties 41
    working with 40

F

fetchWeatherUpdates() function 309
fields
    backing 62
filtering 153
filter operator 153, 154
finally block
    for coroutine cancellation
        exception handling 285-287
first operator 156, 157
flatMap operator 160
floating-point types 21, 22
    numbers representation, on JVM 22
flowables 140
    from observable 142, 143
    usage criteria 142
    using, in Kotlin 140, 141
    versus, observables 141, 142
    with backpressure 144-149
flow constraints 316-318
Flux 221
    using 221-223
for loop 35, 36
function 29
    creating 29
    function arguments 30
    using 29, 30
functional data structure 116
functional reactive programming
    paradigm 108
function arguments
    default arguments 30
    mixing named arguments 31
    named arguments 31
    positional arguments 31

G

generator 290
generic classes
   creating 76, 77
generic constraints 79
   type erasure 81
   upper bound constraint 79-81
generic functions 78, 79
generics 76
   advantages 77, 78
getter method 61, 62
Gradle 202, 207
   build script 209, 210
   installing 207
   Kotlin application, creating 207, 208
   project, building 211
   project, running 211
groupBy operator 165-167
grouping 165

H

HashMap 176
higher-order functions 112, 113

I

if as expression 33
if-else statement 33
if statement 32
inheritance, Kotlin 52-56
   abstract class 59, 60
   parent class methods, overriding 57-59
inheritance, OOP 52
inline functions 113, 114
inner class 69
instantiation 94
integer types 20, 21
integrated development environments (IDE) 3
interfaces, Kotlin 63
IO dispatcher 275

J

Java 13
   advantages 13, 14
   disadvantages 14, 15
JavaServer Pages (JSP) 218
Java Virtual Machine (JVM) 5, 201
Jetpack Compose 335
   Android application, creating 324, 325
   benefits 335
jobs 243
   benefits 243
   creating 243, 244
JUnit 185
   assertions, using 186, 187
   examples 188-191
   setting up 185
   writing 186
   writing, for reactive applications 192, 193
JVM reflection dependency 96
   callable references 97
   in Gradle project 96
   in Maven project 96
   reference, to Kotlin class 96, 97

K

Kotlin 4, 17
   advantages 9-13
   benefits 4
   disadvantages 13
   history 2-4
   inheritance 52-56
   name, from Kotlin Island 5
   overview 18
   smart cast 39, 40
   URL 17
   versus Java 5-9
Kotlin constructor references 98
Kotlin function references 97
Kotlin interfaces 63
   inheritance 63

properties 64, 65
Kotlin multiplatform mobile (KMM) 15
Kotlin property references 98

L

lambda 110
　declaring 110
　lambda type declaration 110
last operator 157
lock-free data structures
　examples 176
Long-Term Support (LTS) 6
loops 34
　do…while loop 36
　for loop 35, 36
　repeat loop 35
　while loop 36

M

main dispatcher 275, 276
map operator 159, 160, 167, 168
mapping 167
message passing
　using 236, 237
meta-annotations 92
methods 45
mixing named arguments 31
Model-View-Controller (MVC)
　　pattern 106
Model-View-ViewModel
　　(MVVM) 347
monitor 175
Mono 221
　using 222, 223
multiplatform development 321, 322
　development environment, setting up 323
multithreading 232, 233
　challenges 233, 234
　features 233
　solutions, to challenges 234

N

named arguments 31
nested class 68, 69
noinline keyword 114
non-blocking linked list 176
non-blocking stack 176
non-suspending function 249
not-null assertion operator (!!) 29
n-tier architectures
　examples 212
n-tier Spring Boot application 212, 213
null safety 28, 29

O

object 50
object-oriented programming
　　(OOP) 45
　advantages 46
　classes 46
　inheritance 52
　Kotlin class 47-50
　objects 46-52
observable factory methods 127-130
observables 126, 140
　versus, flowables 141, 142
　working 126, 127
onErrorResumeNext operator 169, 170
onErrorReturn operator 169
open class 67
operator overloading 41

P

pipeline 292-295
polymorphic functions 114, 115
positional arguments 31
primary constructor 50
primitive type arrays 27
processors 163, 164
　BehaviorProcessor 164, 165
　PublishProcessor 163
　ReplayProcessor 163, 164

producer 302
profiling tool
　using 237
properties 61
PublishProcessor 163
PublishSubject 133-135
pure function 111

R
Reactive Manifesto 109, 110
　URL 109
reactive programming 106-108, 126
ReactiveX (Rx) 153
receive method 297-299
reduce operator 161
reducing operators 161
　average operator 162, 163
　count operator 161, 162
　min and max operators 162
　reduce operator 161
reflection 95, 96
　deserialization 103
　JVM reflection dependency 96
　serialization 99-102
reified-type parameters 84, 85
　type casting 86, 87
　type checking 86, 87
　type reification 85, 86
repeat loop 35
ReplayProcessor 163, 164
ReplaySubject 135
return expression 37, 38
RxKotlin 193
　examples 193
　observables 193, 194
　operators 194, 195
　subject 195
Rx-operators 152
　example 170, 171
　examples 155-159

filter operator 153, 154
reducing operators 161
skip operator 155
skipWhile operator 155
take operator 154
takeWhile operator 154, 155
transforming operators 159

S
safe call operator (?.) 28
scan operator 160, 161
schedulers 177, 178
　with observeOn operator 179-181
　with subscribeOn operator 178, 179
sealed class 70
secondary constructor 50
semaphore 175
send method 295
　example 295, 296
sequence 291, 292
serialization 98-102
setter method 61, 62
simple class 67
singly linked list
　declaration 116-119
　definition 116
skip operator 155
skipWhile operator 155
Spring Boot 202, 203, 211
　key features 204, 205
　n-tier architecture 212
　overview 203
　support of reactive programming 205, 206
Spring Boot application
　creating 213-218
　Mono and Flux, using 221-223
　running 219-221
@SpringBootApplication
　　annotation 215, 216
Spring Data Reactive 224-229

streamOfIntegers() function 308
streams limitations 310
  backpressure, handling 310-313
  cancellation, handling 313, 314
  inefficient resource utilization 314-316
string 23, 24
string functions 24
  compareTo function 25
  get function 25
  indexOf function 25
  length function 24
  lowercase function 25
  plus function 25
  split function 26
  string templates 26
  uppercase function 24
subjects 131
  BehaviorSubject 131-133
  PublishSubject 133-135
  ReplaySubject 135-137
suspendable API 252
  advantages 252-255
  creating 251
  debugging 257-259
  testing 257-259
  thread safety 255-257
suspending functions 248-250
  examples 248
  real-world examples 250, 251
  versus, non-suspending functions 249
synchronization mechanisms
  using 234

T

take operator 154
takeWhile operator 154
task scheduling 270
  coroutine builders 274
  coroutine contexts 273, 274
  coroutine scheduling and execution flow 270-273
TestObserver 198-200
TestScheduler 197, 198
TestSubscriber 196
thread pools
  using 235, 236
thread-safe data structures
  using 234
throttleFirst operator 157, 158
Todo app, in Compose Multiplatform
  App composable, creating 355, 356
  creating 335-340
  database, setting up 341-344
  data model, defining 340
  DataSource, configuring 344-346
  final multiplatform application, testing 357, 358
  InputTaskForm composable, creating 351-353
  platform-specific entry points, setting up 356, 357
  TaskList composable, creating 350, 351
  TaskListItem composable, creating 348-350
  TaskListScreen composable, creating 353-355
  ViewModel, configuring 347, 348
Tomcat 221-223
  benefits 220
transforming operators, Rx-operators 159
  flatMap operator 160
  map operator 159, 160
  scan operator 160, 161
try-catch block
  for coroutine cancellation exception handling 284, 285
tryReceive method
  using 297-299
trySend method 295
  example 295, 296
TypeAlias 72, 73

type arguments 76
type erasure 81
type parameters 76

U

UI threads 244, 245
  real-world examples 245
unit testing 184
  importance 184, 185
upper bound constraint 79-81
use-site target
  using 95
use-site variance
  type projection 83, 84

V

varargs 32
variables 19
  declaration 19
  initialization 19
variance 81, 82
  declaration-site variance 82
visibility modifiers 65
  class 66
  interface 66
  packages 65

W

when statement 33, 34
while loop 36

Z

zipWith operator 163

Printed in France by Amazon
Brétigny-sur-Orge, FR